STATE OF CHANGE

STATE of CHANGE

COLORADO POLITICS

IN THE TWENTY-FIRST CENTURY

EDITED BY

COURTENAY W. DAUM

ROBERT J. DUFFY

JOHN A. STRAAYER

UNIVERSITY PRESS OF COLORADO

Published by the University Press of Colorado
5589 Arapahoe Avenue, Suite 206C
Boulder, Colorado 80303

 The University Press of Colorado is a proud member of
the Association of American University Presses.

The University Press of Colorado is a cooperative publishing enterprise supported, in part, by
Adams State College, Colorado State University, Fort Lewis College, Metropolitan State College
of Denver, Regis University, University of Colorado, University of Northern Colorado, and
Western State College of Colorado.

Library of Congress Cataloging-in-Publication Data

State of change : Colorado politics in the twenty-first century / edited by Courtenay W. Daum,
Robert J. Duffy, and John A. Straayer.
    p. cm.
  Includes bibliographical references and index.
  ISBN 978-1-60732-086-9 (pbk. : alk. paper) — ISBN 978-1-60732-087-6 (ebk.) 1. Colorado—
Politics and government—21st century. I. Daum, Courtenay W. II. Duffy, Robert J. III. Straayer,
John A., 1939– IV. Title: Colorado politics in the twenty-first century.
  JK7816.S73 2011
  320.9788—dc23
                                    2011018035
Design by Daniel Pratt

20 19 18 17 16 15 14 13 12 11   10 9 8 7 6 5 4 3 2 1

Contents

Acknowledgments

Courtenay Daum, Bob Duffy, and John Straayer owe a debt of gratitude to our colleagues and the staff in the Political Science Department at Colorado State University, especially Violet Marquart and Maureen Bruner. Our thanks as well to the good folks at the University Press of Colorado, including Darrin Pratt, Jessica d'Arbonne, Daniel Pratt, and Laura Furney; to our skilled and tenacious copyeditor, Cheryl Carnahan; and to the peer reviewers, including John Redifer of Mesa State College and James Null of the University of Colorado at Colorado Springs. Finally, we thank the contributors to the edited volume for their substantive contributions, as well as their patience and cooperation with various requests and deadlines.

John Straayer is indebted to the many good legislative interns, General Assembly members and staffers, lobbyists, and capitol reporters who over the years have provided cheerful help and friendship. Thanks to Colorado State University for a sabbatical leave that helped make this work possible. On this project, as with others, thanks to Judy Straayer for enduring his endless political jabber.

Bob Duffy thanks David Magleby of the Center for the Study of Elections and Democracy at Brigham Young University for organizing a series of studies of campaign finance and communications in competitive federal elections. The Colorado studies, which were supported by the Pew Charitable Trusts, date back to 2004 and provided the foundation for many of the ideas expressed in this volume. He would also like to thank the many individuals associated with campaigns, parties, and interest groups for speaking with him and answering his questions about Colorado politics. A number of graduate student research associates were also instrumental in collecting data: Mike Roloff, Andy Kear, Christina Farhart, and Erik Mims. Finally, thanks to Debbie, Julia, Marissa, and Sarina for tolerating absences as a result of this and other projects.

Courtenay Daum would like to thank her colleagues in the Political Science Department, especially John Straayer for sharing his vast knowledge of Colorado politics. In addition, she thanks her many undergraduate and graduate students for their inspiration and willingness to serve as a useful sounding board for various research ideas and projects. Finally, she thanks Joe for his incredible support and patience over the duration of this project (and many others) and Zoe and Bodhi for always helping her keep her priorities straight and in check.

STATE OF CHANGE

INTRODUCTION

State of Change:
Colorado Politics in the Twenty-First Century

Courtenay W. Daum, Robert J. Duffy, Kyle Saunders, and John A. Straayer

Over the past several decades, Colorado's political landscape has changed in many ways and in dramatic fashion. This volume identifies and focuses on these changes and seeks to provide some explanations for these shifts by placing them within the larger context of national and regional politics and shifting demographic and partisan patterns in Colorado. These developments include a shift within the Republican Party that led to the end of its dominance in most state and congressional elections, as well as increased use of direct democracy that has resulted in the implementation of term limits, significant changes in fiscal policy, major diminishment of state and local governments' taxing and spending authority, and a variety of unintended consequences of the initiative process. The result is a political landscape in the early twenty-first century that is drastically different from the Colorado politics of a few decades ago. This volume will use these changes as a starting point to present a variety of perspectives on Colorado's recent political evolution.

Courtenay W. Daum, Robert J. Duffy, Kyle Saunders, and John A. Straayer

CONTEXT OF COLORADO ELECTIONS

In 1876 Colorado was admitted to the Union as the thirty-eighth state, and it is known as the Centennial State because its admission coincided with the 100th anniversary of the Declaration of Independence. Similar to constitutions in other states, the Colorado Constitution provides for a three-branch state government that includes an executive branch, a two-house legislature, and a state judiciary (Colorado Constitution, Article III). The governor, thirty-five members of the state senate, and sixty-five members of the state house are elected by the citizens of Colorado, whereas members of the Colorado courts are selected through a hybrid appointment-election system. Judges on the Colorado Supreme Court, the Colorado Appeals Court, district courts, and county courts are initially nominated by nominating commissions and appointed by the governor to serve a provisional two-year term (Lorch 2003: 179). At the conclusion of the provisional term, the justice or judge may run for election on a noncompetitive ballot that asks simply whether the individual should be retained in office; if the public approves, he or she will serve a full term with the option of running for reelection until he or she reaches the mandatory retirement age of seventy-two (Lorch 2003: 180–181).

Yet Colorado's unique history and location have combined to influence the state government and elections in ways that are distinct from other states. For example, Colorado's geography—within the state's borders the eastern plains meet the Rocky Mountains—and abundant natural resources have affected the state's economic and political development.

Historically, the state's natural beauty and abundant natural resources have attracted individuals from out of state as both new residents and tourists; in fact, a majority of Colorado residents are natives of other states (National Journal 2010). The election of Bill Ritter as Colorado governor in 2006 was the first time a native Coloradan had been elected governor in more than thirty-five years. According to the *National Journal*:

> Colorado has been reshaped, economically and politically, by its successive waves of newcomers. The conservative and boosterish Colorado of the 1960s was transformed in the 1970s by a wave of young liberal migrants who swept the state's politics by calling for environmental protections and slow growth . . . Then, in the 1990s, a new wave of migrants—tech-savvy, family-oriented cultural conservatives looking for an environment to prosper—moved Colorado's politics to the right . . . Both of these politically divergent communities have some reason to believe that they exemplify the state. Colorado elections can be viewed as contests to determine which one does. (National Journal 2010)

Early settlers migrated to Colorado after gold and silver were discovered in the Rocky Mountains in the second half of the nineteenth century; for much of Colorado's history the economy was dependent on the exploitation of its natural resources in addition to its strong agricultural tradition. Today, the state's oil and natural gas resources continue to lure businesses and individuals (National Journal 2010), The same geography that provides numerous agricultural and resource extraction opportunities also enabled the development of recreational tourism—such as skiing, rafting, hiking—and real estate as important economic drivers in recent decades. The resulting tension between the "old" and "new" economies generates some interesting politics, as exemplified by the many conflicts on Colorado's western slope over energy exploration. Individuals who rely on recreational tourism to make a living, wealthy homeowners who seek to preserve their pristine environmental surroundings, and political liberals often disagree with farming and mining communities, corporate interests, and political conservatives about environmental regulations and policies and what constitutes appropriate stewardship of Colorado's natural resources and environs (National Journal 2010). These disagreements have contributed to the fluidity in Colorado politics since the 1960s.

In recent decades Colorado, like many other states, has experienced a great deal of anti-tax fervor, which has exacerbated the state's revenue problems and added additional nuances to Colorado electoral politics and governance. These anti-tax tendencies now influence Colorado polities and policy in myriad ways. For example, a University of Colorado–Denver study noted that while Colorado ranked "49th out of 50 states in state taxes paid as a percentage of income, and 44th in state and local taxes combined," with respect to expenditures per $1,000 in personal income, "in 2009 the state ranked 48th in K–12 education, 48th in higher education, and 49th in Medicaid" (Fermanich 2001: i–ii).

The state constitution granted the state government few taxing powers, relying instead on a decentralized local government tax system. As a result, although state taxes are low, Colorado does have relatively high local taxes, notably local property and sales taxes. Colorado ranked twelfth nationally for local taxes ($48.09 per $1,000 in income) in FY 2005–2006. Local sales taxes in Colorado are especially high, ranking second in the nation (Kirk 2009). In short, the state's local governments have an easier time generating revenue than the state government, despite the state's relative prosperity. The anti-tax fervor that has dominated state politics in the last twenty years has only exacerbated the state's revenue problems and added nuances to Colorado electoral politics and governing within the state.

PARTY BALANCE: A RED STATE BEGINS TO TURN BLUE?

During the more than 110 years since 1900, two-party politics in Colorado has been remarkably balanced. There have been extended periods when one party held the upper hand, to be sure, but the big picture is one of considerable party balance. That being said, during the last four decades of the twentieth

TABLE 0.1. Winners of Colorado statewide elective offices and legislature control, 1970–2008

Year	Governor	Attorney General	Secretary of State	Treasurer	HR Majority	Senate Majority
2008	No election	No election	No election	No election	Democrat	Democrat
2006	Ritter-D	Suthers-R	Dennis/ Coffman-R	Kennedy-D	Democrat	Democrat
2002	Owens-R	Salazar-D	Davidson-R	Coffman-R	Republican	Republican
1998	Owens-R	Salazar-D	Davidson-R	Coffman-R	Republican	Republican
1994	Romer-D	G. Norton-R	Buckley-R	Owens-R	Republican	Republican
1990	Romer-D	G. Norton-R	Meyer-R	Schoetler-D	Republican	Republican
1986	Romer-D	Woodard-R/D	Meyer-R	Schoetler-D	Republican	Republican
1982	Lamm-D	Woodard-R	Meyer-R	Romer-D	Republican	Republican
1978	Lamm-D	MacFarlane-D	Buchanan-R	Romer-D	Republican	Republican
1974	Lamm-D	MacFarlane-D	Buchanan-R	Brown-D	Democrat	Republican
1970	Love-R	Dunbar/ Moore-R	Anderson-R	Blue-R	Republican	Republican
Party balance	7-D/3-R	4-D/6-R	0-D/10-R	6-D/4-R	3-D/8-R	2-D/9-R

Source: Colorado Election Records.

century and the early years of the twenty-first century, politics in Colorado generally favored the Republican Party. Republican candidates dominated elections for US president, state treasurer, attorney general, and both houses of the General Assembly. In nine of the past twelve presidential elections, Colorado's electoral votes went to the Republican candidate. The exceptions were Lyndon Johnson in 1964, Bill Clinton in 1992, and Barack Obama in 2008. As shown in table 0.1, between 1970 and 2006 the Republican candidate won every election for secretary of state and six of the ten races for attorney general. Similarly, over a forty-year period from the mid-1960s to 2004, Republicans held the majority in both houses of the General Assembly, save for a single two-year span in each chamber.

During the period of Republican dominance, Democrats did have some successes. In the four decades between 1970 and 2010, a Democrat was governor for twenty-eight of the forty years, most notably during the twenty-four-year run of Richard Lamm and Roy Romer. (See the epilogue for a discussion of Democrat John Hickenlooper's 2010 election.) Democrats have also had the edge in the office of state treasurer, having won six of the past ten contests. In the last several election cycles, the overall tide has turned in the Democratic Party's favor. Whereas Colorado was a red state for most of the past thirty years, it has now become a distinct shade of purple.

TABLE 0.2. Colorado senatorial elections, 1968–2008

Year	Senator Elected	Opposing Candidate
2008	Udall (D) 53%	Schaffer (R) 42%
2004	Salazar (D) 51%	Coors (R) 47%
2002	Allard (R) 51%	Strickland (D) 46%
1998	Campbell (R) 62%	Lamm (D) 35%
1996	Allard (R) 51%	Strickland (D) 46%
1992	Campbell (D) 52%	Considine (R) 43%
1990	Brown (R) 56%	Heath (D) 42%
1986	Wirth (D) 50%	Kramer (R) 48%
1984	Armstrong (R) 64%	Dick (D) 35%
1980	Hart (D) 50%	Buchanan (R) 49%
1978	Armstrong (R) 59%	Haskell (D) 40%
1974	Hart (D) 57%	Dominick (R) 40%
1972	Haskell (D) 49%	Allott (R) 48%
1968	Dominick (R) 59%	McNichols (D) 41%

Source: Colorado Secretary of State.
Note: Totals may not add up to 100%, as minor party candidates are not included; percentages rounded to nearest integer.

Regarding party fortunes in congressional races, Colorado's US Senate elections have been competitive and rather cyclical (see table 0.2). From 1958 to 1998, one of the state's Senate seats was held by a Democrat and the other by a Republican. The Republican Party gained control of both Senate seats in 1998 when Senator Ben "Nighthorse" Campbell switched parties and became a Republican. When Campbell retired in 2004, Democrat Ken Salazar won election to the Senate, and in 2008 Democrat Mark Udall won the state's other Senate seat.

Colorado's delegation to the US House of Representatives has varied dramatically over the years. The state's rapid population growth moved it from a five-seat delegation in 1973 to a seven-seat delegation beginning with the 2003 redistricting. While Colorado did not gain another seat for the 2012 redistricting, some congressional district lines will likely change. The geography of the current congressional districts can be seen in figure 0.1; a more detailed description of each of the districts can be found in the sidebar on p.7.

Clear patterns have emerged in many of the districts: two are very safe Republican districts (the Fifth and Sixth) and two are very safe Democratic districts (the First and Second). As the sidebar on p. 7 illustrates, Colorado's remaining three congressional seats—the Third, Fourth, and Seventh—can be deemed

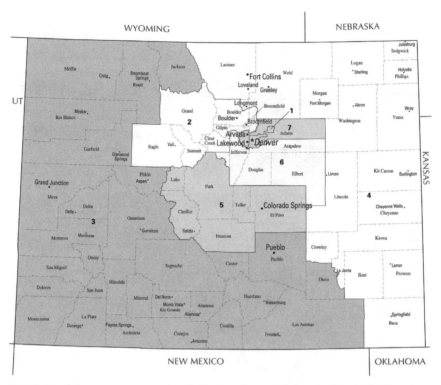

0.1. Colorado's current congressional districts. Source: Colorado Board of Education: http://www.cde.state.co.us/cdeboard/images/map.gif.

"competitive." Table 0.3 shows the election results from these three districts during the years 2002–2008.

STATEWIDE REGISTRATION TRENDS

Much of Democrats' success in recent federal elections in Colorado can be traced to registration and turnout trends over the past decade. For four decades beginning around 1970, a clear majority of affiliated voters—roughly one-third of Colorado voters identify as unaffiliated—were Republican. As table 0.4 indicates, the Republican advantage persisted through the 1990s and into the next decade. In fact, Republicans enjoyed an advantage of nearly 180,000 voters as recently as 2004. By the 2008 presidential election, however, the two parties were at near parity, and unaffiliated voters made up the single largest bloc in the state. Currently, Democrats, Republicans, and unaffiliated voters each constitute one-third of the electorate. Much of the statewide gains for Democrats and the growth in the number of unaffiliated voters have taken place in competi-

First District (2010 Cook Partisan Voting Index[1] D+21, D 1973–present). The First District encompasses much of urban Denver and the surrounding area. Democrat Diana DeGette has held the seat since 1997; it is by far the most Democratic district in Colorado.

Second District (2010 Cook PVI: D+11; R 1973–1975, D 1975–present). The Second District encompasses the northwestern suburbs of Denver, the city of Boulder, and mountain towns such as Vail, Grand Lake, and Idaho Springs. The seat, now held by freshman Jared Polis, has been held by a Democrat since 1975.

Third District (2010 Cook PVI: R+5; D 1973–1985, 1987–1993, 2005–present, R 1985–1987, 1993–2005). The Third District is located in western and south-central Colorado and includes most of the rural western slope, including the cities of Grand Junction and Durango, as well as southern portions of Colorado's eastern plains including the city of Pueblo. Despite its Republican tilt, the seat has been held by Democrat John Salazar since 2004.

Fourth District (2010 Cook PVI: R+6; R 1973–2009, D 2009–present). The sprawling Fourth District is located in eastern Colorado. It includes most of the state's rural eastern plains as well as the larger cities of Fort Collins, Greeley, Loveland and Longmont along Colorado's Front Range. The seat is now held by freshman Democrat Betsy Markey, who was the first Democrat to hold the seat since 1973. Republicans who previously held this seat include former Colorado Senators Hank Brown and Wayne Allard as well as socially conservative firebrands Bob Schaffer and Marilyn Musgrave. This will likely be the most competitive congressional district in 2010.

Fifth District (2010 Cook PVI: R+14; R 1973–present). The Fifth District lies in the center of the state and encompasses Colorado Springs and surrounding areas. The Fifth District is held by Republican Doug Lamborn, who has represented the district since 2007. It is by far the most Republican district in Colorado.

Sixth District (2010 Cook PVI: R+8; R 1983–present). The Sixth District is located in central Colorado; it includes much of the southern part of metropolitan Denver and surrounding areas. The Sixth District is represented by Republican Mike Coffman, former Colorado Secretary of State. The seat has been held by a Republican since its creation after the 1980 Census.

Seventh District (2010 Cook PVI: D+4; R 2003–2007, D 2007–present). The Seventh District, the state's most competitive, encompasses much of the northern counties surrounding Denver. The district is currently represented by Democrat Ed Perlmutter, now serving his second term.

tive congressional districts that contain urban areas, which has contributed to Democratic success in those districts.

As table 0.5 illustrates, this trend is readily apparent if we look at the registration totals in Colorado's five largest counties. Democratic gains were most pronounced in Jefferson and Arapahoe Counties, which had been Republican-dominated; Democrats' advantages also increased in Denver and Boulder Counties. Except for El Paso County, which is strongly Republican, Democrats added to their numbers at rates above the statewide average of 20 percent in

TABLE 0.3. Colorado house elections, 2002–2008

Year	3rd District	4th District	7th District
2008	Salazar (D) 62%	Markey (D) 55%	Perlmutter (D) 63%
	Wolf (R) 38%	Musgrave (R) 45%	Lerew (R) 37%
2006	Salazar (D) 61%	Musgrave (R) 46%	Perlmutter (D) 55%
	Tipton (R) 37%	Paccione (D) 43%	O'Donnell (R) 42%
2004	Salazar (D) 50%	Musgrave (R) 51%	Beauprez (R) 55%
	Walcher (R) 47%	Matsunaka (D) 45%	Thomas (D) 43%
2002	McInnis (R) 66%	Musgrave (R) 55%	Beauprez (R) 47%*
	Berckefeldt (D) 31%	Matsunaka (D) 42%	Feeley (D) 47%

* Beauprez won the 7th District in 2002.
Source: Colorado Secretary of State 2002, 2004, 2006, 2008.
Note: Totals may not add up to 100%, as minor party candidates are not included; percentages rounded to
nearest integer.

TABLE 0.4. Colorado voter registration trends, 1996–2008

	Democrats	*Chg. 2004–2008 (%)*	*Republicans*	*Chg. 2004–2008 (%)*	*Unaffiliated*	*Chg. 2004–2008 (%)*	*Total*
2008	1,051,643	12	1,063,347	−5	1,069,294	3	3,184,284
2006	904,767		1,070,190		1,013,177		2,988,134
2004	942,025		1,118,597		1,024,973		3,085,595
2000	863,749		1,022,019		998,189		2,883,957
1996	719,230		824,222		742,051		2,285,503
2008 Proportion	33.00%		33.40%		33.60%		

Sources: Colorado Secretary of State 2004, 2006, 2008; telephone call to secretary of state's office by Kyle
Saunders, data unknown.

three of these five counties between 2002 and 2008. At the same time, the numbers of Republicans declined precipitously in four of those counties, well below
the flat trend illustrated in table 0.4. Even in El Paso County, where Republicans
added just over 7 percent to their rolls between 2002 and 2008, Democrats outpaced them twofold, at just over 15 percent. In sum, over the time period 2002
to 2008, Democrats gained in each of these five counties and grew by leaps and
bounds in Adams, Larimer, and Weld Counties.

TABLE 0.5. Registration trends in Colorado's five largest counties, 2002–2008

Arapahoe

	Democrats	% of total	% chg from 2002	Republicans	% of total	% chg from 2002	Unaffiliated	% of total	% chg from 2002	Democrats-Republicans
2008	119,454	34.95	31.74	114,078	33.37	−6.33	108,283	31.68	2.61	5,376
2006	100,476			120,179			109,109			−19,703
2004	106,690			133,885			122,970			−27,195
2002	90,674	28.52		121,786	38.30		105,526	33.19		−31,112

Boulder

	Democrats	% of total	% chg from 2002	Republicans	% of total	% chg from 2002	Unaffiliated	% of total	% chg from 2002	Democrats-Republicans
2008	90,382	41.85	26.87	44,377	20.55	−16.63	81,207	37.60	5.63	46,005
2006	77,481			48,311			82,633			29,170
2004	77,717			51,924			83,527			25,793
2002	71,240	35.38		53,231	26.44		76,878	38.18		18,009

Denver

	Democrats	% of total	% chg from 2002	Republicans	% of total	% chg from 2002	Unaffiliated	% of total	% chg from 2002	Democrats-Republicans
2008	200,988	48.89	30.32	71,736	17.45	−8.34	138,386	33.66	25.58	129,252
2006	159,597			70,380			127,231			89,217
2004	169,584			79,074			132,115			90,510
2002	154,228	45.01		78,267	22.84		110,195	32.16		75,961

continued on next page

TABLE 0.5—continued

El Paso

	Democrats	% of total	% chg from 2002	Republicans	% of total	% chg from 2002	Unaffiliated	% of total	% chg from 2002	Democrats-Republicans
2008	85,259	22.92	15.30	165,916	44.60	7.13	120,833	32.48	12.30	−80,657
2006	73,478			162,934			113,052			−89,456
2004	77,485			164,884			112,149			−87,399
2002	73,943	21.98		154,867	46.04		107,599	31.98		−80,924

Jefferson

	Democrats	% of total	% chg from 2002	Republicans	% of total	% chg from 2002	Unaffiliated	% of total	% chg from 2002	Democrats-Republicans
2008	118,114	32.01	13.66	127,215	34.48	−9.53	123,615	33.51	4.64	−9,101
2006	105,950			132,978			119,159			−27,028
2004	110,016			142,925			122,213			−32,909
2002	103,920	28.65		140,610	38.77		118,137	32.57		−36,690

Source: Colorado Secretary of State 2002, 2004, 2006, 2008.

POPULATION GROWTH AND DEMOGRAPHIC CHANGE

The Democratic registration gains were the result of a number of factors, including rapid population growth, demographic changes, and aggressive voter identification and registration campaigns by the party, affiliated interest groups, and candidates. These factors and others will be discussed in greater detail in chapter 2 of this volume.

Colorado's population has boomed in recent decades, increasing by 50 percent since 1990. From 2000–2009, Colorado's population grew by 16.8 percent, making it the seventh–fastest-growing state in the nation (US Census Bureau 2009a). Most of this explosive growth has been concentrated in the increasingly urbanized Front Range communities that stretch between Colorado Springs to the south and Fort Collins to the north. Just over half of the state's population resides in the Denver metropolitan area, the state's largest. Overall, the Denver area grew by 12 percent from 2000–2007, but by far the most explosive growth was in Denver's outer suburbs (Douglas, Elbert, Park, Gilpin, Clear Creek, and Broomfield Counties), which increased by nearly 42 percent, making it the state's fastest-growing region. The city of Denver and its inner suburbs (Adams, Arapahoe, and Jefferson Counties) grew at much lower rates; Colorado Springs, the state's second-largest metropolitan area, has increased by 12.8 percent since 2000; while Boulder, the third-largest, has grown by just 6.8 percent during that period. The population of the sixteen counties in the western and northern parts of the state—including the Fort Collins–Loveland, Greeley, and Grand Junction metropolitan areas—increased by 18.8 percent; this region is now home to approximately one-fifth of the state's residents (Frey and Teixeira 2008: 9–10).

Like other rapidly growing states in the region, Colorado's growth has resulted from a number of developments. About half of the total increase since 2000 was attributable to the number of births exceeding that of deaths, approximately 30 percent resulted from migration from other states, and immigration from other nations accounted for the remainder (US Census Bureau 2009b). As one might expect, the state has thus become more racially and ethnically diverse. In 1990, whites constituted nearly 81 percent of the state's population; by 2008, that figure had shrunk to 71 percent. Conversely, Hispanics increased from 12.9 percent to nearly 20 percent of the state's total population (US Census Bureau 2008). In fact, in the period 2000–2006, the state's minority population grew by 17 percent, nearly double the rate for whites. In Denver's outer suburbs, the state's fastest-growing region, the minority share of eligible voters increased by 66 percent. Moreover, the Hispanic growth rate was much higher in Denver's outer suburbs (a phenomenal 61 percent), Denver's inner suburbs (24 percent), and the state's western and northern regions (23 percent) (Frey and Teixeira 2008: 13; State of Colorado Division of Local Government 2010). In short, the minority vote has steadily grown as a share of the state's eligible voters, while the white vote has declined.

The state's economy has changed as well over the past twenty years. Employment in agriculture and in resource extractive industries such as mining and logging has declined, while tourism, information technology, energy, health and financial services, and real estate have fueled the state's population growth (Lang, Sarzynski, and Muro 2008: 22). As a result, the state's economy is more diversified than in the past. Growth in these industries has contributed to increased demand for educated workers. Census figures (2008) show that the share of the population with at least a bachelor's degree has grown and now constitutes approximately one-third of voting-age residents. In fact, Colorado ranks fourth nationally in the percentage of the population with at least a bachelor's degree (Frey and Teixeira 2008: 5). Statewide, since 2000 the number of white college graduates has increased by 16 percent; the growth has been most pronounced in Denver's outer suburbs, the western and northern regions, and Colorado Springs (Frey and Teixeira 2008: 7). In contrast, the growth rate among the white working class has been much lower, and that group's share of eligible voters has actually declined.

Why does this matter politically? Because the state's population and demographic shifts can partially explain changes in voter registration figures and election results. Part of the reason Colorado has shifted toward the Democrats in recent years is because of rapid population growth in specific counties and demographic groups. The areas of the state that have been growing the fastest have also been experiencing the largest net registration gains for Democrats, in part because of the high growth rates for Hispanics and white college graduates in these areas. In contrast, the demographic group that has been most supportive of Republicans in recent years—white working-class voters—has declined as a share of the state's eligible voters, especially in the aforementioned counties (Frey and Teixeira 2008).

Republicans have done best in the sparsely populated counties on the eastern plains that contain less than 7 percent of the state's population. This region had the lowest population growth rate in the state during the years 2000–2007; in fact, half of the counties in this region registered population declines. Moreover, the eastern part of the state was the only region where the percentage of white working-class voters increased during that same period. According to William Frey and Ruy Teixeira (2008: 20), "One clear pattern is that a good chunk of the counties that gave the GOP big margin gains between 1988 and 2004 are also counties that are losing population . . . In fact, every shrinking county, with a couple of minor exceptions, moved sharply toward the Republicans over this time period."

The fastest-growing groups in the heavily populated and rapidly growing areas around the Denver, Boulder, and Fort Collins–Loveland metropolitan

- Colorado's population is primarily concentrated in its metropolitan areas; in fact, just over half of the state's voters reside in the Denver metropolitan area. Nearly 80 percent of its estimated 5 million residents live in the rapidly growing urban corridor along the Front Range of the Rocky Mountains, most within a two-hour drive of Denver.

- Areas of Democratic strength include: the City of Denver; the college towns of Fort Collins and Boulder; Pueblo; and a few western ski resort counties. The Republicans are strongest in: Colorado Springs, the headquarters of numerous Christian organizations, including Focus on the Family; some Denver suburbs; the sparsely populated rural eastern third of the state; and the rapidly growing metropolitan areas near Greeley and Grand Junction.

- The most hotly contested areas of the state are the populous suburbs surrounding Denver; many of these have trended Democratic in recent elections.

- Colorado's population has increased 50 percent since 1990; only 41.1 percent of current residents were born in state.

- The median income in Colorado is $55,517, twelfth highest in the nation (U.S. Census Bureau 2008).

- Colorado is relatively well-educated, ranking second in percentage of college graduates (32.7 percent) (U.S. Census Bureau 2008).

- Like most states in the Mountain West, Colorado is disproportionately white (71 percent), but the rapidly growing Hispanic population now constitutes 20 percent of the state's overall population. In fact, Colorado has one of the highest proportions of Hispanic citizens of any U.S. state; only five states have a higher percentage.

- Colorado is home to a large proportion of military veterans, who constitute 14 percent of the population.

- Colorado's overall population, like many other Western states, is predominantly Christian (65 percent). Of this group, a plurality (44 percent) is Protestant, 23 percent are evangelicals, 19 percent are Catholic, and nearly one third express no religious affiliation (Pew Forum 2008, The Association of Religion Data Archives 2000). The Catholic population has increased in recent years as the Hispanic share of population has grown.

- Just 10.3 percent of the state's population is over the age of 65, ranking the state 47th nationally (U.S. Census Bureau 2009). The median age in Colorado is 35.8, making it the tenth youngest state.

- Colorado's economy is diverse, but is focused primarily on white-collar technology and energy jobs. 64.5 percent of the Colorado work force is employed in white-collar positions, while 21 percent is employed in blue collar and 14.5 percent in gray collar jobs. The public sector in Colorado is relatively small, constituting just 14 percent of the population. The most prevalent industrial sectors of Colorado's economy include professional (29 percent), trade (15 percent), and manufacturing (14 percent). Construction, finance, and agriculture also play important roles in Colorado's economy.

Source: All information, except where noted, is from Barone and Cohen's *Almanac of American Politics* 2008 on Colorado.

areas are Hispanics and white college graduates (sidebar, p. 13). These are the regions in which voter registration figures have changed dramatically in recent years, at least in part because of demographic shifts. These are also areas where Republicans used to be dominant.

There are other reasons for the shift in party control, some dating back several decades. In the mid-1970s Republican voters began sending increasingly conservative members to the state legislature. An early group of these members was self-identified as the House "crazies." The "crazies" were libertarian in political orientation and pressed relentlessly for ever smaller government. Over several decades this cadre of conservatives grew in number, melded a taste for social and cultural conservatism with its fiscal libertarianism, and eventually dominated the Colorado Republican Party. Over time, these individuals' growing influence became increasingly troublesome for the Republican Party, as reflected in the tension between the party's moderate wing and conservatives who pressed for a social-cultural agenda. Primary battles within the party became nasty and damaged the political fortunes of Republican candidates in general elections. Further, as the state faced increasingly difficult budgetary problems, the fiscal stance of the party's dominant conservative element rendered it incapable of developing a forward-looking agenda for the state.

DIRECT DEMOCRACY, FISCAL POLICY, AND MORE

Paralleling this transformation in party control has been the increasing use of Colorado's initiative process and voter adoption of measures that have altered both the state's policies and its institutions. Paramount among the changes produced by direct democracy are constitutional measures that have impacted state and local finances as well as term limits, especially as they have affected the General Assembly.

Colorado's constitution has provided for the initiative, referendum, and recall since 1910. For some years following the addition of these procedures to the constitution, the initiative was employed with some frequency, but by the late 1920s its use had dropped off considerably. Then, beginning around 1970, political activists seemed to rediscover the process, and 51 percent of initiated measures have been on the ballot since that date. Every general election ballot now includes a string of citizen-initiated proposals.

Post-1970s ballot measures that have affected fiscal policy include the Gallagher Amendment, TABOR, and Amendment 23 addressing K–12 school funding. Collectively, these and other measures with less impact have made budgeting increasingly complicated and difficult. Term limits—adopted for state legislative and executive positions in 1990 and expanded to local governments in 1994—have weakened political leaders, most notably in the General Assembly.

Indeed, one might argue that the combination of popularly enacted fiscal limitations and term limits has stripped Colorado government of its republican character and pushed the lawmaking process into the hands of a 4.5 million-member committee.

This recent use of direct democracy's initiative process has diminished the authority of the state legislature, limited tenure for elected officials in the legislative and executive branches of both the state and local governments, and shifted control of fiscal policy from representative institutions to the broader public. The consequences of these changes have, in the eyes of most close observers of Colorado's government and politics, been damaging and have undermined representative government.

Perhaps in a few years, Colorado's politics will again change in significant fashion. What is clear is that Colorado politics and government today in no way resemble the Colorado of three or four decades ago. The purpose of this volume is to provide a portrait of contemporary Colorado politics and government and place it in the context of the changes that have occurred over the past several decades.

CONTENTS OF THE BOOK

The chapters in this volume focus on several dimensions of the state's politics. Broadly, they address Colorado's apparent shift from a "red" to a "blue" state, the underlying demographic and political forces that help explain this trend, institutional changes produced by increasing use of the initiative process, and the political and institutional consequences of these myriad developments. By situating contemporary events in their historical context, the authors of each chapter are able to go beyond simply describing and analyzing the current state of affairs in favor of explanations rooted in the history of Colorado politics. In addition, this approach makes it clear that the current state of affairs analyzed and discussed by the volume's contributors is certain to change yet again.

The first five chapters examine Colorado elections. In the opening chapter, Robert Loevy paints the broad picture of Colorado's political landscape by tracking partisan shifts over time in both state and national offices. Loevy notes that, on balance, Republicans enjoyed an advantage for several decades—until 2004. Robert Duffy and Kyle Saunders's discussion of federal elections in chapter 2 shows that demographic changes and associated voter registration patterns have subsequently shifted the advantage to the Democrats; they also argue that a Republican move to the political right and a superior Democratic political strategy help explain the current Democratic dominance of Colorado's elective federal offices. In chapter 3, Seth Masket looks at the 2008 presidential race in Colorado through the lens of the state's caucus system and the Obama and Clinton campaigns' quest for Democratic delegates. Masket concludes that the distinction between the Obama and Clinton strategies in the race for delegates is reflected in the vast differences in the number of field offices the two campaigns opened in Colorado. He calls attention to the shifting political winds nationally and the resultant national focus on the Mountain West and Colorado in particular.

In chapter 4, Daniel Smith paints a historical picture of Colorado's use of the initiative process. He describes the state's adoption of direct democracy in the Progressive Era, the impact of its use on minority citizens, and the impact of money on ballot issues. Finally, he provides an interesting look at Douglas Bruce, arguably the best-known user of the initiative in Colorado. Chapter 5, by Larimer County clerk and recorder Scott Doyle, his staff, and John Straayer, examines the logistical changes in the election system at the local level with an in-depth discussion of the development of "vote centers." Vote centers have replaced precincts as voting locations; combined with the increased use of mail balloting and opportunities for voters to submit their ballots early, they have changed campaign tactics and election day routines for local officials.

The next three chapters examine changes in the Colorado legislature. In chapter 6, John Straayer tracks more than two decades of change in the General Assembly and demonstrates how term limits have weakened leadership, increased partisanship, and stripped the legislature of its institutional and policy history; how successful citizen initiatives have removed much of the legislature's fiscal authority; and how Republican domination came to an end. In addition to term limits and successful citizen initiatives, an internal reform known as GAVEL (Give a Vote to Every Legislator) has changed the internal operation of the General Assembly. Mike Binder, Vladimir Kogan, and Thad Kousser describe and analyze the adoption and consequences of GAVEL in chapter 7. They demonstrate that GAVEL has weakened party caucuses and leadership and opened the door for "mavericks" in both parties to join forces and push legislation in a moderate direction. In chapter 8, Courtenay Daum examines the effect of term limits on the composition of the General Assembly. Contrary to expectations, term limits did not result in the election of substantially more women to the General Assembly, but the distribution of women legislators by political party did change dramatically. Daum explains that the rightward ideological migration of the Republican Party appears to have interacted with term limits to decrease the number of female Republicans, while the number of female Democrats increased significantly.

The final two chapters examine Colorado fiscal policy. In chapter 9, John Straayer analyzes the ways increased use of citizen-initiated ballot measures interacted with legislative action to produce contradictory policies and what he calls a "fiscal train wreck." Straayer concludes that current political alignments may preclude any "repair" of the system and the return of fiscal authority to the state legislature. In contrast, chapter 10 casts state fiscal policy in a different light. Scott Moore focuses attention on two specific policy areas—the development of highway funding policy and the Great Outdoors Colorado program—to demonstrate how the "architecture" of Colorado's fiscal policy has developed piece by piece as a result of political victories by a parade of self-interest coalitions. The result is an array of earmarked funding streams that will likely continue to proliferate in coming years.

The volume concludes with a brief epilogue by the editors that discusses and evaluates the results of the 2010 election. That election proved to be significant at both the national and state levels, and the epilogue revisits and updates many of the chapter authors' contributions in light of these latest political and electoral developments.

This volume demonstrates that changes are afoot in Colorado politics, but this story is not over. Just as twenty-four years of Democratic control of the governorship ended with the election of Republican Bill Owens in 1998 and the forty-year Republican reign in the General Assembly ended in 2004, the events and patterns described in this volume will give way to new developments. Indeed, in the context of continued wars, deep divisions over federal spending, health care, and severe state budget problems here in Colorado, the political winds continue to swirl. The key question is whether the changes noted here have enhanced or detracted from our political institutions' ability to address serious issues.

NOTES
....

1. The Cook Partisan Voting Index (CPVI), sometimes referred to simply as the Partisan Voting Index (PVI), is a measurement of how strongly an American congressional district or state leans toward one political party compared to the nation as a whole. It was developed in 1997 by Charlie Cook of the *Cook Political Report*, a nonpartisan political newsletter, working with Polidata, a political statistics analysis firm. The index for each congressional district is derived by averaging its results from the prior two presidential elections and comparing them to national results. The index indicates which party's candidate was more successful in that district, as well as the number of percentage points by which its results exceeded the national average. The index is formatted as a letter + a number; for example, in a district whose CPVI score is R+2, recent Republican presidential candidates received 2 percentage points more votes than the national average. Likewise, a CPVI score of D+3 shows that the Democrats received 3 percentage points more votes than the national average.

REFERENCES
....

Association of Religion Data Archives. 2000. "State Membership Report, Colorado (2000)." Available at http://www.thearda.com/mapsreports/reports/state/08–2000. asp. Accessed December 12, 2008.

Barone, Michael, and Richard E. Cohen. 2008. *The Almanac of American Politics*. Washington, DC: National Journal Group. Available at http://www.nationaljournal.com/almanac/2008/states/co. Accessed December 2, 2008.

Colorado Constitution.

Colorado Secretary of State. 2002. "December 2002 Voter Registration Numbers by Party." Copy faxed to authors from the secretary of state's office.

———. 2004. "December 2004 Voter Registration Numbers by Party." Available at http://www.elections.colorado.gov/Default.aspx?tid=480&vmid=134. Accessed November 25, 2008.

———. 2006. "December 2006 Voter Registration Numbers by Party." Available at http://www.elections.colorado.gov/Default.aspx?PageMenuID=1961&ShowVM =1451TitleVM=2006%20Voter%20Registration%20Numbers. Accessed November 25, 2008.

———. 2008. "December 2008 Voter Registration Numbers: Voter Recap by Party." Available at http://www.elections.colorado.gov/WWW/default/2008%20Voter%20 Registration%20Numbers/October_22_2008/vr_stats_by_party_10.22.2008.pdf. Accessed November 25, 2008.

Fermanich, Mark. 2011. "Colorado's Fiscal Future: We Get What We Pay For." Fiscal Policy Series Report 2011-100-01. Denver: School of Public Affairs, University of Colorado at Denver.

Frey, William H., and Ruy Teixeira. 2008. *The Political Geography of the Intermountain West: The New Swing Region*. Washington, DC: Brookings Institution.

Kirk, Ron. 2009. How Colorado Compares in State and Local Taxes. Colorado Legislative Council Staff Memorandum, July 6.

Lang, Robert E., Andrea Sarzynski, and Mark Muro. 2008. *Mountain Megas: America's Newest Metropolitan Places and a Federal Partnership to Help Them Prosper*. Washington, DC: Brookings Institution.

Lorch, Robert S. 2003. *Colorado's Government: Structures, Politics, Administration and Policy*. Colorado Springs: Center for the Study of Government and the Individual.

National Journal. 2010. "The Almanac of American Politics: Colorado." Available at http://www.nationaljournal.com/almanac/area/co/. Accessed May 25, 2010.

Pew Forum on Religious and Public Life. 2008. "US Religious Landscape Survey." Available at http://religions.pewforum.org/reports. Accessed December 12, 2008.

State of Colorado Division of Local Government, State Demography Office. 2010. "Race and Hispanic Origin for Colorado and Counties." Available at http://dola.colorado. gov/dlg/demog/population/race/colraceper.pdf. Accessed January 10, 2010.

US Census Bureau. 2008. "Quick Facts: Colorado." Available at http://quickfacts.census. gov/qfd/states/08000.html. Accessed January 10, 2010.

———. 2009a. "Cumulative Estimates of Resident Population Change for the United States, Regions, States, and Puerto Rico and Region and State Rankings: April 1, 2000 to July 1, 2009 (NST-EST2009–02)." Available at http://www.census.gov/ popest/states/NSTpop-chg.html. Accessed January 10, 2010.

———. 2009b. "Estimates of the Components of Resident Population Change for the United States, Regions, States, and Puerto Rico: July 1, 2008 to July 1, 2009 (NST-EST2009–05)." Available at http://www.census.gov/popest/states/NST-comp-chg. html. Accessed January 10, 2010.

CHAPTER ONE

Colorado: Sometimes Red and Sometimes Blue

Robert D. Loevy

This chapter provides a historical overview of Colorado electoral politics, including both federal and state elections, and demonstrates that the state of Colorado is very much available to either political party. Over the long term, the state has voted for both Democrats and Republicans in major statewide contests such as US president, state governor, and US Senate. From 2004 to 2008, there was a discernable Democratic trend in Colorado voting. This trend, which paralleled a nationwide shift to the Democratic Party, was not unusual for the state and fit with traditional Colorado voting behavior.

In the years since the end of World War II, Republicans have won more elected offices than Democrats. Notably, in Colorado, Republicans have done particularly well at winning presidential elections and since 1967 have controlled both houses of the state legislature for long periods. The Democrats, however, controlled the governorship for twenty-four years from 1975 to 1999, and both Democrats and Republicans have had success winning election to the US Senate and House of Representatives.

In elections from 2004 to 2008, Colorado Democrats made solid gains. In 2004 the Democrats elected a US senator (after a Republican retired) and gained control of both houses of the state legislature from the Republicans. Two years later, in 2006, Democrats won the governorship (replacing a term-limited Republican) and maintained control of the state legislature. Then, in 2008 the Democrats won Colorado's nine electoral votes for president, captured a second US Senate seat (again after a Republican retired), and continued to hold both houses of the state legislature. Along with all these gains, from 2004 to 2008 the Democrats switched Colorado's delegation to the US House of Representatives from a ratio of five-to-two Republican-Democratic to five-to-two Democratic-Republican.

The 2010 elections blunted the Democratic Party's recent winning record in Colorado, although not completely. Despite a nationwide tide in favor of the Republican Party, Democrats in Colorado succeeded in defending a seat in the US Senate and retaining control of the state governorship. Republicans won all the other major statewide races, however, and gained two seats in the US House of Representatives. Republicans also gained a one-vote majority in the state house of representatives, but Democrats remained in control in the state senate.

Colorado tends to follow national voting patterns while, during the forty-two years from 1962 to 2004, slightly favoring the Republican Party. The Republicans' advantage in Colorado politics resulted in Colorado being identified as a red state for the past several decades. Given recent Democratic successes, however, the question now becomes: is Colorado a blue state? That is, were the impressive Democratic gains in Colorado from 2004 to 2008 merely the result of a national trend toward the Democrats in the final years of Republican George W. Bush's presidency, or do they represent a significant and permanent shift to the Democrats in Colorado partisan voting behavior?

COLORADO GOVERNORS: WHERE DEMOCRATS DOMINATE

In the long sweep of Colorado history, from statehood in 1876 to 2010, Colorado elected more Democrats (twenty-three) than Republicans (eighteen) as governor. Starting in 1974, Democrats dominated the Colorado governorship. For over three-and-a-half decades, from 1974 to 2010, there were four Democratic governors, who were elected to a total of thirty-two years, and only one Republican governor, who served just eight years (see table 1.1). Two Democratic governors, Richard Lamm (1974–1986) and Roy Romer (1986–1998), each served twelve years in office, back-to-back. For all but two of those twenty-four years, however, Lamm and Romer had to deal with a Republican state legislature.

Richard Lamm first emerged on the Colorado political scene when he led the opposition to holding the 1976 Winter Olympics in Colorado. State financing for the Olympics was petitioned onto the general election ballot in 1972, and

TABLE 1.1. Colorado gubernatorial elections, 1974–2010

Year	Republican %	Democratic %
1974	46.2	53.8
1978	39.6	60.4
1982	32.5	67.5
1986	41.3	58.7
1990	36.4	63.6
1994	41.1	58.9
1998	50.5	49.5
2002	65.0	35.0
2006	41.3	58.7
2010	17.9	82.1
Average percentages, 1974–2010	41.2 R	58.8 D (10 elections)
Average percentages, 1994–2010	43.2 R	56.8 D (5 most recent elections)

Sources: Colorado Secretary of State. 2010 data. Available at http://www.sos.state.co.us/pubs/elections. Accessed March 31, 2011; CQ Press Voting and Elections Collection. 1960–2008 data. Available at http://0-library.cqpress.com.tiger.coloradocollege.edu/elections. Accessed March 31, 2011.

voters rejected state participation and terminated the Olympics proposal. Lamm clearly had established himself as a leading spokesperson for environmental and "anti-growth" sentiments in Colorado.

Lamm ran for governor on the Democratic ticket in 1974, the year of the Watergate sweep in US electoral politics. Republican president Richard M. Nixon had resigned the presidency because of his role in covering up a Republican break-in and robbery at Democratic National Headquarters in the Watergate Hotel in Washington, DC. Voter revulsion over Watergate caused Democrats to be elected over Republicans throughout the nation, and Lamm rode that Democratic tide into the governor's office in Colorado.

As governor, Lamm's legislative priorities often ran into resistance from the Republican-controlled legislature. Notably, Lamm's efforts to preserve the environment, as well as his efforts to address runaway population growth and urban development in Colorado, were frustrated by Republican legislators. His major victory was stopping plans to build an interstate belt highway around the city of Denver through the Denver suburbs. The Republican legislature trumped that victory by building much of the belt highway as a state highway (Colorado 470) and a toll highway.[1]

Maximizing the power of incumbency, Lamm was easily reelected to a second term in 1978 and a third term in 1982. Despite those convincing victories, Lamm had no coattails, and the Republicans continued to dominate both houses of the state legislature. He spent much of his third term giving speeches about the long-range effects of unrestricted population growth, fueled by lax enforcement of immigration laws, on government finances. His dreary view of the future earned him the nickname "Governor Gloom."[2]

Richard Lamm declined to run for a fourth term as governor in 1986, although most observers argued that he would have had no problem being reelected a fourth time. His successor was another Democrat, state treasurer Roy Romer, who benefited from the fact that 1986 was the sixth year of Republican Ronald Reagan's presidency. Opposition to Reagan that had built up over his first six years in the White House helped Romer win as a Democrat in Colorado.

Roy Romer appeared to genuinely enjoy being Colorado's governor, even though he never had the political luxury of a Democratic majority in the state legislature. He cast himself as the major advocate of economic development in Colorado. To that end, he played a leading role in helping the city of Denver build a new and larger airport (Denver International Airport, usually referred to as DIA). In addition, he intervened in, and helped settle, a public schoolteachers' strike in Denver. Romer seemed to be going everywhere and doing everything in Colorado, despite the notable lack of cooperation from the Republican-controlled state legislature.[3]

With his colorful persona and activist attitude, Romer had no trouble getting reelected to a second term in 1990 and a third term in 1994. He could have easily been reelected to a fourth term in 1998, but state voters had adopted a two-term limit (eight years) for the Colorado governorship in the early 1990s, which applied to Romer beginning with his second term in office. Roy Romer was thus the first Colorado governor to be forced to relinquish the gubernatorial office because of term limits. Republicans regained the governorship in 1998 in a very tight contest. Former state legislator and state treasurer Bill Owens was elected and then easily reelected in 2002. During his first six years in office, Republicans controlled both houses of the state legislature. In 2004, however, Democrats won both the Colorado House of Representatives and the Colorado Senate. Thus during his last two years in office, Bill Owens was forced to work with a state legislature dominated by the opposition political party.

One highlight of Owens's governorship was gaining state voter approval for financing a major statewide highway rebuilding program, the centerpiece of which was T-Rex, a major reconstruction and expansion of I-25 south of Denver. Late in his second term in office, Owens joined with the Democratic majority in the state legislature in getting voters to approve Referendum C, a so-called time-out from tax limitation in Colorado that strengthened the state's finances.

In 2006 the Democrats regained the governorship while retaining majorities in both houses of the General Assembly. For the first time in decades, Democrats had unified control of the governorship and both houses of the Colorado legislature. The victorious Democrat was Bill Ritter, who first came to political attention as the Denver district attorney. Similar to both Lamm and Romer, Democratic candidate Ritter benefited from running for governor during a big year for Democratic candidates nationwide. In 2006, voter dissatisfaction with Republican president George W. Bush, who had served for six years, contributed to Democratic electoral victories across the United States.

After three years in office, Governor Ritter made a surprise announcement in January 2010: he was stepping down and would not seek the Democratic nomination for Colorado governor. Ritter cited family responsibilities as the main reason for leaving the race, but another factor was the large budget deficits facing Colorado's state government because of the 2008–2009 economic recession.

As it turned out, the Democrats succeeded in nominating a strong candidate to run in Ritter's place. Denver's popular mayor, John Hickenlooper, took up the Democratic gubernatorial cause in the 2010 election. A hard-fought and divisive Republican primary produced a right-wing, inexperienced Republican nominee. The situation was complicated further when former Republican US representative Tom Tancredo ran as a third-party candidate, thus splitting the Republican vote. Democrat Hickenlooper won easily on election day.

If the Colorado governorship shows one strong historical pattern, it is that Democrats tend to win in the sixth year of a Republican presidential administration: Democrat Dick Lamm was elected in 1974, the sixth year of the Nixon-Ford Republican presidential administration; Democrat Roy Romer won his first term as chief executive of the Centennial State in 1986, the sixth year of Republican Ronald Reagan's presidency; and Democrat Bill Ritter was elected to the Colorado governorship in 2006, the sixth year of Republican president George W. Bush's eight years in the White House. This rule also works for the two most recent Republicans who were elected governor. John Love was reelected in 1966, the sixth year of the Kennedy-Johnson Democratic presidential administration, while Bill Owens was elected in 1998, the sixth year of Democrat Bill Clinton's presidency. This leads to some advice for those who would be governor of Colorado: try to schedule your initial run for the office in the sixth year of an opposition-party presidency (Loevy 2006).

THE STATE LEGISLATURE: SURPRISING UPSET

In the twenty-four years from 1976 to 2000, the Republicans controlled both houses of the Colorado legislature by comfortable margins, but in 2000 the Democrats gained control of the Colorado Senate. Republicans regained control of the state senate in 2002, but in 2004 the Democrats took control of both houses and maintained that control through the 2006 and 2008 legislative elections.

A contributing factor in the Democratic takeover of both houses of the Colorado state legislature was the fact that the Democrats gained control of the state legislative redistricting process following the 2000 US Census. Colorado uses a bipartisan reapportionment commission to draw state legislative district boundaries. The Democrats gained a six-to-five majority on the reapportionment commission and proceeded to redistrict the state legislative seats to the Democratic Party's advantage.

It took only two elections, in 2002 and 2004, for the pro-Democratic redistricting to take full effect and put the Democrats in control of both houses of the state legislature in 2004. Other factors were in play, but redistricting was a major factor in the Democrats' sudden rise to power over both houses of the Colorado legislature for the first time in many years.

Following the 2010 election, Coloradans experienced something that rarely occurs in their state: split political party control of the state legislature. Republicans gained control of the lower house by just one vote, while Democrats remained in charge in the upper house. Perhaps no event better illustrated the even balance between the two political parties in contemporary Colorado than the fact that one party had narrow control of the state house of representatives while the other party still dominated the state senate.

COLORADO AND THE US SENATE: AN EVEN STRUGGLE

Both Democrats and Republicans have done well at winning US Senate elections in Colorado. For instance, between 1972 and 2010, the Democrats won eight US Senate elections in Colorado and the Republicans won six (see table 1.2).

In 1992 Democratic incumbent Tim Wirth retired from the US Senate after only one six-year term. He was succeeded by Democrat Ben Nighthorse Campbell, a Native American from western Colorado. In a spirited Democratic primary, Campbell, then a member of the Colorado House of Representatives, surprised many Colorado election observers by defeating former governor Richard Lamm.

Ben Nighthorse Campbell was one of Colorado's more colorful US senators. He manufactured and sold Native American jewelry and drove a Harley-Davidson motorcycle. After the Republicans gained control of the US Senate in 1994, Campbell switched to the Republican Party, ostensibly to have more power and influence as a member of the majority party. Campbell was easily reelected as a Republican in 1998.

In 1996, incumbent Republican US senator Hank Brown of Colorado joined Tim Wirth in retiring after only one six-year term. He was succeeded by Republican Wayne Allard, a veterinarian from northern Colorado. Allard was reelected to a second term in the Senate in 2002.

Colorado's 2004 senatorial election began with a shock when Campbell withdrew from his reelection campaign for health reasons. The Democrats nom-

TABLE 1.2. Colorado US Senate elections, 1972–2010

Year	Republican %	Democratic %
1972	49.5	50.5
1974	40.8	59.2
1978	59.3	40.7
1980	49.2	50.8
1984	65.0	35.0
1986	49.2	50.8
1990	57.2	42.8
1992	45.2	54.8
1996	52.6	47.4
1998	64.1	35.9
2002	52.3	47.7
2004	47.6	52.4
2008	44.6	55.4
2010	49.1	50.9
Average percentages, 1972–2010	51.8 R	48.2 D (14 elections)
Average percentages, 1998–2010	51.5 R	48.5 D (5 most recent elections)

Sources: Colorado Secretary of State. 2010 data. Available at http://www.sos.state.co.us/pubs/elections. Accessed March 31, 2011; CQ Press Voting and Elections Collection. 1960–2008 data. Available at http://0-library.cqpress.com.tiger.coloradocollege.edu/elections. Accessed March 31, 2011.

inated the incumbent Colorado attorney general, Ken Salazar, a Hispanic from southern Colorado. The Republicans recruited Pete Coors, a leading member of the family that owned the Coors brewery in Golden, Colorado. In a hard-fought election, Salazar defeated Coors.

In 2008 Republican incumbent US senator Wayne Allard kept a campaign promise and retired after two six-year terms. Senator Allard was proud of keeping his pledge to serve only twelve years in the US Senate. "I moved on and kept my commitment to voters," Allard concluded (Mulkern 2009).

US representative Mark Udall, a Democrat from the Boulder area, ran for the open seat against former US representative Bob Schaffer of northern Colorado. Udall had a liberal reputation within Colorado politics, while Schaffer was known as a dedicated conservative. Udall benefited from the strong 2008 Democratic trend and easily defeated Schaffer.

Thus in early 2009, Colorado had two Democratic US senators: Ken Salazar and Mark Udall. From 1995, when Campbell switched parties, to 2004, when Salazar prevailed over Schaffer, Republicans held both Senate seats. With Udall's election in 2008, Colorado went from having two Republican US senators to two Democratic US senators in just a four-year span.

There was a surprise development in Colorado's all-Democratic delegation to the US Senate, however. Newly elected US president Barack Obama appointed Colorado's Ken Salazar to be the new secretary of the interior. The Senate vacancy was quickly filled when Bill Ritter, Colorado's Democratic governor, appointed a political neophyte, Democrat Michael Bennet, to serve the last two years of Salazar's term. Bennet had never held elected office and was little-known outside the Denver area.

The Republicans nominated Ken Buck, the district attorney from Weld County in northern Colorado, to run for the US Senate in 2010. Buck ran as a staunch conservative in the Republican primary and succeeded in defeating a more moderate competitor, but in the course of doing so, Buck took a number of extreme positions that Bennet was able to attack in the general election. Despite the national Republican tide flowing throughout the United States in 2010, Democrat Michael Bennet eked out a narrow US Senate victory over the Republican Buck. When the dust cleared, Colorado still had two Democratic US senators.

How long will Colorado have two Democratic US senators? There is good reason to believe the situation will not endure. Throughout history, Colorado voters have demonstrated fluidity in Senate elections, as demonstrated by the fact that at any time it is normal for Colorado to have two Democratic US senators or two Republican US senators or one Democratic and one Republican US senator.

COLORADO AND THE US HOUSE OF REPRESENTATIVES: A THREE-SEAT SWITCH, THEN A SWITCH BACK

Following the 2000 US Census, Colorado was awarded a seventh US representative because of rapid gains in the state's population. In the 2001 redistricting process, Colorado Democrats sued the Republicans in an effort to gain a more favorable redistricting. The suit was successful when, for the first time in Colorado history, a Denver district court determined the US House redistricting plan for the state. Ordinarily, that job would have been done by the state legislature and the governor, at that time mainly dominated by Republicans (Brown 2001; Loevy 2002). Instead, the district court adopted a plan that had been prepared by the Democratic Party. The judge's reasoning was that the plan submitted by the Democrats was more equitable and contained less of a partisan bias than the one submitted by the Republicans (Martinez 2002; Martinez and Soraghan 2002; Quillen 2002).

As would be expected, the Democratic Party's redistricting plan bolstered its political prospects in US House of Representatives elections. In the four years from 2004 to 2008, the split in Colorado US House seats shifted from five-to-two Republican to five-to-two Democratic.

In the Fifth and Sixth US House Districts in Colorado, Democrats packed Republican voters, thereby minimizing the effect of the Republican vote in those two heavily Republican areas. In the First and Second Districts, Democrats packed as many Democrats as possible, thus creating two super-safe seats for the Democrats. In District Three, Democrats added a significant number of Democratic voters from the city of Pueblo, giving the district more of a Democratic flavor. A conservative Democrat, John Salazar, brother of former senator and Secretary of the Interior Ken Salazar, won the seat for the Democrats when it became open in 2004.

In US House District Four, the Democrats took a rural Republican district and added in voters from the northern part of the state who were somewhat more moderate. The seat stayed Republican until 2008, when the arch-conservative Republican incumbent Marilyn Musgrave was narrowly defeated by Democrat Betsy Markey. In District Seven, a newly created House district for Colorado following the 2000 Census, the Democrats linked a number of working-class and minority neighborhoods north and west of Denver. This seat stayed Republican for four years until the Republican incumbent vacated the seat to run for governor. A Democrat won the open seat in 2006.

But two-thirds of these Democratic gains in the Colorado delegation to the US House of Representatives from 2004 to 2008 were wiped out in the Republican electoral sweep of 2010. John Salazar, the Democratic incumbent in the Third District in southern Colorado, was defeated by Scott Tipton, a Republican from Cortez. In the Fourth District in eastern Colorado, Democratic Betsy Markey was ousted by Republican Cory Gardner. But in the Seventh District, the new seat in the US House created following the 2000 US Census, Democratic incumbent Ed Perlmutter was easily reelected.

It thus appears that gerrymandering, the drawing of district lines to favor one political party over the other, can be a factor in determining which party wins US House of Representatives elections in Colorado. It does not seem to matter whether the redistricting plan is adopted by a court or by the legislature and the governor. US House districts in Colorado are generally biased by gerrymandering to favor one political party over the other.

COLORADO AND THE PRESIDENCY: REPUBLICANS SHINE

In the thirteen presidential elections between 1960 and 2008, Republican candidates received an average of 53.9 percent of the vote in Colorado, compared to 46.1 percent for the Democrats. In those thirteen presidential elections, Republicans won Colorado ten times and Democrats prevailed only three times. Nationwide, Republicans won seven of those thirteen presidential elections and Democrats won six.

TABLE 1.3. Colorado voting in US presidential elections, 1960–2008

Year	Republican %	Democratic %
1960*	54.9	45.1
1964†	38.4	61.6
1968	55.0	45.0
1972	64.4	35.6
1976*	55.9	44.1
1980	63.9	36.1
1984	64.4	35.6
1988	54.0	46.0
1992	47.2	52.8
1996*	50.8	49.2
2000	54.5	45.5
2004	52.4	47.6
2008†	45.4	54.6
Average percentages, 1960–2008	53.9 R	46.1 D (13 elections)
Average percentages, 1992–2008	50.1 R	49.9 D (5 elections)

* Years in which the United States voted Democratic but Colorado voted Republican.
† Years in which the percentage of the Democratic popular vote in Colorado exceeded that of the United States as a whole. In all other years, the percentage of the Republican popular vote exceeded the US percentage.
Sources: Colorado Secretary of State. 2010 data. Available at http://www.sos.state.co.us/pubs/elections. Accessed March 31, 2011; CQ Press Voting and Elections Collection. 1960–2008 data. Available at http://0-library.cqpress.com.tiger.coloradocollege.edu/elections. Accessed March 31, 2011.

Democrats have fared better in the last five presidential elections. During this shorter period, from 1992 to 2008, Republicans averaged only 50.1 percent of Colorado's presidential vote compared to 49.9 percent for Democrats. These data suggest that by 2008, Colorado was beginning to lose some of its heavy Republican bias in presidential elections (see table 1.3).

Clearly, Colorado does not vote with the United States as a whole in every presidential contest. It has tended to favor Republican candidates for president, particularly if the national presidential election is close. On three occasions between 1960 and 2008, Colorado voted for the Republican candidate for president when the Democrat was winning nationally. The Republican candidates who won Colorado but lost the race for the White House were Richard Nixon in 1960, Gerald R. Ford in 1976, and Robert Dole in 1996.

Republican candidates for president can have long coattails in Colorado. The Republican presidential candidate with the longest coattails was former California governor Ronald Reagan, who swept Colorado in both the 1980 and 1984 presidential elections. Republicans dominated both houses of the state legislature in Colorado in the 1980s and early 1990s thanks to Reagan's great vote-getting power on Colorado's "down ballot."

That being said, presidential coattails are not always effective in Colorado. In 2004 incumbent Republican president George W. Bush was reelected to the White House and carried Colorado with 52.4 percent of the two-party vote. In that same election, however, the Democrats surprised nearly everyone by winning control of both the Colorado House of Representatives and the Colorado Senate. It was one of the first signs that the solid Republican grip on Colorado elections might be weakening, at least for a while.

In 2008 Democratic presidential candidate Barack Obama easily won the White House and swept Colorado with 54.6 percent of the two-party vote. Obama's popularity in Colorado helped the Democrats maintain the firm control of the state legislature they originally achieved in 2004.

Prior to the election of President Barack Obama in 2008, only two Democrats had won Colorado's electoral votes in the previous fifty-six years. In both those instances, Colorado voted heavily for the Republicans in the legislature two years later. Democratic president Lyndon Johnson won Colorado with 61.6 percent of the vote in 1964, but two years later Colorado Republicans took control of the lower house of the state legislature from the Democrats. Democratic president Bill Clinton carried Colorado in 1992 with 52.8 percent of the two-party vote, but two years later Republicans strengthened their control of the Colorado legislature in the nationwide 1994 anti-Clinton Republican sweep.

This pattern was half-broken in the 2010 state legislative elections. It was two years after Obama had won the presidential election in Colorado, but Republicans only succeeded in taking back the lower house of the state legislature. The state senate remained firmly in Democratic hands. This was simply more evidence that Colorado had truly become a competitive state between the two major political parties and was no longer a one-party or even a generally Republican state.

THE 2008 PRESIDENTIAL ELECTION:
COLORADO'S PRESIDENTIAL CAUCUSES

The quest for the Democratic presidential nomination in 2008 was a spirited contest. Former first lady Hillary Clinton, the wife of former president Bill Clinton and a US senator from New York, was running. Her major opponent was Illinois US senator Barack Obama, the first African American to make a competitive run for president of the United States.

Colorado's Iowa-style presidential caucuses were held on Super Tuesday, February 5, 2008, the earliest date allowed by national Democratic Party rules. Although many other states held presidential caucuses and primaries that evening, interest in the Democratic contest in Colorado was intense. Record numbers of Democrats (only registered Democrats were allowed to participate) turned out to support their candidates. The activist Democrats who attend precinct caucuses in Colorado tend to be very liberal and progressive; since Barack Obama was viewed as the more liberal of the two candidates, he easily defeated the more moderate Hillary Clinton in Colorado. In contrast, Colorado's Democratic primary election voters tend to be more moderate and middle of the road than Democratic caucus goers. There was good reason to argue that if Colorado had held a Democratic primary rather than caucuses in 2008, the more centrist Hillary Clinton would have won.

For the Republicans in 2008, there was considerable interest in the presidential caucuses but nothing to match the excitement on the Democratic side. The Republican caucuses in Colorado tend to attract highly conservative voters; as a result, former Massachusetts governor Mitt Romney—a newly converted conservative—easily defeated centrist Arizona US senator John McCain in Colorado's Republican presidential caucuses.

Colorado's presidential caucuses received considerable media attention, which, coupled with the enthusiasm of Obama's supporters, contributed to the Democratic Party's success in Colorado in 2008. Thousands of Coloradans took the opportunity to work and vote for Obama in the caucuses. Undoubtedly, many of them also supported him in the general election in November.

THE 2008 DEMOCRATIC NATIONAL CONVENTION

In the early 2000s, leading Democratic Party elected officials in Denver campaigned to lure the 2008 Democratic National Convention to Colorado. Recent public improvements in Denver, such as the building of the Pepsi Center sports arena and the remodeling of the downtown convention center, had given Denver the facilities it needed to compete to be the Democrat's 2008 convention city. The final choice came down to Denver or New York. Thanks in part to the energetic campaign by Colorado Democrats and the national party's desire to broaden its appeal geographically, Denver was chosen.

The 2008 Democratic National Convention turned out to be one of the greatest political events in Colorado history. Barack Obama, who won the Democratic nomination for president, was a colorful campaigner who brought his charisma and great speaking ability to Denver. The convention ran smoothly, with virtually none of the intra-party fights that can ruin a national political party convention. The highlight was Obama's acceptance speech in Denver's new outdoor football stadium, Invesco Field at Mile High. The weather cooperated, and the speech was given under perfect conditions. Most of the people in the giant stadium that evening were Coloradans.

The 2008 Democratic National Convention in Denver further strengthened Obama's popularity in Colorado, enabling him to build on the momentum he received in the state by winning Colorado's presidential caucuses. The final payoff came in the general election in the fall of 2008, when Barack Obama became only the third Democrat to win Colorado's electoral votes since the 1940s.

COLORADO'S PRESIDENTIAL VOTING PATTERNS

Colorado's population has been growing since World War II, and that high growth rate continued in the first decade of the 2000s. At the time of the 2008 presidential election, the US Census Bureau estimated that Colorado's population was approximately 4.95 million. By July 2009, Colorado's estimated population had zoomed past 5 million for the first time in the state's history. From 2008 to 2009 the growth rate was 1.8 percent, the fourth-highest rate in the United States. From 2000 to 2009 Colorado's population increased by 16.8 percent, ranking the state seventh nationally in growth rate (Hubbard 2009)

In the one-year period 2008–2009, 40 percent of the population increase resulted from migration into Colorado from other US states, compared with a 20 percent migration from other states during the previous years in the decade. Colorado thus remained a desirable location to which people in other states wanted to move. The remainder of the state's population growth came from natural increase (births over deaths) within the state (Hubbard 2009).

Voter registration in Colorado has been very consistent for many decades. The numbers change from year to year, but generally one-third of Coloradans register Democratic, one-third register Republican, and one-third register unaffiliated with either of the two major parties.

The Colorado secretary of state keeps two sets of figures. One is for active voters, who voted in recent elections and have remained at one address. The other set is for inactive voters, who registered at one time but have not voted recently and have moved away. Among inactive voters, there are more Democrats than Republicans. Among active voters (those who actually vote), there are more Republicans than Democrats. In November 2009 there were approximately 832,000 active Republicans and 800,000 active Democrats in Colorado. The other third of Coloradans, the unaffiliated voters, are said to swing the balance of power between the two major parties and determine the outcome of elections in the state (Brown 2009).

Similar to a number of other states, most of Colorado's population is concentrated in a super-city. In the case of Colorado, that super-city, or megalopolis, is located along the eastern slope of the Rocky Mountains. This section of Colorado, which extends from the city of Pueblo to the south to the cities of

Greeley and Fort Collins to the north, is called the Front Range. It contains more than 80 percent of Colorado's statewide electorate. Newcomers often think the term "Front Range" refers to the mountains. It can, because there is a Front Range of mountains to the west of Boulder, Colorado. To most Coloradans, however, the Front Range is the great population mass at the eastern foot of the Rocky Mountains.

The Front Range, similar to other megalopolitan strips in the United States, contains a wide variety of populations and community types. Denver (which has a combined city-county government) is typical of most major US cities in that it contains large numbers of minority groups and some of the least wealthy neighborhoods in the state. There is an inner ring of Denver suburbs, some of which are fairly upscale in terms of family incomes and education levels. Then there are the smaller cities, such as Colorado Springs and Greeley, which tend to be very middle class and conventional in their political attitudes. In other words, the Colorado Front Range is a typical stretch of urban-suburban America. Statewide election campaigns in Colorado are conducted mainly along the Front Range. People often refer to a statewide campaign in the state as primarily an "I-25 campaign" because Interstate 25 runs up the middle of the Front Range from north to south. Candidates for statewide office in Colorado spend most of their time driving I-25 from one Front Range political event to another. Table 1.4 lists Colorado's ten major Front Range counties and the vote margins by which Democrats or Republicans won those counties in the three most recent presidential elections.

Table 1.4 indicates that Denver is the powerhouse of Democratic voting strength in Colorado. Its 142,315-vote margin for Democrat Barack Obama in 2008 far exceeded any other number on the chart. In addition, the Democratic vote margin in Denver more than doubled from 2000 to 2008 because Denver is home to many working-class Coloradans, Hispanics, and African Americans— groups that traditionally have favored the Democratic Party, both in Colorado and in the nation at large.

The second-strongest county for Democrats in Colorado is Boulder County, which comprises the northwestern portion of the Denver metropolitan area and contains the main campus of the University of Colorado. Boulder County was once regarded as a swing county, likely to vote Democratic or Republican in presidential elections, but in recent decades it has trended strongly Democratic. In 2008 Boulder County's vote margin of 79,255 Democratic was about half the size of Denver's.

The third-most-consistently Democratic county in Colorado is Adams County, an industrial suburban area northeast of Denver. Adams County contains many middle-class industrial workers, an electorate that traditionally has been Democratic but that began trending somewhat toward the Republicans in

TABLE 1.4. Presidential elections: Vote margins in major Front Range counties, 2000, 2004, 2008

County	Margin, 2000	Margin, 2004	Margin, 2008	Shift, 2004–2008
Adams	6,571 D	3,210 D	29,469 D	26,259 D
Arapahoe	15,154 R	9,213 R	34,356 D	43,569 D
Boulder	19,110 D	53,978 D	79,255 D	25,277 D
Denver	61,469 D	96,232 D	142,315 D	46,083 D
Douglas	28,931 R	40,990 R	26,148 R	14,842 D
El Paso	66,495 R	83,713 R	51,419 R	32,294 D
Jefferson	19,168 R	14,086 R	26,530 D	40,616 D
Larimer	16,374 R	7,618 R	16,181 D	23,799 D
Pueblo	6,061 D	4,252 D	10,840 D	6,588 D
Weld	13,973 R	23,723 R	9,234 R	14,489 D

D = Democratic margin; R = Republican margin

Note: Colorado's newest county, Broomfield, is not included because it did not exist at the time of the 2000 presidential election.

Sources: Colorado Secretary of State. 2010 data. Available at http://www.sos.state.co.us/pubs/elections. Accessed March 31, 2011; CQ Press Voting and Elections Collection. 1960–2008 data. Available at http://0-library.cqpress.com.tiger.coloradocollege.edu/elections. Accessed March 31, 2011.

the early years of George W. Bush's presidency. The group swung back strongly to the Democrats in the 2008 presidential election.

Pueblo County, similar to Adams County, has been consistently Democratic over the years. Also similar to Adams County, it is industrial and manufacturing in character. The city of Pueblo is located 110 miles south of Denver on the Front Range and is known to longtime Coloradans as Colorado's "Steel City" because of the large steel mill located there. At one time Pueblo ranked only behind Denver as Colorado's second-most Democratic county, but in recent years its commitment to the Democrats had weakened, and the county's population has not increased significantly. Pueblo County did follow Adams County in swinging strongly back to the Democrats in 2008.

Table 1.4 indicates that the major area of Republican voting strength in Colorado has been El Paso County, which contains most of the Colorado Springs metropolitan area. Two other strong Republican locations, both on the Front Range, are Douglas County (county seat is Castle Rock) and Weld County (county seat is Greeley). Of the three, Douglas is the only county in the Denver metropolitan area, although it is somewhat distant from Denver, located in what could best be described as the outer ring of Denver suburbs.

From 2000 to 2004, the Republican vote margins in all three of these counties increased substantially, thereby helping Republicans overcome the simultaneous Democratic gains in Denver and Boulder Counties. In fact, the substantial Republican gains in El Paso, Douglas, and Weld Counties in 2004 enabled Republican candidate George W. Bush to win Colorado that year.

In 2008, however, all three of these counties failed to deliver the high Republican margins of 2004. As seen in table 1.4, El Paso County shifted 32,294 votes to the Democrats between 2004 and 2008, Douglas County shifted 14,842 votes, and Weld County shifted 14,489 votes. This major weakening of Republican support in El Paso, Douglas, and Weld Counties was a major factor in the Democrats winning Colorado with relative ease in the 2008 presidential election.

Heavily populated Front Range counties that sometimes switch from one party to the other are the Denver suburban counties Arapahoe and Jefferson. These two counties were once strongly Republican, but they slowly evolved into swing counties. In the 2008 presidential election, Arapahoe and Jefferson Counties surprised many observers by voting strongly for the Democratic candidate Barack Obama—the first time in many years that either county had produced a Democratic vote margin in a presidential election.

Most observers cited the Republican Party's increasing emphasis on religious conservatism for the Republican presidential candidate's loss of Arapahoe and Jefferson Counties in 2008. Issues such as opposing abortion, criticizing gays and lesbians, and wanting to halt stem-cell research were thought to be unpopular with the well-educated, upscale suburban residents of Arapahoe and Jefferson Counties.

To sum up, El Paso County (Colorado Springs), Douglas County (Castle Rock), and Weld County (Greeley) currently produce the highest Republican vote margins in Colorado. For the Democrats, the two strongest areas are Denver and Boulder Counties. Democrats also often enjoy large vote margins in Adams and Pueblo Counties. The central arena of competition between the two major political parties is the Denver suburbs, principally Arapahoe and Jefferson Counties. In those two counties, Republican vote margins declined from 2000 to 2004 and then shifted to Democratic margins between 2004 and 2008.

Major changes thus occurred in Front Range voting behavior in Colorado in the early 2000s. The general pattern was that the heart of the Denver metropolitan area (Denver, Boulder, Adams, Arapahoe, and Jefferson Counties) was becoming more Democratic, while three of the Front Range counties more distant from Denver (El Paso, Douglas, and Weld) were becoming the new Republican base in Colorado. The increasing strength of the Democratic Party in the Denver metropolitan area (the city and surrounding suburbs) suggested that Denver political interests might become unusually well represented in Colorado state politics and government.

At the time of the 2008 presidential election, there was clearly a strong Democratic trend along Colorado's Front Range, particularly in the Denver metropolitan area. Republican hopes for the future rested on maintaining strength in strongly Republican counties such as El Paso, Douglas, and Weld. Critical for the Republicans, however, was winning back Republican support in Arapahoe and Jefferson Counties in the Denver suburbs.

WHY COLORADO WENT DEMOCRATIC

A number of reasons have been given as to why the Republicans, after such a long period of dominating both presidential elections and state legislative elections in Colorado, began to lose so many elections to the Democrats between 2004 and 2008.

REDISTRICTING

One explanation is that the Democrats gained control of the state legislative redistricting process at the time of the 2000 US Census and succeeded in gerrymandering the state so more Democrats would be elected to the state legislature. The same thing happened with Colorado's delegation to the US House of Representatives, where the Democrats filed a suit to gain court-ordered redistricting that favored the Democratic Party. More than partisan redistricting was at work, of course, but gerrymandering was an important factor in explaining how Democrats improved their electoral position in Colorado.

TERM LIMITS

Another explanation is the adoption of a constitutional amendment that set eight-year term limits for the governor and the state legislature. The amendment was adopted in the early 1990s and thus first began forcing legislators to retire in the late 1990s and early 2000s. Significant numbers of Republican incumbents, who would likely have been easily reelected to the legislature, were forced out of office by term limits. This gave the Democrats ample opportunity to compete for so-called open seats, which are easier targets for the non-incumbent party.

Term limits represent a two-edged sword for the Democrats, however. The Democrats won many seats in the state legislature in 2002, 2004, 2006, and 2008, as they gained and maintained their tight grip on control of the legislature. This meant that in succeeding elections, large numbers of Democrats rather than Republicans would be forced out of office by term limits, thereby creating many open-seat opportunities for the Republicans.

CAMPAIGN FINANCE REFORM

Colorado voters have instituted strict campaign finance limits. Democrats have proved considerably more adept than Republicans at getting around these

limits. The Democrats quickly formed "independent expenditures" committees that spent large sums of money on negative advertising that discredited
Republican candidates. Colorado Republicans lagged behind the Democrats
in developing similar techniques and ended up woefully behind in spending on
state legislative elections.

Wealthy Contributors

Another reason cited for the state's shift to Democratic voting was the "Gang
of Four," four wealthy Democratic campaign contributors who poured considerable amounts of their personal funds into financing Democratic campaigns for
the legislature and many other campaigns in Colorado. The Democratic Party's
success in adapting to the changes in campaign finance rules made these four
super-rich contributors' donations particularly effective at the ballot box.

Social Conservatism

An additional cause was the Republican Party's tendency to choose candidates for public office who were staunch right-wing social conservatives.
These candidates strongly opposed abortion, gay and lesbian rights, and stem-
cell research. These religious conservatives had little appeal to well-educated,
upscale Republicans, many of whom are concentrated in Denver's inner suburbs
and voted Democratic in protest.

Presidential Coattails

Candidates for president of the United States have traditionally had long
coattails in Colorado, even as far down the ballot as the state legislative level.
Beginning in 1992 and continuing through 2008, Democrats were more effective
in winning presidential elections in Colorado. As a result, Democrats running
for the US Senate, the US House, and the Colorado state legislature received an
added lift.

Whatever the reason, which was likely a combination of all the reasons cited
in this section, by 2009 the Democratic Party was enjoying a full plate of political victories. The party had carried Colorado for the Democratic presidential
candidate in 2008, won one US Senate seat in 2004 and the second seat in 2008,
enjoyed a five-to-two advantage over the Republicans in the state's delegation to
the US House of Representatives, and firmly controlled both houses of the state
legislature. It was one of the greatest periods of Democratic dominance in state
elections in Colorado history.

CONCLUSION

Between the 1960s and the 1990s, Colorado earned a reputation as a Republican-leaning or red state. The Democrats, however, always won a share of statewide elections, and they dominated gubernatorial elections in the state. The Democrats also carried Colorado in the 1992 and 2008 presidential elections. Thus Colorado voting has tended to follow the United States as a whole, and the fact that Democrats did well both nationally and in Colorado in the 2008 presidential election was not a coincidence. An apt political description of Colorado might be: it is a two-party state that was characterized by a drift toward the Republicans during the thirty years from 1960 to 1990, with a counter-drift toward the Democrats in the late 1990s and 2000s.

The Republican Party's surging national comeback in the 2010 elections took some, but not all, of the bloom off the Democratic electoral rose in Colorado. Democrats in the state had much to cheer about that year. They won the election's two top prizes—the US Senate seat and the state governorship. They held on to the District Seven seat in the US House, one of three US House seats they picked up from the Republicans between 2004 and 2008. In addition, they retained solid control of the state senate.

The Democrats gave up significant ground to the Republicans further down the ballot, however. They lost the races for state treasure, state attorney general, and state secretary of state. They failed to defend successfully two seats in the US House of Representatives, and they lost control of the state house of representatives, even if by only one vote.

These ambivalent results in the 2010 elections in Colorado confirm that the state is no longer a Republican stronghold, as many believed it was for many years. In an election year in which Republicans swept many offices in numerous other states, Colorado Republicans managed only modest results. The likeliest assumption appears to be that Colorado is now truly competitive between the two major political parties but is dominated by neither of them.

NOTES

1. I encountered Richard Lamm at a panel discussion in Pueblo, Colorado, several years after Lamm left the governorship. In response to my questions, Lamm confirmed that the Republicans in the state legislature had blunted his plans for increasing environmental concerns in Colorado. He also acknowledged that the Denver belt highway had indeed been constructed despite his efforts to prevent it. Author's personal recollection.

2. For a lengthier discussion of Richard Lamm's governorship, see Cronin and Loevy (1993: 220–223).

3. For a fuller discussion of the first six years of Roy Romer's governorship, see ibid., 223–224. For a scholarly account of Roy Romer's campaign for reelection in 1994, see Loevy (1996: 255–326).

Robert D. Loevy

REFERENCES

Brown, Fred. 2009. "Candidates Wise to Stay in the Middle." *The Denver Post*, December 13, 5D.

———. 2001. "Judge John Coughlin, Cartographer." *The Denver Post*, December 21, B7.

Colorado Secretary of State. 2010 data. Available at http://www.sos.state.co.us.pubs/elections. Accessed March 31, 2011.

CQ Press Voting and Elections Collection. 1960–2008 data. Available at http://0-library.cq.press.com.tiger.coloradocollege.edu/elections. Accessed March 31, 2011.

Cronin, Thomas E., and Robert D. Loevy. 1993. *Colorado Politics and Government: Governing the Centennial State*. Lincoln: University of Nebraska Press.

Hubbard, Burt. 2009. "5,024,748." *The Denver Post*, December 24, 1A.

Loevy, Robert D. 1996. *The Flawed Path to the Governorship 1994: The Nationalization of a Colorado Statewide Election*. Lanham, MD: University Press of America.

———. 2002. "It's Time for Judicial Redistricting." *The Denver Post*, December 21, B27.

———. 2006. "Beauprez and the Six-Year Jinx." *The Denver Post*, October 22, 4E.

Martinez, Julia C. 2002. "Court Upholds Redistricting; Federal Appeal Rated Unlikely." *The Denver Post*, February 27, B4.

Martinez, Julia C., and Mike Soraghan. 2002. "Remapping to Bring Changes, Big and Small, Across State." *The Denver Post*, January 27, B6.

Mulkern, Anne. 2009. "Tancredo, Allard Ride off into Political Sunset." *The Denver Post*, January 5, A1.

Quillen, Ed. 2002. "Some Win and Some Lose in Congressional Remapping." *The Denver Post*, January 29, B9.

Chapter Two

What's Going On? The Shifting Terrain
of Federal Elections in Colorado

Robert J. Duffy and Kyle Saunders

As recently as 2002, Colorado appeared to be reliably Republican: George W. Bush won the state 51–42 in 2000, and in 2002 Governor Bill Owens—who won a close contest in 1998—was reelected by almost two-thirds of the electorate. That same year Senator Wayne Allard, after trailing in many polls, was reelected by a five-point margin. Republicans also retained control of the General Assembly by regaining a majority in the state senate and won Colorado's newly created Seventh Congressional District—designed to be competitive for both parties—by 121 votes (Barone and Cohen 2008). In short, Republicans controlled both chambers of the state legislature, the governorship, both US Senate seats, and five of the state's seven US House seats.

Just two years later, however, Democrats began to make dramatic gains at every level of government. Although George Bush again carried the state in the presidential race, his margin was cut nearly in half. In an otherwise bad year for Democrats nationally, Ken Salazar won a hotly contested race for the US Senate, and his brother John captured the Third Congressional District seat. Perhaps most surprising, Democrats gained control of both chambers of the state legislature for the first time in forty years. In 2006, Democrats easily won the governorship and the Seventh District House seat. Democrats did even better in 2008, winning three competitive races by surprising margins. Barack Obama defeated John McCain 54 percent to 45 percent, doubling George W. Bush's margin of victory over John Kerry just four years earlier. Mark Udall beat former congressman Bob Schaffer by ten points in an open-seat race to succeed retiring Republican Wayne Allard. In the Fourth Congressional District, Betsy Markey defeated three-term incumbent Marilyn Musgrave by twelve points, 56 percent to 44 percent.

This chapter seeks to explain the Democratic winning streak in federal elections, focusing on the two Senate seats as well as the Democratic gains in Congressional Districts 3, 4, and 7. Although some Republicans have suggested that a small cabal of wealthy Democrats developed a secret "Colorado Model" that was responsible for Democratic success in the state, the truth is both less mysterious and more complicated (Barnes 2008; Witwer 2009). To be sure, the wealthy donors did play a direct role in one US House race, but it would be more accurate to say that a mix of demographic changes, Democratic successes, Republican failures, and national political and economic factors explain the dramatic shift. Since 2004, Democratic candidates for federal office have enjoyed significant financial and organizational advantages, offered candidates more appealing to the state's large bloc of unaffiliated voters, and benefited from two successive "wave" elections that swept Republicans from office nationwide. Long-term demographic changes, including the growth of the Hispanic population, have also helped Democrats.

EXPLAINING DEMOCRATIC SUCCESS IN
FEDERAL ELECTIONS SINCE 2004

THE "GANG OF FOUR" AND OUTSIDE GROUPS

In seeking to explain Democrats' recent electoral success, some have focused on the actions of a small group of wealthy liberal donors, sometimes called the "Gang of Four" (Tim Gill, Jared Polis, Pat Stryker, and Rutt Bridges) (Barnes 2008; Fender 2008; Schrager and Witwer 2010; Witwer 2009). As described by conservative pundit Fred Barnes, the group's so-called Colorado Model depends in part on "wealthy liberals spending tons of money not only on 'independent expenditures' to attack Republican office-seekers but also to create a vast infrastructure of liberal organizations that produces an anti-Republican, anti-conservative echo chamber in politics and the media" (Barnes 2008). In the same vein, former Republican legislator Rob Witwer has argued that the donors worked through the Colorado Democracy Alliance, an organization that helped build a network of nonprofit entities to replace the Colorado Democratic Party, which had been "rendered obsolete" by campaign finance reform (Schrager and Witwer 2010). As described rather breathlessly in *The Denver Post*, this "epic and mysterious" group of "progressive power brokers" devised an "ingenious scheme" to create a "vast progressive infrastructure" that would "skirt" federal election rules and direct money to races and causes "almost entirely out of the public eye" (Fender 2008). Most important, according to Witwer (2009), they "put aside their policy differences to focus on the common goal of winning elections," primarily at the state level. To that end, the group met in early 2004 to identify vulnerable Republicans and design strategies to defeat them. A central element of the plan was to put huge amounts of cash into state legislative races, through nonprofits and newly created 527 organizations.[1]

The problem with this story, however, is that it overemphasizes the importance of wealthy donors, minimizes the role of the state's Democratic Party, and largely ignores the failures of the Republican Party. Aside from an aggressive effort to oust Republican Marilyn Musgrave in the Fourth District, described later, there is no evidence that Gill and the others played a significant direct role in the other federal races. At most, one could argue that their 2004 efforts at the state level played an indirect role in helping Ken Salazar in his Senate race because several of the legislative seats targeted by the 527s were located in the Denver suburbs, an area also targeted by the Salazar campaign. In fact, several of the 527 groups had field staff working to boost interest and turnout in those districts, so there may have been some synergistic effects from the overlapping campaigns.

It is the case, though, that beginning in 2004, Gill, Stryker, and Polis devoted significant time and money trying to defeat Musgrave. That year the three funded Coloradans for Plain Talk, a 527 group, which ran a very controversial television ad campaign attacking Musgrave. One ad depicted a Musgrave look-alike in a bright pink dress stealing a watch from a corpse in a funeral parlor, while the voiceover detailed her votes to allow nursing homes to charge families after a patient's death. A second ad showed "Musgrave" picking the pocket of a soldier in combat and noted her votes against "supporting the troops." In 2006 Stryker and Gill helped fund another 527, Coloradans for Life, which spent $1.5 million on television and radio ads against Musgrave (Campaign Money 2006). Despite the attacks, Musgrave won reelection both times, but her victory margins were smaller in each successive race.

Musgrave, whose favorability ratings had taken a beating over the years, was not so lucky in 2008, when challenger Betsy Markey defeated her. The Fourth District again attracted a considerable amount of independent spending by organized groups that year, virtually all of it attacking Musgrave. By far the biggest spender was Defenders of Wildlife, whose 501(c)(4) and 527 entities spent a combined $1.6 million. Stryker donated $175,000 to the Defenders of Wildlife on July

25, three days before the group made a television ad buy for the same amount. Stryker also gave $225,000 to Majority Action, a 527 organization funded largely by organized labor, on October 1—one day before the group spent $220,000 on television ad buys against Musgrave (Moore 2008a). In a conversation with reporters after her first debate with Markey, Musgrave denounced the Defenders of Wildlife, saying the group "hates our way of life" (Moore 2008b) and claiming that the race was close "because of 527s and 501c4s that have thrown $10 million in garbage against me. I have to break through that when I run again and do the best I can to present my case to the citizens of the Fourth District" (Kosena 2008b). But in her first public comments a month after the election, Musgrave spread the blame more widely, citing "vicious attacks and lies" by wealthy "leftist special interests," notably "pro-abortion radicals and liberal activists" (Moore 2008c). Although it would be hard to deny that the attacks by outside groups played a role in her defeat, it is also fair to say that Markey, who was a good candidate and ran an effective campaign, was also a factor. As noted later in this chapter, voters had grown weary with Musgrave's confrontational style of politics, which was out of sync with voter sentiments given the nation's economic problems in 2008.

While the Gang of Four has not been a major player in federal races, other outside groups have spent considerable sums of money in the state. This is largely a reflection of the state's growing importance at the federal level. As might be expected, most of the spending has occurred in open-seat races, the most likely to be competitive. In the 2004 US Senate race, for example, groups supporting Democrat Ken Salazar outspent those supporting Peter Coors, especially late in the race. The League of Conservation Voters made approximately $1.1 million in independent expenditures against Coors, branding him "Polluter Pete." Citizens for a Strong Senate, a 527 organization, spent more than $900,000 on television and direct mail campaigns. Spending by Republican groups amounted to less than $2 million, with Americans for Job Security, a 501(c)(6) organization, spending approximately $1 million criticizing Salazar's environmental record and the US Chamber of Commerce spending approximately $500,000 on a direct mail effort (Saunders and Duffy 2005a). Arguably, one of the most effective 527s that year was Colorado Conservative Voters, a 527 organization headed by former members of Bob Schaffer's campaign: Schaffer had lost to Coors in a nasty primary that spring. The group spent nearly $1 million during the primary attacking Coors from the right. The group's message, that Coors's positions on drinking and other social issues were insufficiently conservative, was eventually picked up by both Citizens for a Strong Senate and the League of Conservation Voters and used against Coors in the general election.

Finally, significant outside money was spent on the US Senate race in 2008, but the vast majority of that spending was by Republican groups attacking

Democratic candidate Mark Udall. In fact, with just about a month to go in the race, interest groups had spent more in Colorado than in any other Senate contest nationwide, with Republican-affiliated organizations outspending Democratic ones by an almost three-to-one margin (Riley 2008a). Five separate groups supporting Bob Schaffer spent more than $1 million each: the US Chamber of Commerce spent $1.97 million, Freedom's Watch spent $1.71 million, American Future Fund spent $1.5 million, Employee Freedom Action Committee spent $1.21 million, and ABC–Free Enterprise Alliance spent $1.04 million (Riley 2008a). Among the groups supporting Udall, the top spenders were the League of Conservation Voters ($946,000), the National Education Association ($845,000), and Colorado First Project ($642,000) (National Public Radio 2008).

POPULATION, DEMOGRAPHY, AND VOTER REGISTRATION TRENDS

As noted in the Introduction to this volume, although Republicans out-numbered Democrats in Colorado by approximately 180,000 as recently as 2004, the parties are now at parity. The Colorado electorate is roughly one-third Democratic, one-third Republican, and one-third unaffiliated. Some of the Democrats' recent success in Colorado can be traced to demographic shifts and registration trends over the past decade. Although there are many reasons for this sudden and dramatic shift in registration, some of it can be traced to population growth and demographic changes.

According to William Frey and Ruy Teixeira (2008), rapid population growth among Hispanics and white college graduates, coupled with the relative decline of the white working class, helps explain the state's partisan shift. The growth in both groups, they contend, is concentrated in the state's metropolitan areas and has made the electorate more Democratic. Hispanics have always been a Democratic constituency, but their rapid growth means their share of the elec-torate has increased dramatically. This has occurred at a time when they have become even more strongly Democratic, at least in part because of the anti-immigrant rhetoric and actions of Republican politicians such as Tom Tancredo. According to a post-election analysis by Project Vote (2008), Latino voters were critical to both Obama's and Udall's 2008 victories. Obama won 61 percent of the Latino vote, and Udall won 63 percent. Although both John Kerry and John Salazar did better among Latinos, the group cast approximately 123,000 more votes in 2008 than it had in 2004—an increase of more than 70 percent. Indeed, Latinos made up 13 percent of the total vote in 2008, compared to just 8 percent four years earlier. The Udall and Obama campaigns made concerted efforts to mobilize Latinos, a strategy that yielded ample dividends.

The share of the vote cast by white college graduates has also increased, and this group has been trending Democratic as well. Frey and Teixeira (2008:

11) caution however, that white college graduates' affinity for Democrats is less pronounced, more recent, and thus subject to change. In 2008, exit polls revealed that Barack Obama won 56 percent of the vote among white college graduates, slightly less than Mark Udall (Cable News Network 2008a, 2008b). Both men, however, won a larger share of this group than did John Kerry or Ken Salazar. The 2008 election results provided few bright spots for McCain and Schaffer, but one was their performance among voters who did not attend college. McCain won 57 percent of this group, while Schaffer won 55 percent (Cable News Network 2008a, 2008b).

More generally, in 2008 Obama and Udall carried the traditional Democratic voting blocs along with some groups that normally voted Republican. Obama won among women (56–41) and Democrats (92–7), and he even carried the white vote (50–48), a group Bush had won by 15 points in 2004. Obama carried every age group except those sixty-five and over; in another sign of his strength, he won 13 percent of the state's Republicans and 18 percent of self-described conservatives. Obama also carried unaffiliated voters by a decisive 54–44 margin, and he won self-described moderates—just under half of the state's voters—by an even larger 63–35 margin. The exit polls revealed very similar results for Mark Udall in his Senate victory over Bob Schaffer (Cable News Network 2008a, 2008b).

In fact, in 2008 Democrats improved upon their 2004 performance in all parts of the state. Perhaps most important, in every one of the state's ten most populous counties, which contain approximately 77 percent of registered voters, Barack Obama outperformed John Kerry. For example, Obama received 46,000 more votes in Denver than did Kerry. Obama carried Arapahoe, Jefferson, and Larimer Counties by at least 10 points, while George W. Bush had carried them in 2004. In addition to his huge but expected wins in the state's urban areas, Obama also won among suburban voters (50–48), as well as those in the state's rural regions (50–49). McCain, on the other hand, did very well only in the sparsely populated counties on the eastern plains, although his margins fell well short of George Bush's in 2004. Moreover, although the state's eastern plains is reliably Republican, its lower population growth rate means these counties cast relatively fewer votes in each election cycle (Frey and Teixeira 2008).

In addition, the Obama campaign's efforts to limit McCain's margins in traditionally Republican areas worked. The clearest example was in El Paso County, where McCain won by only 52,000 votes, compared to Bush's 2004 margin of nearly 84,000. Similarly, Bush won 63 percent of the vote in Weld County, while McCain received just 54 percent (Cable News Network 2004, 2008a).

Population growth rates and demographic shifts have been highest in those counties where Democrats have made the biggest registration gains. Table 2.1

demonstrates that much of the Democratic registration gains statewide occurred in the three competitive House districts in Colorado. In the Third Congressional District, Democrats (151,773) actually trailed Republicans (161,201) by about 10,000 registrants going into the 2008 election, yet John Salazar, after winning the district by three points in 2004, was reelected with 61 percent of the vote. Part of the explanation for Salazar's success is that Democrats have the momentum in registration, even in this Republican-leaning district. Democrats gained just under 7 percent (9,814) in registrants since 2002, compared with a gain of 4 percent (6,671) for Republicans. The number of unaffiliated voters in the district has grown even faster, at just under 14 percent overall and at more than 20 percent in the district's urban counties. Like other Democrats in recent years, Salazar's success among unaffiliated voters has contributed to his large reelection margins (Colorado Secretary of State 2002, 2004, 2006, 2008).

Going into the 2008 election, voter registration figures in the Fourth District showed that registered Republicans (168,689) outnumbered registered Democrats (123,281) by about 45,400 voters, down 15,000 in just two years (see table 2.1). The second-largest bloc of voters in the district (154,516) was unaffiliated, and statewide those voters have been trending Democratic. Further, since 2002 the Democrats had added 15,000 voters to their rolls (or 14 percent), while Republicans lost more than 5,000 voters (a decline of 3 percent). Meanwhile, the number of unaffiliated voters increased by 12 percent since 2002 (Colorado Secretary of State 2002, 2004, 2006, 2008). Table 2.2 shows that these trends are even more apparent when viewed by county. The largest of the counties, Larimer, had a more than 25 percent increase in Democratic registrants between 2002 and 2008, while Republican registration declined by just under 2 percent over the same time period in a county that had been markedly Republican for the past forty years. In part, these changes have occurred because the area is increasingly urbanized and has attracted a growing number of college graduates, but Democratic efforts at increasing registration are also paying off. Similarly, Democrats have gained in Weld County as well—a traditionally Republican area—and in Boulder County, which has become increasingly Democratic in recent years.

The Seventh District has also shown marked gains for the Democrats. In 2002 the two parties were at parity in the district, with Democrats outnumbering Republicans by 110. Republican Bob Beauprez ultimately won the 2002 election, one of the closest in Colorado history (Smith 2003). But as table 2.1 shows, going into the 2008 election, registered Democrats (144,505) outnumbered registered Republicans (108,642) in the Seventh District by about 35,800, a gain of 26,000 for the Democrats since 2006. In addition, the district has a large bloc (130,286) of unaffiliated voters. Democratic registration in the Seventh District increased 17 percent between 2002 and 2008, the largest gain in the state. At the

TABLE 2.1. Registration trends in select Colorado congressional districts by election year, 2002–2008

CD3 Registration Totals by year

	Democrats	% of total	% change from 2002	Republicans	% of total	% change from 2002	Unaffiliated	% of total	% change from 2002	Democrats-Republicans
2008	151,773	32.98	6.91	161,201	35.03	4.25	147,161	31.98	13.32	−9,428
2006	141,728			161,097			137,864			−19,369
2004	145,195			161,799			133,045			−16,604
2002	141,959	33.29		154,630	36.26		129,866	30.45		−12,671

CD4 Registration Totals by Year

	Democrats	% of total	% change from 2002	Republicans	% of total	% change from 2002	Unaffiliated	% of total	% change from 2002	Democrats-Republicans
2008	123,281	27.61	13.90	168,689	37.78	−3.08	154,516	34.61	12.24	−45,408
2006	108,534			170,146			145,409			−61,612
2004	111,225			174,148			142,256			−62,923
2002	108,240	25.77		174,041	41.44		137,664	32.78		−65,801

CD7 Registration Totals by Year

	Democrats	% of total	% change from 2002	Republicans	% of total	% change from 2002	Unaffiliated	% of total	% change from 2002	Democrats-Republicans
2008	144,505	37.69	17.27	108,642	28.33	−11.57	130,286	33.98	5.09	35,863
2006	123,911			113,914			127,074			9,997
2004	133,595			126,762			136,529			6,833
2002	123,221	33.30		122,857	33.20		123,975	33.50		364

Source: Colorado Secretary of State 2002, 2004, 2006, 2008.

TABLE 2.2. Registration trends in three largest counties in CD4, 2002–2008

Larimer

	Democrats	% of total	% change from 2002	Republicans	% of total	% change from 2002	Unaffiliated	% of total	% change from 2002	Democrats-Republicans
2008	60,295	28.80	25.52	74,453	35.56	-1.66	74,613	35.64	17.75	-14,158
2006	51,582			74,739			68,923			-23,157
2004	52,288			78,087			68,565			-25,799
2002	48,035	25.67		75,706	40.46		63,367	33.87		-27,671

Weld

	Democrats	% of total	% change from 2002	Republicans	% of total	% change from 2002	Unaffiliated	% of total	% change from 2002	Democrats-Republicans
2008	29,822	25.56	18.24	45,160	38.70	13.03	41,715	35.75	26.77	-15,338
2006	26,069			44,848			39,901			-18,779
2004	26,331			44,137			36,358			-17,806
2002	25,222	25.71		39,954	40.73		32,907	33.55		-14,732

Boulder

	Democrats	% of total	% change from 2002	Republicans	% of total	% change from 2002	Unaffiliated	% of total	% change from 2002	Democrats-Republicans
2008	17,857	32.51	26.75	16,900	30.76	-7.07	20,178	36.73	8.69	957
2006	15,493			17,898			19,770			-2,405
2004	15,469			18,518			19,658			-3,049
2002	14,088	27.71		18,186	35.77		18,564	36.52		-4,098

Source: Colorado Secretary of State 2002, 2004, 2006, 2008.

Note: Registration data in this table are only from the portion of the county inside congressional district borders.

same time, Republican registration declined by 12 percent, approximately 14,000 voters. Unaffiliated voters also increased in the Seventh District, but only at a rate of 5 percent (a gain of just over 6,000 registrants) (Colorado Secretary of State 2002, 2004, 2006, 2008).

Table 2.3 shows similar trends at the county level in the Seventh District. In each county, especially in Adams and Arapahoe, Democrats made well over double-digit percentage gains in voter registration between 2002 and 2008; Republicans lost registrants in every county except Adams, where they increased by 17 percent. The numbers in Jefferson County are particularly striking because as recently as 2002 it was a Republican stronghold. By 2008, though, Democrats outnumbered Republicans by 6,000.

Colorado and the Republicans Circa 2004

As noted previously, the Democrats' good fortunes began in 2004, when Ken and John Salazar won their races for the US Congress and Democrats gained control of both chambers of the state legislature for the first time since 1960. Although each of the state legislative races was unique, it seems fair to say that Colorado voters were unhappy with the performance of the state government and the Republicans who controlled it. The state's economy, which had been booming a few years earlier, had turned sour: unemployment rates were up, revenues were down, and the Taxpayer's Bill of Rights (TABOR)–imposed budget restrictions had forced the state to cut $1 billion in spending in each of the prior two years. On the largely Republican western slope, the growing conflict over the Bush administration's push to dramatically expand natural gas exploration angered many surface owners, who felt the state government was not doing enough to protect their property rights from being trampled by energy companies. As election season approached, there was a palpable sense that the state was facing very serious problems. At the same time, though, the state's Republican leadership seemed preoccupied with championing divisive social issues such as abortion and gay marriage and with trying to engineer a controversial redistricting scheme to guarantee more Republican congressional seats. It is not that voters' views of the Republican governor and state legislators directly affected their votes in that year's federal elections; rather, it is that voters' general unhappiness over state affairs created a context favorable to Democrats at all levels. This was particularly true for unaffiliated voters, who cast a disproportionate share of their votes for Democrats—at least in part because Republicans were seen as responsible for the state's ills and for ignoring them to push a partisan social agenda demanded by the party's right wing. Democrats, on the other hand, were at least talking about issues that mattered to voters.

TABLE 2.3. Registration trends in three largest counties in CD7, 2002–2008

Jefferson

	Democrats	% of total	% change from 2002	Republicans	% of total	% change from 2002	Unaffiliated	% of total	% change from 2002	Democrats-Republicans
2008	75,675	34.58	12.11	69,102	31.57	-13.29	74,093	33.85	3.96	6,573
2006	67,537			72,864			71,686			-5,327
2004	70,722			79,585			74,038			-8,863
2002	67,501	30.90		79,693	36.48		71,269	32.62		-12,192

Adams

	Democrats	% of total	% change from 2002	Republicans	% of total	% change from 2002	Unaffiliated	% of total	% change from 2002	Democrats-Republicans
2008	28,973	38.89	21.60	18,943	25.43	16.96	26,580	35.68	27.78	10,030
2006	23,714			17,878			23,512			5,836
2004	26,203			19,036			24,564			7,167
2002	23,827	39.17		16,196	26.63		20,801	34.20		7,631

Arapahoe

	Democrats	% of total	% change from 2002	Republicans	% of total	% change from 2002	Unaffiliated	% of total	% change from 2002	Democrats-Republicans
2008	39,857	44.25	24.97	20,597	22.87	-23.62	29,613	32.88	-7.18	19,260
2006	32,660			23,172			31,876			9,488
2004	36,670			28,141			37,927			8,529
2002	31,893	35.14		26,968	29.71		31,905	35.15		4,925

Source: Colorado Secretary of State 2002, 2004, 2006, 2008.
Note: Registration data in this table are only from the portion of the county inside congressional district borders.

GEORGE W. BUSH, IRAQ, AND THE ECONOMY: WAVE ELECTIONS

By 2006, national trends began to copy those in Colorado. The Democrats gained twenty-two seats in the US House and seven seats in the US Senate, giving them control of both houses of Congress, and Democrats won almost every major contest in Colorado as well. Bill Ritter handily won the race for governor, and Ed Perlmutter won an easy victory in an open-seat race in the very competitive Seventh District. The trend continued in 2008; Democrats won the White House and gained twenty-four additional House seats and eight more Senate seats. In Colorado, Mark Udall easily defeated Republican Bob Schaffer in the US Senate race, and Betsy Markey defeated Marilyn Musgrave in what should have been a very competitive race in the Fourth District.

These historic shifts were the result of the public's antipathy toward President Bush and the Republican Party. The war in Iraq, the nation's growing economic ills, and a host of scandals (including the indictment of a number of Republican legislators tied to jailed lobbyist Jack Abramoff) were largely responsible for the Republican Party's defeats. In addition, the incumbent party often falls out favor after eight years in office, as voters invariably blame problems on those in power. Whatever the root cause, Colorado Democrats were the beneficiaries of national factors that lifted Democrats everywhere.

Although it is difficult to distinguish between candidate effects and the national discontent with the Bush administration, it is abundantly clear that in 2006 and 2008 the Perlmutter, Udall, and Markey campaigns successfully tied their opponents to the sitting administration, arguing that they—like Bush— were responsible for the nation's ills. Indeed, in 2006 the Perlmutter campaign and the Democratic Congressional Campaign Committee (DCCC) were remarkably effective at nationalizing the race by linking the Republican Rick O'Donnell to George Bush and depicting him as just "another vote for Bush's agenda" on Iraq, Social Security privatization, and stem-cell research. Perlmutter also succeeded in portraying O'Donnell as an out-of-the-mainstream, right-wing ideologue, assailing him for his radical ideas, especially on Social Security. In a 1995 essay written for a Washington think tank, O'Donnell had claimed that it was "time to slay" Social Security and argued that the program sent "the un-American message that it is not your responsibility to take care of yourself" (O'Donnell 1995). O'Donnell spent three months of his campaign disavowing those remarks and eventually asked voters to "forgive" him. Still, the damage was done, and Perlmutter won handily.

Exit polls in 2008 made it clear that national political and economic factors were significant in Obama's and Udall's victories in Colorado. Most important, fewer than 70 percent of Colorado voters approved of the way President Bush was handling his job, and both Obama and Udall won 73 percent of the vote in their respective races. The exit polls also revealed that the economy (54 percent), Iraq (13 percent), and terrorism and health care (10 percent each) were the most important issues for Coloradans. Obama won 64 percent of the votes among those who said Iraq was the most important issue, 56 percent of the votes of those who said the economy was the most important issue, and 78 percent of those who said health care was the top issue. The only group McCain carried was the one that cited terrorism as the top issue (Cable News Network 2008a). In short, George W. Bush was a significant drag on McCain and other Republicans.

THE CANDIDATES: PRAGMATIC MODERATES OR IDEOLOGICAL CONSERVATIVES?

Another reason Democrats won in Colorado is because they offered socially and fiscally moderate messages that appealed to Colorado voters, especially unaffiliated voters. In a contentious race in the Republican-leaning Third District in 2004, Democrat John Salazar, running against Greg Walcher who was seeking to replace retiring Republican Scott McInnis, emphasized nonpartisanship and local issues—including his opponent's support for a controversial plan to divert district water to the Denver area. "I think I have a proven track record; I have a record of being a moderate and pulling the middle," said Salazar. "There is no room for partisanship—conservative versus liberal—we need to stand up for the district" (quoted in Vlahos 2004).

Ken Salazar, a candidate in Colorado's Senate race that year, also ran as a fiscal and social moderate who understood the concerns of ranchers, farmers, and small business owners. As was the case with his brother, Ken Salazar's emphasis on water issues was particularly important to farmers and ranchers, who were concerned about losing water rights to the rapidly growing Front Range suburbs. To reinforce his moderate, populist agenda, Salazar often talked about the struggles of the working class and promoted tax cuts for the middle class rather than for millionaires, affordable health insurance, and affordable prescription drugs; he also supported the death penalty and gun rights. This combination of issues allowed Salazar to hold on to the Democratic base and win over unaffiliated voters and a larger-than-normal share of Republicans (Couch and Crummy 2004).

Another reason Democrats have been successful among unaffiliated voters in recent elections is that they have offered pragmatic and moderate candidates, whereas Republicans have run several conservative ideologues, including a number of unapologetic social conservatives such as Bob Schaffer and Marilyn Musgrave. Others, like Pete Coors, were forced to veer to the right to win contested primaries and to embrace positions that were problematic in the general election, especially for unaffiliated voters. Faced with significant economic problems and an increasingly unpopular war, voters seemed to tire of the relentless drumbeat on abortion, gays, stem-cell research, and other elements of the culture wars. Republican efforts to paint the two Salazars, Perlmutter, Udall, and Markey as liberals hell-bent on spending taxpayer money were rejected, largely because they had little connection to reality. Beginning with the Salazar brothers, all of these Democrats campaigned as pragmatic, non-ideological problem solvers—which, given the growing unpopularity of the Republican brand, was a decided plus. In addition, with the exception of Betsy Markey, all were known quantities, having previously served in elective office.

In contrast, during their time in public life, both Schaffer and Musgrave had established reputations as strong conservatives: they were committed to cutting taxes and spending and protecting gun rights, and they opposed abortion and gay rights. In 2008, they both tried to downplay social issues in their campaigns, but it was nearly impossible for them to escape those issues, given their long records. Schaffer's campaign downplayed social issues, noting only that he was a "good family man." Instead, Schaffer relentlessly attacked Mark Udall as a "Boulder liberal" in an attempt to brand Udall as hopelessly out of touch with average Coloradans. Like the other Democrats discussed here, Udall cast himself as a centrist and emphasized his bipartisan work in Congress on veteran's issues. Although Udall was known as a strong environmental voice, when gas prices spiked in the summer of 2008 he signaled a willingness to consider nuclear power and offshore drilling and spoke of balancing the environment against the need to develop the state's energy resources (Riley 2008b). As Ken Salazar had done in 2004, Udall's television ads and direct mail emphasized issues rather than attacks and highlighted populist and folksy themes designed to cast him as a regular Coloradan.

Musgrave decided to run for the US Congress in 2002 when Schaffer, the incumbent, term-limited himself after six years in office. Once elected, Musgrave's record in the House reinforced her conservative credentials and raised her public profile. The American Conservative Union, for example, ranked Musgrave as one of the most conservative members of the House—with a 99.2 lifetime rating based on her record of votes on guns, abortion, embryonic stem-cell research, gay rights, and more (American Conservative Union 2009). Musgrave became best known for sponsoring the Federal Marriage Amendment, which would have amended the US Constitution to prohibit same-sex marriage. In remarks that would later be used against her, Musgrave told an audience at the Family Research Council that "as we face the issues that we are facing today, I don't think there's anything more important out there than the marriage issue" (quoted in Giroux 2006).

Over time, voters in the Fourth District grew weary of Musgrave's controversial stances. Her victory margins decreased in every election; by early 2008, 51 percent of voters in the district had an unfavorable impression of her. Her unfavorable rating among self-identified independents was 62 percent; among ideological moderates it was 66 percent. Because independents accounted for more than a third of the district's voters, Musgrave was clearly in trouble (Survey USA 2008).

Her opponent understood this and devoted considerable time and effort to visiting heavily Republican parts of the district in an effort to show voters that she understood their concerns (Kosena 2008b). From the outset of the campaign, Markey cast herself not as a partisan Democrat but instead as pragmatic and moderate on nearly every issue, from spending, taxes, and energy policy to the social issues that so strongly defined her opponent. In the end, Markey's win owed much to her ability to win over a large majority of the district's unaffiliated voters.

MONEY

Colorado Democrats have also fared better in recent years because they have raised more money than in prior years and have benefited from significant support from the party's campaign committees, which had not always been the case. This was especially important because campaign costs have escalated—in fact, each of the races discussed here set a record for total spending. In the US Senate races, both Ken Salazar and Mark Udall outspent their Republican opponents, while John Salazar, Ed Perlmutter, and Betsy Markey each raised about the same amount as their opponents in their initial open-seat races, and all of these candidates benefited from substantial party support. Perlmutter and Salazar have subsequently far outpaced their challengers in their reelection campaigns and have required little financial help from the party.

It was not always thus, as shown in table 2.4, which illustrates campaign finance trends for candidates and campaign committees from 2002 to 2008. In their 2002 rematch for the US Senate, incumbent Republican Wayne Allard and Democratic challenger Tom Strickland were fairly evenly matched, with each spending just over $5 million. It was a very different story in 2004, when Ken Salazar raised $9.9 million to Pete Coors's $7.6 million, despite Coors's great personal wealth. Most important, Salazar outspent Coors 2–1 in the final weeks of the campaign, providing a vital edge in television advertising. Salazar's financial advantage was enhanced by help from the Democratic Senatorial Campaign Committee (DSCC), which outspent the National Republican Senatorial Committee (NRSC) $2.3 million to $1.1 million. In a sign of the race's national importance, the DSCC spent more in Colorado than in any other state that year (Saunders and Duffy 2005a).

Democrats enjoyed an even bigger advantage in the 2008 Senate race, when Mark Udall raised and spent nearly $13 million—the most by any candidate

TABLE 2.4. Campaign spending in Colorado House and Senate races by candidates and campaign committees, 2002–2008

	2002	2004	2006	2008
Third District				
Democratic candidate	*	$1,661,486	$2,028,066	$1,335,166
Republican candidate	$567,940	$1,638,304	$821,303	$21,704
Democratic campaign committees	*	$1,905,065	$29,693	*
Republican campaign committees	*	$3,682,410	*	*
Fourth District				
Democratic candidate	$955,654	$869,007	$1,977,177	$2,893,744
Republican candidate	$1,249,564	$3,422,482	$3,160,640	$2,862,907
Democratic campaign committees	*	*	$353,593	$1,111,300
Republican campaign committees	*	$1,049,831	$1,809,938	$983,366
Seventh District				
Democratic candidate	$1,147,759	$1,156,413	$2,984,171	$1,770,087
Republican candidate	$1,827,119	$2,967,373	$2,818,132	$34,048
Democratic campaign committees	$682,185	$61,850	$1,993,266	*
Republican campaign committees	$1,900,000	$608,393	$556,029	*
Colorado Senate				
Democratic candidate	$5,206,080	$9,925,778	NR	$12,867,562
Republican candidate	$5,334,115	$7,642,839	NR	$7,387,843
Democratic campaign committees	$295	$2,752,983	NR	$4,644,386
Republican campaign committees	$0	$2,489,181	NR	$3,530,825

Source: Center for Responsive Politics 2004a, 2004b, 2006, 2008a, 2008b, 2008c, 2008d. Available at http://opensecrets.org.
Note: An asterisk (*) indicates that no data were available; NR indicates that there was no senate race in 2006.

in Colorado history (Federal Election Commission 2008). Bob Schaffer, who trailed in the polls throughout, raised nearly $7.4 million and spent just under $7.1 million, a respectable amount but far short of Udall's totals. As in 2004, the DSCC was a major player, making just over $4.6 million in independent expenditures in the race and contributing another $2.6 million to the state party's coordinated campaign (Center for Responsive Politics 2008b; Waak 2009a). The NRSC, which was plagued by poor fundraising that year, spent more than $3.5 million—well short of its initial budget of $4.8 million (Center for Responsive Politics 2008c). In fact, the NRSC shifted its dwindling resources to other states in mid-October, when it became convinced that Schaffer could not win (Bartels 2008).

The story is more complicated in the three House seats that changed hands between 2004 and 2008, as can be seen in table 2.4. In Colorado's Third District, Republican Scott McInnis won in a landslide in 2002, but his retirement created an open seat and touched off a spending frenzy in the 2004 race ultimately won by John Salazar. Both Salazar and Greg Walcher, the Republican candidate, raised more than $1.6 million. Salazar won despite the NRCC spending $3.6 million against him, roughly twice the amount spent by the DCCC (Saunders and Duffy 2005b). As noted later, spending by interest groups may have helped mute the disparity in party spending; in any event, Salazar had raised enough money on his own to wage a competitive race and get his message out. In 2006 Salazar was reelected with 61 percent of the vote and outspent his opponent, Scott Tipton, $2 million to $821,000 (Center for Responsive Politics 2006). In 2008 Salazar again captured 61 percent of the vote, this time spending $1.335 million to his opponent's paltry $21,704 (Center for Responsive Politics 2008d). In each subsequent election cycle, then, Salazar has enjoyed a tremendous financial edge over his opponents; because his seat seemed safe, neither party's congressional campaign committees spent any money in the district.

In 2002 Republican Bob Beauprez won Colorado's newly created Seventh District by 121 votes. "Landslide Bob," as he came to be known, raised more than $1.8 million, compared to less than $1.2 million for Democrat Mike Feeley. Beauprez's advantage was magnified when party spending is taken into account. The NRCC far outspent its Democratic counterpart, $1.9 million to $682,185, and combined spending by the Republican state and federal parties totaled $2.5 million, compared to just $830,000 by the Democrats. According to Daniel Smith (2003), the flood of party money was a critical element in Beauprez's razor-thin win because Feeley was short on cash toward the end of the campaign.

Similarly, Beauprez cruised to an easy win in 2004, in part because he enjoyed a huge financial edge over his opponent, Dave Thomas. Incumbents typically raise and spend more money than challengers, and that year Beauprez raised $2.96 million, compared to Thomas's $1.16 million. As before, the NRCC far outspent the DCCC, $608,393 to $61,850 (Saunders and Duffy 2005b).

Beauprez's surprise decision to run for governor created an open seat in 2006. As in the Third District two years earlier, the two major party candidates raised and spent roughly the same amount. Democrat Ed Perlmutter raised over $2.9 million, and Republican Rick O'Donnell raised $2.8 million. In a departure from previous cycles, the DCCC made $2 million in independent expenditures, compared to just $556,000 by the NRCC (Saunders and Duffy 2007). Perlmutter won rather easily, clearly benefiting from both the financial superiority and the national wave that handed Democrats control of the US House for the first time since 1994 (Saunders and Duffy 2007).

Until Democrat Betsy Markey won a surprisingly easy victory over embattled incumbent Marilyn Musgrave in 2008, Republicans had represented the state's Fourth District for nearly four decades. During Musgrave's previous campaigns, she raised and spent far more than her opponents, and, as her victory margins declined, she was backed by increasingly large expenditures by the NRCC. In fact, as table 2.4 indicates, the organization made $1,049,831 in independent expenditures in the district in 2004 and $1,809,938 in 2006 (Center for Responsive Politics 2004a).

Heading into 2008, in what was another bad year for Republicans, Musgrave was clearly vulnerable. In the end, Musgrave and Markey spent a combined $5.75 million, surpassing the $5.1 million spent by Musgrave and Democrat Angie Paccione in 2006. As indicated in table 2.4, Markey raised $2.85 million and spent $2.89 million, both records for a Democrat in the Fourth District. Markey's fund-raising increased each quarter as her chances of winning improved. During the crucial month of October, Markey raised more than $1 million, most of it in the final two weeks (Caprara 2008).

Musgrave's fundraising lagged prior cycles, as a number of previous donors sat out the race, turned off by her polarizing positions and negative campaigning. In the end, Musgrave raised $2.86 million and spent $2.83 million. Although this was a significant sum, it was less than the nearly $3.2 million she spent in 2006 and the $3.4 million she spent in 2004 (Center for Responsive Politics 2004b, 2006).

According to Federal Election Commission records, the DCCC made $1.1 million in independent expenditures in the contest, its first major foray into the Fourth District (see table 2.4). The DCCC also contributed about $225,000 to the coordinated campaign in Colorado (Waak 2009a). The NRCC ended up spending just over $983,000 in the race, less than the $1.2 million it had originally planned. Indeed, in late October the organization notified Denver television stations that it was canceling a $400,000 ad buy for the last week of the campaign. The NRCC's decision came just two days after early voting began and was reflective of Musgrave's dismal polling as well as the group's severe cash shortage (Chacon 2008). The decision to write her off and shift resources to other states came shortly after the leak of an internal Republican "death list" of endangered House incumbents, which characterized Musgrave as exceptionally vulnerable. Nationally, the DCCC outspent the NRCC by a three-to-one margin in 2008, and Democratic candidates subsequently won thirty-seven of the sixty districts in which the DCCC spent more than the GOP (Wilson 2009).

WE'RE NOT DEAD YET, OR WHY REPORTS OF THE COLORADO DEMOCRATIC PARTY'S DEMISE ARE GREATLY EXAGGERATED

Although some have argued that campaign finance reforms have rendered state parties obsolete, we suggest that they have played an important yet overlooked role in the Democrats' recent success (Witwer 2009). A number of state Democratic Party organizations, including Colorado's, underwent significant changes at about the same time Howard Dean became head of the Democratic National Committee (DNC). In Colorado, Pat Waak replaced Chris Gates as party chair and charted a new direction for the organization, which became more strategic and focused on capacity building for itself and for county and local party organizations as well. Previously, the state party had focused primarily on the Denver metropolitan area, which is where most of the state's Democratic voters were located. But Waak, along with a new group of party officers, thought more could be done to bolster the party's presence throughout the state. As a result, the party instituted a "64-county strategy" that mirrored Dean's controversial "50-state strategy" at the DNC. The goal, of course, was to maximize Democratic votes statewide. In an effort to signal that every county and every voter mattered, Waak visited with the county chairs and asked them to name three things they needed most. Their answers were better voter files, better training, and better communications and messaging.

Beginning in 2005, according to Waak, the party invested significant time and money in improving its voter files. This involved hiring a voter file manager, assembling a technology committee of approximately 180 people, and testing "every single voter contact program" in existence at the time (Waak 2009b). The party selected the Voter Activation Network (VAN), a program used by many other state Democratic parties, to help manage its voter contact programs. VAN, which Waak described as the party's "most valuable asset," helps the party with essential tasks like voter identification, persuasion, and getting out the vote (Waak 2008). More specifically, it merges voter files with sophisticated programs for canvassing, collecting and importing new information about voters, organizing events, and other volunteer management and mobilization activities. As an example, VAN allows users to produce precinct maps that display concentrations of voters, showing exactly where specific groups of voters live along with their voting histories, their group affiliations, whether they have been contacted before, and how often. These tools, which are available to the county parties as well, allow users to more effectively focus their resources and efforts. The DNC assumed the cost of VAN starting in 2006.

VAN has also made it much easier for the party to improve its early voting efforts, which, as discussed in chapter 5, is a crucially important task in Colorado elections. The voter file makes it much easier to target those who have voted early in prior elections; the party can contact them to encourage them to again cast an early ballot. In fact, in recent years the state party has moved to a two-pronged get out the vote (GOTV) program. Part one involves getting the early vote in, while part two focuses on turning out the vote on election day. VAN, in short, provides the Democrats with the technology to adapt to the numerous changes in state election laws, such as early and absentee voting. By 2008, in fact, Democrats had eliminated the traditional Republican advantage in early voting (Duffy, Saunders, and Dunn 2009).

The state party's capacity-building efforts have also yielded results at the county level. In 2005 the party initiated training programs for county parties and local activists. The programs emphasized how to recruit better candidates, how to conduct effective get out the vote programs, and more. As part of the 64-county strategy, the DNC provided money for rural field directors, which allowed the state party to hire Colorado residents to work with county parties in traditionally Republican areas. Here the goal was not necessarily to turn the counties Democratic but rather to cut into the Republican advantage and give Democrats running statewide a better shot at winning. These efforts laid the groundwork for statewide campaigns in 2006 and for the Obama and Udall campaigns in 2008 (Waak 2009b).

Voter registration efforts in Arapahoe County provide an excellent illustration of the party's efforts. In 2004 there were 27,000 more registered Republicans than Democrats in the county. The leaders of the county's Democratic Party made it their mission to change the registration figures and embarked on an ambitious voter registration program. By election day in 2008, Democrats outnumbered Republicans by more than 5,000, a stunning turnabout in just four years.

The state party has also taken a major role in recruiting candidates at all levels. Sometimes this has meant convincing candidates to run for office; at other times, it has meant talking them out of running (Waak 2009a). Since 2004, Democrats have largely succeeded in avoiding divisive primaries. Although several prominent Democrats coveted the open US Senate seat in 2004, the field cleared quickly for Ken Salazar. Mark Udall ran unopposed for the Senate in 2008, and Betsy Markey ran unopposed in the Fourth District's primary after former candidate Angie Paccione withdrew. In all of these cases, the Democratic candidate was spared a potentially destructive intra-party squabble and was able to save campaign cash for the general election.

The state party has also done a good job working with federal candidates and the national congressional committees. The state party has held retreats with candidates for offices at all levels and has done a better job in coordinating messaging with candidates. In 2008, for example, the party's coordinated campaign, known as Forward Colorado, was better funded and far more effective than the Republicans' effort. The state party spent more than $500,000 in coordinated expenditures (Federal Election Commission 2008), while the DCCC contributed approximately $225,000, the DSCC sent $2.6 million, and the DNC provided $3.5 million (Waak 2009a). The Republican National Committee contributed just over $1.2 million to its state party's coordinated campaign, less than one-fifth the amount available to the Democrats (Duffy, Saunders, and Dunn 2009).

With so much more money than the Republicans had, the Democrats' coordinated campaign was able to do much more, and for a much longer period of time, than the Republican effort, which only became fully operational in the campaign's final weeks. The Democrats had twelve offices statewide, with approximately 100 employees—again, far more than their opponents (Duffy, Saunders, and Dunn 2009).

COLORADO REPUBLICANS REPLAY THE GOLDEN OLDIES: NAME CALLING, ATTACK POLITICS, AND FIGHTING THE LAST WAR

While Colorado Democrats have done some things well, Colorado Republicans have made some mistakes. Unlike the Democrats, the Republican Party experienced significant leadership turnover in the middle of the decade, which left the organization without direction. Republicans were also guilty of fighting the last war—they assumed their technological advantage in voter files and GOTV would last forever, and they failed to adapt to the state's changing registration landscape. As a result, they assumed that campaign tactics that had worked in previous election cycles would continue to work in the future. The problems with these approaches became manifest in 2008 in both the Marilyn Musgrave and Bob Schaffer campaigns.

Musgrave ran the same campaign in 2008 as she had in her prior races: relentlessly attacking her opponent and providing little substance as to her own priorities. In her first two races she caricatured former state senate president Stan Matsunaka as "Stan Taxanaka," then followed with a nasty campaign focusing on Angie Paccione's personal bankruptcy. In none of these races did Musgrave's television ads offer insights into what she would do about important issues. In 2008, all but one of Musgrave's seven television ads attacked Markey for using her staff position with Senator Salazar to boost her family business. Each subsequent ad upped the ante and used increasingly heated rhetoric, culminating in the two most controversial ads of the campaign.

Musgrave's penultimate ad began, "Like the worst on Wall Street, Betsy Markey gamed the system and got rich with taxpayer money. But Millionaire Markey got caught." The narrator states that "Markey broke the rules. The [US] Justice Department has been asked to investigate whether Markey broke the law. She could spend five years in prison." While technically true, the ad failed to mention that the request for a Justice Department investigation had been filed by a Republican operative who had prepared it with the help of Musgrave's campaign. Moreover, the ad failed to disclose that the same man had filed a similar charge against Angie Paccione, Musgrave's opponent in 2006. Not surprisingly, the ad's claim that Markey could do prison time raised some eyebrows because it seemed to cross a line in a campaign marked by attack ads, even for a candidate known for running tough campaigns.

Although that ad was harsh, it seemed tame in comparison to Musgrave's "Lie Detector" commercial, which featured images of a woman who is supposed to be Betsy Markey strapped to a lie detector under an overhead light. A man in the foreground is administering a lie detector test. The announcer says, "We've attached a lie detector to Betsy Markey." The man administering the lie detector then asks, "Did you violate Senate ethics rules to make millions in government contracts for your family business?" "Markey" answers "no," which is followed by loud beeping sounds and red letters flashing the words "false detection." The ad continues in this vein, with the interrogator asking "Markey" if she had falsified information and if she had told the truth. Each time, her answer is followed by the beeping sound and the flashing words "false detection."

The reaction to this ad was immediate and severe. Senator Ken Salazar held a conference call with reporters the next day to denounce Musgrave as an "an agent of hate," saying she should be "ashamed of herself" and that voters "should be appalled by her blatant disregard for the truth" (quoted in Moore 2008d). The ad was so over the top that a number of Republicans in the district, including a former US House member and a former state representative, issued statements condemning the ad and saying they would vote for Markey. One stated that the "Musgrave campaign has violated whatever is left of campaign ethics by accusing Markey of being a criminal. That's too much! Musgrave wants the election so badly she has lost her way, her sense of propriety, her very decency" (quoted in Kosena 2008d; Moore 2008d).

Similarly, Bob Schaffer was plagued throughout his race by high negatives—that is, voters did not like him very much. Schaffer rarely spoke during the campaign, and when he did speak, he often attracted bad publicity because he was seen as belligerent or petulant. His appearance on *Meet the Press*, as a case in point, was widely criticized because he frequently interrupted and talked over Udall. His refusal to begin another televised debate unless he was allowed to use notes, despite his campaign's prior agreement that notes would not be allowed, reinforced Schaffer's negative image. Most of the time, Schaffer let Dick Wadhams, his colorful and combative campaign manager, do the talking. Wadhams, who had run Wayne Allard's successful reelection campaign in 2002 and later John Thune's run in South Dakota against then Senate majority leader Tom Daschle, was known for his take-no-prisoners approach to politics. Wadhams had relentlessly criticized Tom Strickland, Allard's 2002 opponent, as a "lawyer lobbyist." It was no surprise, then, that Wadhams tried the same tactic in 2008, endlessly referring to Schaffer's opponent as "Boulder liberal Mark Udall." In fact, Wadhams used the term so often that reporters began to joke about it.

Part of the reason the old tactic failed to work was that Republicans no longer outnumbered Democrats by 180,000 registered voters. In addition, 2008 was not a normal election—George Bush and the Republican brand were in disrepute, the nation was facing serious economic problems, and voters were more interested in candidates who offered solutions rather than in negative personal attacks. Republicans, in rerunning campaigns from the old playbook, either failed to recognize the changed circumstances or were unwilling to try something different.

CONCLUSION

There is no single explanation for the Democratic success in recent federal elections. Rather, Democrats have won in Colorado for a variety of reasons: population growth and demographic shifts; financial and organizational advantages, including a resurgent state party; and because they offered pragmatic, non-ideological candidates who proved more appealing to the state's unaffiliated voters. Perhaps most important, in 2006 and 2008 Colorado Democrats were helped by national economic and political factors that resulted in two successive wave elections.

The lesson for students of Colorado politics is this: the playbook has changed, and the Democrats are the ones writing the new playbook. However, politics are dynamic, and circumstances can change quickly. As the epilogue shows, 2010 is shaping up to be a bad year for Democrats everywhere. The economy remains in poor shape, unemployment rates are very high, and voters appear to be blaming President Obama and Democrats in general because they are now the majority party in Washington. In particular, the Democrats' mishandling of health care reform—the president's top legislative priority—has renewed questions about the party's competence and ability to govern. With health care, congressional Democrats have struggled publicly to balance the concerns of moderates such as Markey against those of their more liberal members. If these trends continue, purple states like Colorado and swing districts like the Third, Fourth, and Seventh could easily go Republican again.

If Republican candidates are to succeed in Colorado, they will need to find new ways of appealing to unaffiliated voters as well as stemming the Democratic momentum in registration and turnout over the last decade. Until recently, the Republican recipe for success in Colorado was fairly straightforward: mobilize the base, and compete for a respectable share of independents. But as Democratic gains first reduced and then eliminated the Republican edge in voter registration, that formula no longer worked. In 2010 the Republican strategy of saying "no" to all things Obama was enough to win elections. Although voters do seem angry, there is little evidence at this point that Coloradans are rushing to embrace Republicans, especially the stridently anti-government rhetoric voiced by the party's more conservative members. Nor is there any evidence that the state's sizable and growing bloc of unaffiliated voters has suddenly developed an affinity for ideology-based politics. For the foreseeable future, then, whichever party's candidates can turn out their own supporters and win among unaffiliated voters will have the edge.

NOTES

1. Most organizations involved in political activities are usually classified under their section in the US Tax Code, which regulates the financial activities of all political groups whose intent it is to influence political outcomes. Section 501(c)(3) organizations are subject to limits or absolute prohibitions on engaging in political activities, while 501(c)(4) organizations can lobby for legislation and are allowed to participate in political campaigns and elections through contributions and other regulated activities, as long as such activities do not become their "primary purpose." In contrast, 527 organizations are independent political groups that are also exempt from federal taxation. While these entities existed prior to the Bipartisan Campaign Reform Act (BCRA) of 2002, they have since become much more common. Political parties and candidates used to be able to accept unlimited and unregulated donations from corporations, unions, and individuals for party-building activities, a practice commonly known as "soft money." The BCRA prohibited this practice, but it left independent 527s comparatively unregulated. So long as there is no coordination among the parties, candidates, and 527 groups, the 527s can raise unlimited amounts of money to spend on vote mobilization, issue advocacy, and the like, as long as those advertisements do not explicitly support or oppose the election of any federal candidate or engage in "electioneering communications." For more information, see http://www.opensecrets.org/527s/index.php.

REFERENCES

American Conservative Union. 2009. "Ratings of Congress." Available at http://www. acuratings.org/. Accessed January 6, 2009.

Barnes, Fred. 2008. "The Colorado Model: The Democrats' Plan for Turning Red States Blue." *The Weekly Standard* 13(42), July 21.

Barone, Michael, and Richard E. Cohen. 2008. *The Almanac of American Politics.* Washington, DC: National Journal Group. Available at http://www.nationaljournal.com/almanac/2008/states/co. Accessed December 2, 2008.

Bartels, Lynn. 2008. "GOP Committee Pulls Schaffer TV Ads." *The Rocky Mountain News*, October 24. Available at http://www.rockymountainnews.com/news/2008/oct/24/gop-committee pulls-schaffer-tv-ads/. Accessed October 24, 2008.

Cable News Network. 2004. "Colorado Presidential Voting History." Available at http://www.cnn.com/ELECTION/2004/pages/pre/CO/history.html. Accessed December 2, 2008.

———. 2008a. "President/Colorado/Exit Polls." Available at http://www.cnn.com/ELECTION/2008/results/polls/CO/epolls.0.html. Accessed November 19, 2008.

————. 2008b. "Senate/Colorado/Exit Polls." Available at http://www.cnn.com/ELEC-TION/2008/results/polls/#COS01p1. Accessed November 19, 2008.

Campaign Finance Institute. 2008. "A First Look at Money in the House and Senate Elections," November 6. Available at http://www.cfinst.org/pr/prRelease.aspx?ReleaseID=215. Accessed January 7, 2009.

Campaign Money. 2006. Coloradans for Life 527 Political Organization Filing Information. Available at http://campaignmoney.com/political/527/coloradans-for-life.asp. Accessed March 20, 2011.

Caprara, Anne. 2008. Campaign manager, Markey for Congress. Interview with Robert Duffy and Kyle Saunders, Fort Collins, CO, November 11.

Center for Responsive Politics. 2004a. "National Republican Congressional Committee Independent Expenditures." Available at http://www.opensecrets.org/parties/ind-exp.php?cycle=2004&cmte=NRCC&cycle=2004. Accessed January 7, 2009.

————. 2004b. "Congressional Elections: 2004 Race: Colorado District 04, Total Raised and Spent." Available at http://www.opensecrets.org/races/summary.php?id=CO04&cycle=2004. Accessed January 7, 2009.

————. 2006. "Congressional Elections: 2006 Race; Colorado District 04, Total Raised and Spent." Available at http://www.opensecrets.org/races/summary.php?id=CO04&cycle=2006. Accessed January 7, 2009.

————. 2008a. "Colorado: Party Transfers." Available at http://www.opensecrets.org/states/other.php?cycle=2008&state=CO. Accessed January 6, 2009.

————. 2008b. "Democratic Senatorial Campaign Committee: Independent Expenditures." Available at http://www.opensecrets.org/parties/indexp.php?cycle=2008&cmte=DSCC&cycle=2008. Accessed December 17, 2008.

————. 2008c. "Republican Senatorial Campaign Committee: Independent Expenditures." Available at http://www.opensecrets.org/parties/indexp.php?cycle=2008&cmte=NRSC&cycle=2008. Accessed December 17, 2008.

————. 2008d. "Congressional Elections: 2008 Race: Colorado District 3, Total Raised and Spent." Available at http://www.opensecrets.org/races/summary.php?id=CO03&cycle=2008. Accessed January 7, 2009.

Chacon, Daniel. 2008. "Committee Cuts Ad Buys for Musgrave." *The Rocky Mountain News*, October 23. Available at http://www.rockymountainnews.com/news/2008/oct/22/party-pulling-tv-ad backing-musgrave/. Accessed October 24, 2008.

Colorado Secretary of State. 2002. "December 2002 Voter Registration Numbers by Party." Copy faxed to authors from Secretary of State's office.

————. 2004. "December 2004 Voter Registration Numbers by Party." Available at http://www.elections.colorado.gov/DDefault.aspx?tid=480&vmid=134. Accessed November 25, 2008.

————. 2006. "December 2006 Voter Registration Numbers by Party." Available at http://www.elections.colorado.gov/Default.aspx?PageMenuID=1961&ShowVM =1451TitleVM=2006%20Voter%20Registration%20Numbers. Accessed November 25, 2008.

————. 2008. "December 2008 Voter Registration Numbers: Voter Recap by Party." Available at http://www.elections.colorado.gov/WWW/default/2008%20Voter%20Registration%20numbers/October_22_2008/vr_stats_by_party_10.22.2008.pdf. Accessed November 25, 2008.

Couch, Mark P., and Karen E. Crummy. 2004. "Senate Seat Goes Blue as Salazar Ices Coors." *The Denver Post*, November 3, 1A.

Duffy, Robert J., Kyle L. Saunders, and Joshua Dunn. 2009. "Colorado 2008: Democrats Expand Their Base and Win Unaffiliated Voters." In *The Change Election: Money, Mobilization, and Persuasion in the 2008 Federal Elections*, ed. David B. Magleby. Provo, UT: Center for the Study of Elections and Democracy, Brigham Young University, 224–261.

Federal Election Commission. 2008. "Candidate Summary Reports: December 31, 2008." Available at http://query.nictusa.com/cgi-bin/cancomsrs/?_08+S8CO00172. Accessed May 16, 2009.

Fender, Jessica. 2008. "Colorado Democratic Scheme Called Ingenious." *The Denver Post,* October 3. Available at www.denverpost.com/ci_10623568. Accessed October 4, 2008.

Frey, William H., and Ruy Teixeira. 2008. *The Political Geography of the Intermountain West: The New Swing Region*. Washington, DC: Brookings Institution.

Giroux, Greg. 2006. "Musgrave's Priorities at Issue in Increasingly Close Colorado 4 Race." *The New York Times*, September 28. Available at http://www.nytimes.com/cq/2006/09/28/cq_1520.html. Accessed January 4, 2009.

Kosena, Jason. 2008a. "E-mailed Plans Aim to Unseat Musgrave." *The Fort Collins Coloradoan*, February 3, A1.

———. 2008b. "Environmental Group Rejoices over Musgrave Loss." *The Colorado Independent*, November 6. Available at http://www.coloradoindependent.com/14396/environmental group-rejoices-over-musgrave-loss. Accessed November 7, 2008.

———. 2008c. "A Stunning Markey Win Marks a Blue Era in Colorado's 4th CD." *The Colorado Independent*, November 5. Available at http://www.coloradoindependent.com/14277/a-blue era-begins-anew-in-colorados–4th-cd. Accessed November 5, 2008.

———. 2008d. "Citing Musgrave Smear Tactics, Republicans Come out for Markey." *The Colorado Independent*, October 17. Available at http://www.coloradoindependent.com/11751/citing-musgrave-smear-tactics-republicans-come-out-for-markey. Accessed October 17, 2008.

Moore, Robert. 2008a. "Report: Markey, Allies Reversed GOP's Historic Money Advantage." *The Fort Collins Coloradoan*, December 5, A1.

———. 2008b. "Group Meets Objective of Unseating Musgrave." *The Fort Collins Coloradoan*, November 10, A1.

———. 2008c. "Marilyn Musgrave Blames Election Loss on 'Leftist Special Interests.' " *The Fort Collins Coloradoan*, December 2, A1.

———. 2008d. "Salazar Blasts Musgrave as Agent of Hate." *The Fort Collins Coloradoan*, October 16, A1.

National Public Radio. 2008. "Secret Money Project: August 15, 2008." Available at www.npr.org/blogs/secretmomey/outside_groups/colorado_first_project.html. Accessed December 1, 2008.

O'Donnell, Rick. 1995. "For Freedom's Sake, Eliminate Social Security." *American Civilization* (February).

Project Vote. 2008. "The Demographics of Voters in America's 2008 General Election: A Preliminary Assessment." Available at http://www.projectvote.org/images/publications/reports on the electorate/demographics-of-voters-in-the-2008-election. PDF. Accessed March 29, 2010.

Riley, Michael. 2008a. "Attack Ads Inundate State Race for Senate." *The Denver Post*, September 25. Available at http://www.denverpost.com/senate08/ci_10550738. Accessed September 25, 2008.

———. 2008b. "Udall Whittles away at Colorado's GOP Strongholds." *The Denver Post*, October 26, B1.

Saunders, Kyle, and Robert Duffy. 2005a. "The 2004 Colorado U.S. Senate Race." In *Dancing without Partners: How Candidates, Parties, and Interest Groups Interact in the New Campaign Finance Environment*, ed. David B. Magleby, J. Quin Monson, and Kelly D. Patterson. Provo, UT: Center for the Study of Elections and Democracy, Brigham Young University, 180–197.

———. 2005b. "The 2004 Colorado 7th Congressional District Race." In *Dancing without Partners: How Candidates, Parties, and Interest Groups Interact in the New Campaign Finance Environment*, ed. David B. Magleby, J. Quin Monson, and Kelly D. Patterson. Provo, UT: Center for the Study of Elections and Democracy, Brigham Young University, 264–274.

———. 2007. "The 2006 Colorado 7th Congressional District Race." In *War Games: Issues and Resources in the Battle for Control of Congress*, ed. David B. Magleby and Kelly D. Patterson. Provo, UT: Center for the Study of Elections and Democracy, Brigham Young University, 69–85.

Schrager, Adam, and Rob Witwer. 2010. *The Blueprint: How the Democrats Won Colorado (and Why Republicans Everywhere Should Care)*. Golden, CO: Speakers Corner.

Smith, Daniel A. 2003. "Strings Attached: Outside Money in Colorado's Seventh Congressional District." In *The Last Hurrah? Soft Money and Issue Advocacy in the 2002 Congressional Elections,* ed. David Magleby and Quin Monson. Washington, DC: Brookings Institution, 180–204.

Survey USA. 2008. Available at http://www.surveyusa.com/client/PollReport.aspx?g=1c cadc3d–8b8d 43b3-a671–939370c87ca3. Accessed January 3, 2009.

US Census Bureau. 2008. "Quick Facts: Colorado." Available at http://quickfacts.census. gov/qfd/states/08000.html. Accessed December 17, 2009.

Vlahos, Kelley Beaucar. 2004. "Water Tempts Thirsty Voters in Colorado's 3rd District." Available at http://www.foxnews.com/story/0,2933,135001,00.html. Accessed November 29, 2009.

Waak, Pat. 2008. Colorado Democratic Party chair. Interview with Robert Duffy, Denver, CO, November 14.

———. 2009a. Colorado Democratic Party chair. Personal e-mail communication to Robert Duffy, January 7.

———. 2009b. Colorado Democratic Party chair. Telephone interview with Robert Duffy, December 29.

Wilson, Reid. 2009. "NRCC Fundraising Woes Continue." *Hotline on Call*. Available at http://hotlineoncall.nationaljournal.com/. Accessed December 18, 2009.

Witwer, Rob. 2009. "Rocky Ride: The Republicans' Fall from Power in Colorado—and How the Democrats Hope to Replicate It." *National Review*, March 23. Available at http://nrd.nationalreview.com/article/?Q=odjmywrimdkxmzyxmzm/nty3ymmwzdc/mzzmmmyzmgu=. Accessed June 8, 2009.

Chapter Three

Colorado's Central Role in the 2008 Presidential Election Cycle

Seth E. Masket

The 2008 presidential nominations process was an unusual one for Colorado.[1] After years of holding largely ceremonial presidential caucuses and primaries in which the nominations had already been effectively decided, 2008 presented the state with a rare chance to be consequential. The nominations contests in both major political parties were far from settled, and the state's decision to join twenty other states in an early February election date had compelled candidates to devote campaign resources and candidate time to winning the delegates from the Centennial State.

The state's increasing importance in presidential nominations paralleled its rising significance in general elections. While recent presidential elections had elevated the stature of populous industrial states such as Ohio, Pennsylvania, and Florida, evidence was mounting that the Mountain West was increasingly becoming the key to presidential elections, and Colorado was the key to the Mountain West. The state's importance in presidential elections was crystallized by national Democrats' decision to hold the 2008 presidential nominating convention in Denver.

The Democratic presidential caucuses, held in February 2008, proved highly competitive, with the candidates and their surrogates spending considerable time crisscrossing the state. The nomination process, however, revealed an even more interesting dimension in the weeks following the caucuses. During the complex translation of caucus-night votes into actual Democratic delegates, both major candidates—Senators Hillary Rodham Clinton and Barack Obama—sought to make inroads in Colorado. Similarly, the state proved competitive in the general election as well, with both major campaigns devoting considerable resources and candidate time to wooing Colorado voters. In both contests, the campaigns' deployment of field offices proved important. To an extent not seen previously in the state's recent history, the presidential campaigns opened offices all across Colorado, dispatching volunteers to contact voters and distribute literature in both dense urban areas and sparsely populated rural regions.

This chapter examines several aspects of Colorado's role in the 2008 presidential selection process. It begins with a discussion of Colorado's increasing importance to both nominations and general national elections in recent years. It then examines the particularities of the caucus system in presidential nominations and the impact of this form of nomination contest on the 2008 race. From there, it turns to an examination of the power of field offices to affect election results, from efforts by the Clinton and Obama campaigns to increase their share of delegates after Colorado's presidential caucus to work by the Obama and McCain campaigns to win over voters from county to county. This study helps shed light on the power of the ground game to affect election results and also on the importance of the delegate selection process, which receives only sporadic attention from journalists and scholars. The chapter concludes with a reflection on the significant, if limited, effects of campaigns on election outcomes and a note on the role Colorado now plays in national politics.

COLORADO AND PRESIDENTIAL ELECTIONS

Colorado proved its relevance to presidential elections very early in its history. It was granted statehood on August 1, 1876, with insufficient time to organize a statewide election for that year's presidential contest. The state legislature thus took on the task of selecting the state's three Electoral College members, all three of whom cast their votes for Republican Rutherford B. Hayes in an election he won by a single electoral vote.

It would be difficult for the state to be that consequential to the outcome of a presidential election again. Nonetheless, the state has received increasing attention from both major political parties throughout the past decade, in part because of demographic factors. Simply put, the state is growing. Colorado went from six to seven congressional districts after the 2000 census, and its population grew by 17 percent between 2000 and 2010 (Hubbard 2009). The state's growing size alone makes it worthy of attention by presidential campaigns.

Also of note, however, is the fact that Colorado is increasingly competitive in statewide elections. For years, although moderate Democrats occasionally occupied the governor's mansion, the state was considered a safe haven for Republicans. Between 1952 and 2004, Colorado voted for a Democratic presidential candidate only twice. Republicans had also enjoyed control of the state legislature for decades. This began to change in 2004, when Democrats took over both state legislative bodies for the first time in forty years and Democrat Ken Salazar won the state's US Senate contest. This was followed by the victory of a Democratic gubernatorial candidate in 2006 and the state's other Senate seat going from red to blue in 2008. Meanwhile, Colorado's delegation to the US House of Representatives went from five Republicans and two Democrats in 2003 to five Democrats and two Republicans in 2009.

This sudden shift in state voting patterns is at least in part a result of national trends—the Republican Party grew steadily less popular during President George W. Bush's tenure—but also of regional ones. National Republicans' increasing cultural focus (fostered in part by the prominence of southern conservatives in that party's leadership) tended to alienate more libertarian-minded conservatives in the West.

Another cause of the state's shifting political stripes has been the reactions (or lack thereof) of the two political parties to recent campaign finance regulations. Several recent studies suggest that the Democrats have been quicker to develop alternative systems of channeling funds to preferred candidates and more adept at recruiting wealthy private benefactors (Loevy 2009; Masket 2010; Schrager and Witwer 2010). Finally, perhaps the most important cause of increased party competition in the state concerns demographics: more liberal residents of coastal states have been flocking to urban and suburban communities in the Denver metropolitan area (Masket 2009b; Perry 2003).

The national parties have recently been portraying Colorado as the key to the Mountain West, an area that is increasingly a battleground for the national political parties. Indeed, as the South has become increasingly Republican and the Northeast increasingly Democratic in recent decades, the West is one of the last areas to have real competition between the parties. As Democratic National Committee chair Howard Dean said when the party decided to hold its 2008 convention in Denver: "There is no question that the West is important to the future of the Democratic Party. The recent Democratic gains in the West exemplify the principle that when we show up and ask for people's votes and talk about what we stand for, we can win in any part of the country" (quoted in AP 2008: A1). Dean concluded, "If we win the West, we will win the presidency" (quoted in Riccardi 2007).

THE CAUCUS

The presidential nominating caucus, as practiced in Colorado and a dozen other states, is strikingly different from primary elections. Rather than casting a simple, secret ballot, participants in a caucus engage in a very public and communal form of politicking. Meeting at the precinct level, fellow partisans gather to proclaim their support for candidates and to debate the relative merits of their choices. In some cases, candidates who fail to meet a viability threshold are dropped, and caucus goers attempt to woo their supporters. The caucus typically lasts a minimum of ninety minutes and culminates with a vote for the various candidates. The vote counts are then aggregated at the state level and reported by the media, much as with primaries.

Unlike primaries, however, caucus contests are only the beginning of the process of assigning delegates to candidates. During the caucus, participants elect delegates to attend the next nominating event, usually a county convention that occurs some weeks later. Participants at that convention then elect delegates to another convention, usually held at the state or congressional district level, where participants elect national delegates. At each of these stages, candidate preference votes are held. The entire process usually takes several months, and the final tally of pledged delegates may differ significantly from the reported levels of candidate support on caucus night.

Colorado has not always picked presidential nominees in this fashion. State political leaders of both parties pushed the state to abandon the caucus system in favor of a presidential primary for the 1992 cycle, arguing that it would give more Coloradans a chance to participate in the nominee selection process (Gavin 1990). However, Colorado's primary votes never proved pivotal, and the state moved back to the caucus/convention system prior to the 2004 presidential election cycle, largely as a cost-saving measure (*Daily Camera* Staff 2003). Canceling the primary saved the state an estimated $2.7 million that year, as caucuses are comparatively inexpensive to run and their costs are borne by the parties (*Daily Camera* staff).

In 2007, leaders of both parties rejected the idea of switching back to primaries—again because of cost considerations—but proposed moving the caucuses from their previous April date to February 5, the earliest date allowed in 2008 under the national parties' rules. The state's nominating contests would thus coincide with those of twenty other states in what became known as "Super Duper Tuesday" (Crummy 2007). If the early contests (Iowa and New Hampshire) proved indecisive, Colorado's choices could again become consequential.

The decision to hold a caucus in lieu of a primary is a consequential one for a state party. Caucuses are often praised for their participatory nature; instead of casting a private vote, people meet and debate with their neighbors, theoretically improving the quality of decisions and promoting the development of social capital (Karlin 2008). Many observers, however, criticize caucuses for their inherent turnout biases. Because of the time commitment necessary to participate in a caucus, turnout tends to be much lower than for primaries and to preclude participation by poorer, less-educated people and by those who have difficulty leaving home at night, such as the elderly or parents of young children (Pearson 2008).

There is little doubt that the electorate in a primary is very different from that in a caucus (Marshall 1978; although see Hersh 2010). Not surprisingly, these differences tend to produce different voting outcomes. In 2008, for example, Barack Obama tended to do about 12 percentage points better in caucuses than he did in primaries. This is not solely a result of the fact that the Obama campaign devoted more campaign resources to the caucus states than the Clinton campaign did. Providing a convenient natural experiment, Texas has a peculiar nominating system in that the state holds a primary and a caucus on the same day. In the Democratic contest there, Hillary Rodham Clinton bested Obama in the primary by a vote of 52–48 but lost to Obama in the caucus 44–56. Similarly, in the early stages of the Republican nomination contest, while John McCain prevailed in the primaries, Mitt Romney dominated the caucus states. Back in 1984, Colorado senator Gary Hart was the darling of caucus states even while the primary states went overwhelmingly to the eventual Democratic nominee, Walter Mondale. As should be clear, the type of nominating system a state chooses can have a substantial impact on the party's eventual choice of a nominee.

The caucus is a fascinating venue for politics in the United States, but it is one that does not lend itself well to quantitative political research and has not been thoroughly studied by political scientists. Moreover, with the exception of Iowa's caucus, the media tend to devote little attention to these contests, suggesting that it might be a ripe venue for campaign influence. That is, given the low media environment and the relatively low turnout, a particularly well-organized campaign could make significant inroads in a caucus by packing the event with its supporters and training volunteers to exploit caucus rules. Yet we have little sense of whether campaigns attempt to influence caucus outcomes or, if they do, to what extent they succeed. Indeed, as the next section suggests, our entire understanding of the influence of local campaigns on election outcomes is extremely limited.

THE GROUND GAME

Political pundits frequently laud successful campaigns for their ground games (see, for example, Jarmin 2008; Sherry 2008). This is certainly understandable—campaign offices and volunteers are measurable, tangible things, while the impact of an advertisement or a speech is much harder to quantify. Yet claims of the effectiveness of campaign field organizations are rarely subjected to empirical scrutiny. To be sure, a number of important experimental research projects have tested the impact of fieldwork (Eldersveld 1956; Eldersveld and Dodge 1954; Gerber and Green 2000, 2005; Gosnell 1927; Imai 2005), suggesting that campaigns can substantially affect voters' perceptions about a campaign and their likelihood of voting. These various studies, however, all share a common limitation: they use nonpartisan campaign messages to try to affect voters. In an effort to avoid tainting the election on behalf of a particular candidate or party, scholars generally avoid using explicitly partisan messages in their field experiments (although see Nickerson, Friedrichs, and King 2006), making them notably dissimilar to much of the campaign activity that actually occurs within an election year.

In an effort to address this shortcoming, other scholars have focused on observational studies of campaign field organizations. Some of these are focused on campaign contact (Hillygus 2005; Kramer 1970; Rosenstone and Hansen 1993; Silver 2008; Verba, Schlozman, and Brady 1995; although see Sides 2008), while others examine a wider range of ground game activities, including direct mail, telephone calls, and personal canvassing (e.g., Magleby, Monson, and Patterson 2007; Monson 2004).

The bulk of campaign studies are focused on general elections. A smaller subset of scholarly work examines the nominations stage of campaigns. Larry Bartels's (1988) examination of momentum and Marty Cohen and others' (2008) study of pre-primary endorsements have shed much light on this murkier area of American candidate selection, but they devote little attention to the study of actual primary and caucus campaign activity.

Only a handful of studies have delved into this area, with mixed findings. Lynn Vavreck and colleagues (2002), for example, found that fieldwork in the form of campaign contact has affected New Hampshire primary voters, boosting their ability to evaluate candidates and their affect toward them. Conversely, Barbara Trish's (1999) detailed study of the 1996 Iowa caucus found surprisingly modest and qualified effects of field organization in that contest. This finding was echoed in 2004 when *The New York Times* lauded the organizational superiority of Richard Gephardt's and Howard Dean's campaigns prior to the Iowa Democratic caucus, only to see those candidates lose to the less organized John Edwards and John Kerry in that contest (Cohen et al. 2008: 294; Purdum 2004: 1).

FROM CAUCUS TO CONVENTION

After the 2008 Iowa caucus and New Hampshire primary, the Democratic presidential nomination contest very quickly boiled down to just two candidates:

Senators Barack Obama and Hillary Rodham Clinton. As has been widely reported (Green 2008), the Clinton campaign chose a very targeted path to the Democratic nomination. It largely bypassed the caucus states, determining that it could effectively lock up the nomination by running strong in the early primaries. The Obama campaign, meanwhile, capitalized on its fundraising prowess to essentially compete everywhere; it sought to run up large delegate totals in the caucus states, since Clinton had largely ceded those, while limiting the size of Clinton's bounty of delegates in the primary states. (Notably, as Senator Clinton observed, the results of this competition would have been very different had the Democrats used winner-take-all delegate rules, as the Republicans do, rather than a more proportional system of delegate allocation. "If we had [the] same rules as the Republicans, I would be the nominee right now," she remarked in May [quoted in Broder 2008.])

The consequences of the two campaigns' strategic approaches could be seen in Colorado in the month before the state's February 5 caucuses. By the time of that contest, Obama had opened twelve field offices across the state, located in Arapahoe, Boulder, Denver, El Paso, La Plata, Larimer, Mesa, Pueblo, San Miguel, and Weld Counties. Clinton, meanwhile, had established just one, in the capital city of Denver. Tyler Chafee, Clinton's state campaign director, derided the Obama approach as misguided: "Clearly, they've taken the Starbucks approach to the campaign . . . Pretty soon, they'll have one [office] on every corner" (quoted in Montero 2008).

It is difficult to say to what extent Obama's 12–1 advantage in campaign offices in Colorado translated into votes. However, the available evidence suggests at least a modest effect. A *Denver Post*/Mason-Dixon poll conducted two weeks prior to the caucus reported 34 percent of likely voters supporting Obama, 32 percent backing Clinton, and 17 percent in favor of John Edwards, with the rest undecided (Booth and Riley 2008). Obama ultimately bested Clinton in the state's caucus 67–33.[2] Of course, such a discrepancy may be explained by the biases associated with caucus participation, which favor younger, wealthier, more educated voters who were already supportive of Obama. Yet Obama tended to do only about 12 points better in caucuses than in primaries. If we make the somewhat risky assumption that the Edwards supporters and undecided voters in the January poll split their support evenly between the two leading candidates, then we can conjecture that Obama would have defeated Clinton 52–48 in a Colorado primary. (This is admittedly an unreliable prediction based on a single poll of likely voters.) Obama, however, won the caucus 67–33. That is a 15-point difference—3 points higher than we might expect from the use of a caucus alone.

We have somewhat better evidence that Obama's field offices helped boost participation in the caucus. Voter turnout in the 2008 caucuses vastly exceeded turnout four years earlier. Roughly 120,000 Coloradans participated in the state's Democratic caucuses in 2008, about eight times the number in 2004 (Riley 2008). This dramatic rise in turnout was attributable both to the competitive nature of the 2008 contest relative to 2004 and to Colorado's decision to move its contest to an earlier date (Kerry was all but assured of the 2004 nomination by the time Coloradans voted in April of that year).

Yet the rise in turnout was not evenly distributed across Colorado's counties. Figure 3.1 shows the distribution of the increase in turnout in the Democratic presidential caucuses between 2004 and 2008 in counties both with and without Obama or Clinton field offices. (The increase is measured as a factor. For example, 969 Democrats showed up for the caucuses in Jefferson County in 2004, and 14,563 Democrats showed up in the same county four years later. Thus turnout increased there by a factor of 15.) The two distributions are strikingly different. In counties without field offices, caucus participation increased by an average factor of 5. The increase was twice that in counties with field offices. This difference is statistically significant ($p \leq .05$), even when controlling for growth in county population between the two election cycles.

Another area in which field offices seemed to matter was in the translation of those caucus-night votes into delegates. As mentioned previously, precinct caucus attendees send delegates to the county conventions (held several weeks later), where those delegates select people to attend state- or district-level conventions, where those delegates elect national delegates. Much of this selection occurs with little media attention and among people without great political experience or stature. This underreported feature of caucus states is actually a venue for considerable activity by campaigns (Marshall 2008). In 1984, according to Democratic strategist Tad Devine, Gary Hart actually lost a number of delegates he thought he had won at caucuses when those delegates flipped their support to Walter Mondale at state conventions (Hennessey and Ohlemacher 2008).

A similar sort of delegate flipping occurred in Colorado in 2008. Again, the night of the state's caucus, Obama received 67 percent of the vote to Clinton's 33 percent. Caucus attendees then elected delegates to the county conventions, which elected delegates to the state convention, held in Colorado Springs in May. Of the approximately 6,000 state convention delegates, only 63 percent were pledged to Obama, and 36 percent were pledged to Clinton. (The remaining 1 percent were uncommitted.) Somehow, Clinton had modestly increased her share of delegates above that which would be predicted from her caucus-night performance.

This shift in delegates may have been a function of the nature of each candidate's supporters. Clinton drew much of her support from longstanding Democratic Party activists who were familiar with the party system in the state

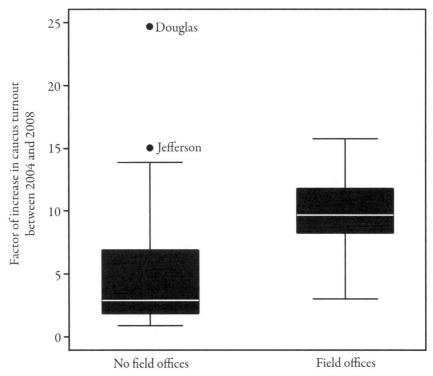

3.1. Distribution of voter turnout increase between 2004 and 2008, by county. Note: Data on caucus turnout provided by the Colorado Democratic Party. Results for ten counties were not available for 2004, so those counties were excluded from the analysis.

and understood that the multi-tiered delegate selection system required attendance at multiple conventions months apart. The core Obama activists, meanwhile, were relatively new to the political process and might not have been aware of these details (Marshall 2008).

On the other hand, the Clinton campaign may have had a far more aggressive post-caucus campaign in some states than the Obama team did. There is limited evidence that the Clinton campaign had paid operatives in several states with multi-tiered delegate selection systems whose mission was to flip pledged Obama delegates, win over unaffiliated delegates, and ensure that Obama delegates who failed to show up were replaced with Clinton-leaning alternates (Bowers 2008).

No direct information is available on how either the Clinton or the Obama post-caucus strategy was executed. However, we do know that throughout this time, Clinton maintained only one campaign office, located in Denver. Thus we would expect that any effects of this post-caucus activity would be the most

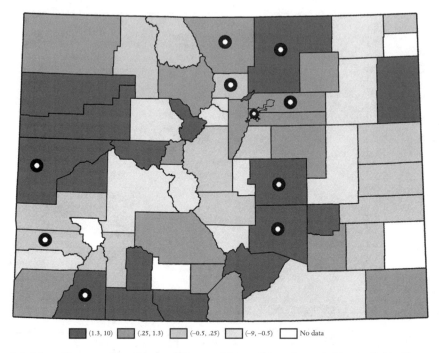

(1.3, 10)   (.25, 1.3)   (–0.5, .25)   (–9, –0.5)   No data

3.2. Map of post-caucus Obama delegate gains and locations of Obama field offices, 2008. Note: Darker-shaded counties are those in which Obama's post-caucus delegate gains were greater. Hollow circles indicate counties with Obama field offices.

concentrated in Denver or in the suburban counties immediately surrounding it. Conversely, the Obama campaign's twelve field offices were scattered throughout the state (although they were concentrated in the counties surrounding the state's major cities—Denver, Colorado Springs, Boulder, Pueblo, Fort Collins, Durango, and Grand Junction).

This presents an opportunity to examine an effect of field offices: were post-caucus delegate gains more concentrated in counties where the two campaigns maintained staff? I examine this question by calculating an expected share of state convention delegates from each county. This was calculated by determining the share of the total vote each candidate received on caucus night and multiplying that figure by the total number of delegates each county sent to the state convention.[3] Then I simply subtracted this expected number of delegates from the actual number of state delegates each candidate brought to the state convention.[4] I term the resulting number the candidate's "post-caucus delegate gains."

Figure 3.2 shows a map of Colorado's counties, with the location of Obama field offices at the time of the precinct caucuses indicated by solid dots. (Counties

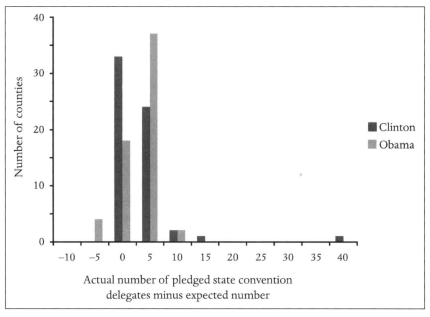

3.3. Obama and Clinton post-caucus delegate gains, 2008, histogram

with multiple Obama offices still receive only one dot.) The counties are color-coded such that darker-shaded counties are those in which Obama's post-caucus delegate gains were greater. While there is not a perfect correlation between post-caucus delegate gains and the location of field offices, the geographic pattern suggests such a relationship.

Figure 3.3 displays a histogram of the two candidates' post-caucus delegate gains by county. In this figure, positive numbers indicate that the candidate received a greater number of pledged delegates to the state convention than would have been expected given his or her share of the caucus vote in that county. Unsurprisingly, the two distributions hover close to zero, indicating that in the vast majority of counties, the candidates received almost exactly their expected shares of delegates. However, the Obama distribution is centralized, while the Clinton distribution skews somewhat to the right. In one county (Denver) Clinton received fifteen more delegates than expected, and in another (Adams, a Denver suburb) she received thirty-five more than expected.

Since there were no counties in which Obama lost potential delegates to the extent that Clinton gained them, a tentative conclusion from this figure is that her delegates came from the ranks of the uncommitted rather than from his supporters. However, figure 3.4 undermines this conclusion. This scatterplot reveals a strong and statistically significant ($p \leq .001$) negative relationship

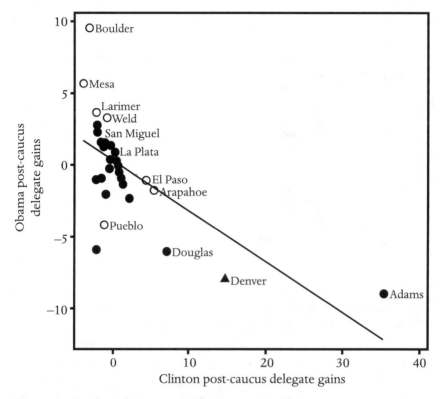

3.4. Obama and Clinton post-caucus delegate gains, 2008, scatter-plot. Note: Hollow dots indicate counties in which Obama staffed a field office prior to the February 5 caucus. Solid dots are counties with no field offices prior to February 5. The triangle (Denver) is the one county in which both campaigns staffed field offices. Counties of interest are labeled.

between Clinton's and Obama's post-caucus delegate gains. (This high level of statistical significance remains even if the high-leverage points of Denver and Adams Counties are removed from the calculation.) It also shows that Obama's delegate gains hovered around zero overall, while Clinton's were almost entirely positive.

This means that Clinton tended, on average, to pick up more delegates after the caucus than Obama did and that her gains came largely at his expense. The counties where she made her strongest gains in delegates were all counties in which Obama lost them, while Obama's delegate gains were made largely without any penalty to Clinton.

Another lesson from this figure can be seen in the location of campaign offices. Hollow dots indicate counties in which Obama had staffed a field office

TABLE 3.1. Variables predicting post-caucus increases in Colorado state convention delegates pledged to Obama

Variable	Coefficient
Obama county field office	3.837*
	(1.286)
Log of number of registered Democrats	−0.459
	(0.501)
Percent urban	0.483
	(1.627)
Percent with college degree	−5.963
	(5.408)
Percent making more than $75,000	1.107
	(6.383)
Percent African American	−59.99*
	(17.31)
Percent Latino	−4.939
	(4.123)
Percent Evangelical	−4.189
	(3.773)
Percent Catholic	−1.411
	(2.913)
Constant	9.455
	(4.990)
Observations	60
R-squared	0.315

Note: Cell entries are ordinary least squares coefficients. Standard errors appear in parentheses. Statistical significance is indicated by an asterisk (* $p < 0.01$).

prior to the caucus. The triangle (Denver) marks the one county in which both campaigns had field offices. As can be seen, counties with Obama field offices (and without Clinton offices) tended to have more Obama delegate gains than those without. Notably, all the Obama field office counties are on or above the trend line, and most are well above zero. It appears that having an uncontested Obama office in the county is positively correlated with Obama's post-caucus delegate gains.

A regression analysis confirms this. Table 3.1 shows a regression of Obama's post-caucus delegate increases on a dummy variable charting whether each county had an Obama field office at the time of the caucus. A host of county control variables was included to ensure that these results are not a function of demographic features of the county populations. County size was controlled for using the log of the number of registered Democrats in each county. Variables were included for the percentages of the county that are urban, are college edu-

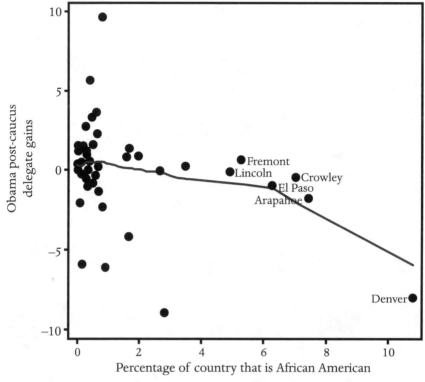

3.5. Obama post-caucus delegate gains by African American percentage of the population, 2008

cated, make more than $75,000 per year, are African American, are Latino, identify as Evangelical Christian, and are Catholic.

The field office variable is both substantively and statistically ($p \leq .01$) significant, suggesting that in every county in which Obama had opened a field office, he garnered roughly four additional state convention delegates. (These results hold even if Denver, the one county with a presence by both campaigns, is removed from the analysis.) Given that he had offices in ten counties, this translates to an additional forty state convention delegates.

Interestingly, the only control variable that reaches statistical significance is the percentage of the county that is African American. The coefficient is negative, suggesting that the counties with the largest numbers of African Americans produced delegates who were less likely to stay with Obama over the course of the multi-tiered process. This relationship is spelled out graphically in figure 3.5. Although Denver is obviously a high-leverage data point, the coefficient is borderline statistically significant ($p = .051$) even without that county.[5]

While this section merely charts evidence from one state and from just one stage of a presidential nomination campaign, it suggests an important role for campaign organization. In a part of the campaign that was largely out of the public spotlight—the conversion of caucus votes to delegates—having a field office nearby made a difference. Those county-level offices seemed to give the campaigns a greater ability to affect the county delegate selection process. The Clinton team did this effectively in Denver and neighboring Adams County, while the Obama team did this (on a somewhat smaller scale) in the ten counties where it had established a staff presence.

THE GENERAL ELECTION

For the general election contest, Senator Obama's financial resources allowed him to dramatically expand his field offices in Colorado and many other states. By the time of the November election, he had established field offices in 27 of Colorado's 64 counties. By contrast, McCain only had 11 offices in the state, and John Kerry had only established 9 four years earlier (Masket 2009a). This advantage in field offices was typical across the battleground states; in 11 competitive states,[6] Obama established offices in 43 percent of counties compared to McCain's 18 percent.

As it had during the nomination stage of the election cycle, the Obama campaign's use of field offices substantially affected the vote in the Colorado general election. These findings are explained more elaborately in a companion piece to this one (Masket 2009a). To summarize, the results suggested that the establishment of an Obama field office in Colorado in 2008 was associated with roughly 2 additional percentage points in the Democrats' presidential vote share in that county. As demonstrated in figure 3.6, in Colorado counties without Obama field offices, the Democratic presidential vote share increased by roughly 4.5 percent between 2004 and 2008; that figure was 6.3 percent in counties with an Obama field office. No county with an Obama field office had less than a 3 percent increase in the Democratic vote between 2004 and 2008.

Further examination of these voting patterns in other battleground states showed that the field office effect was determinative of the outcome in three states: Florida, Indiana, and North Carolina. Had voters contacted by the local Obama office decided instead to vote for McCain, those states would have gone Republican, bringing their fifty-three Electoral College votes with them. The research found no comparable effect for the McCain campaign's offices.

DISCUSSION

As the evidence presented in this chapter suggests, the establishment of a local field office by a presidential campaign can yield substantial dividends for a candi-

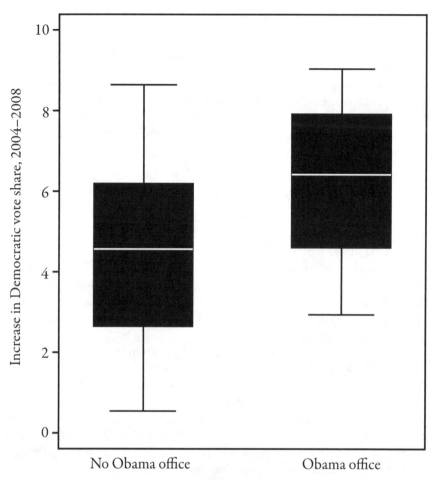

3.6. Democratic vote share increase in Colorado counties between 2004 and 2008. Note: Reproduced from Masket 2009.

date. During the nominations stage of the campaign discussed here, the location of field offices was related to increases in both candidate delegate shares and voter turnout. In Colorado, Senator Clinton increased her share of pledged state convention delegates in the areas immediately surrounding her one campaign office in Denver. Meanwhile, Senator Obama made some delegate gains of his own in smaller counties where he had established offices. In the general election stage, it appears that a judicious deployment of field offices helped Obama gain a few percentage points of the vote, although not enough to be determinative in Colorado.

When analyzing any campaign effect, it is worth asking whether that effect matters. The post-caucus battle for delegates appears to have mattered very little in the case described here. Yes, Hillary Rodham Clinton managed to increase her share of pledged delegates at the Colorado state convention by 3 percentage points. The real payoff for her, however, would have been to have actually increased her share of national delegates, and, at least in Colorado, that did not happen. On caucus night, Obama received 67.3 percent of the Obama + Clinton vote. If we used that percentage to predict Obama's share of the 48 pledged national delegates who would go to the August convention, we would have expected him to control 32 of those delegates. In the end, he got 31. On top of that, all of the alternates who went to the national convention were pledged Obama supporters. So Clinton's post-caucus campaign managed to flip 1 delegate at best. Even if that had happened in all the caucus states, it would not have come close to changing the outcome of the nomination race. While I do not have actual figures on how much money and personnel Clinton invested in Colorado after the caucus, it is hard to believe that it was a better investment of the campaign's efforts than such activity would have been prior to the caucus.

That said, it is not difficult to envision a scenario in which such post-caucus jockeying for delegates is pivotal. Delegate selection methods are not expected to be perfectly representative of party voters' will, but given the criticism caucuses have received for their small and skewed participation (Pearson 2008), the possibility that the results of a caucus could be essentially reversed by post-caucus machinations is cause for reflection. As officials in both major parties consider reforms to produce better nominees and to honor the participation and preferences of their rank-and-file voters, the poorly understood events that occur between a caucus and a convention merit more attention and study.

In the general election, although Obama's deployment of field offices in Colorado was associated with a larger vote share increase over Kerry's from four years earlier, Obama won the state by roughly 8 percentage points—a much larger spread than any field office effect. The field office effect did appear to be determinative in three other states, however. The implication is that campaign efforts *can* change the outcome of a race, although they seldom actually do so. Usually, the effect is a matter of a percentage point or two, and few elections are decided by such a close margin. Still, as any veteran of the 2000 presidential election will attest, close elections do happen, and the effects of those elections may be felt for years or decades.

The results of the 2008 elections in Colorado appeared to vindicate Howard Dean's claims about both the importance of the West and the payoff that can come from simply asking people to vote. At least for the near term, the national parties are continuing to focus on Colorado. Both parties fought fiercely during the 2010 US Senate race in Colorado. Senator Michael Bennet (D) was narrowly reelected in a race that featured some of the highest outside spending in the country. It is difficult to foresee political patterns further into the future, but all signs suggest that Colorado will continue to be a competitive battleground between the major parties.

NOTES

1. The author thanks David Ciepley, Sunshine Hillygus, John Sides, Wayne Steger, Jing Sun, Nancy Wadsworth, and the students in his spring 2008 state and local politics class for their valuable comments, suggestions, and insights.

2. Edwards dropped out of the race a few days prior to the caucus.

3. Three counties—Jackson, Pitkin, and Rio Blanco—did not make their Democratic state caucus delegate information available and were thus excluded from this analysis. Broomfield County was also excluded because of a lack of demographic information.

4. Obviously, this measure is sensitive to the size of counties. For example, Obama won 77 percent of the caucus vote in Hinsdale County (population 790) but only 75 percent of the county's state delegates, not because of any serious delegate poaching effort but because the county only sent four delegates to the state convention. The calculated discrepancy in the actual number of delegates versus the predicted number in such a county is therefore negligible.

5. There are a number of interpretations of this unexpected finding that counties with large numbers of African Americans produced delegates who were less likely to stick with Obama throughout the selection process. African Americans may be disproportionately likely to hold working-class jobs and may possess lower levels of political information, all of which would suggest lower attendance rates at multiple political conventions. Or, African American political activists may have been reacting to their experiences with black presidential candidates (specifically, Jesse Jackson) and been more likely than whites to expect their candidate to lose. One should probably not make too much of this finding, however, since a considerable ecological inference problem is at work here. Since the unit of analysis is the county rather than the individual voter, and since Colorado's African American community is concentrated in just a few counties (roughly a third of the state's African Americans live in Denver alone), it is difficult to be sure that what we are seeing here actually reflects the actions and preferences of African American Democratic voters.

6. Colorado, Florida, Indiana, Iowa, Missouri, Nevada, New Mexico, North Carolina, Ohio, Pennsylvania, and Virginia.

REFERENCES

AP. 2008. "Democrats Pick Denver for '08." *The Colorado Springs Gazette*, January 12, A1.

Bartels, Larry M. 1988. *Presidential Primaries and the Dynamics of Public Choice*. Princeton, NJ: Princeton University Press.

Booth, Michael, and Michael Riley. 2008. "Obama, Clinton Split Colo. Voters." *The Denver Post*, January 27, A01.

Bowers, Chris. 2008. "Politico Misses the Point on Pledged Delegates" [weblog cited February 19]. Available at http://www.openleft.com/showDiary.do?diaryId=4019. Accessed October 1, 2010.

Broder, John M. 2008. "Clinton: 'This Is Nowhere Near Over.' " *The New York Times*, May 19. Available at http://thecaucus.blogs.nytimes.com/2008/05/19/clinton-this-is-nowhere-near-over. Accessed October 1, 2010.

Cohen, Marty, David Karol, Hans Noel, and John Zaller. 2008. *The Party Decides: Presidential Nominations before and after Reform*. Chicago: University of Chicago Press.

Crummy, Karen E. 2007. "Colorado Caucuses May Move to Feb. 5." *The Denver Post*, March 18, C3.

Daily Camera Staff. 2003. "Primary Question—Will Budget Cuts End State's Presidential Contest?" *The Daily Camera* [Boulder, CO], January 24, A4.

Eldersveld, Samuel J. 1956. "Experimental Propaganda Techniques and Voting Behavior." *American Political Science Review* 50(1): 154–165.

Eldersveld, Samuel J., and Richard W. Dodge. 1954. "Personal Contact or Mail Propaganda? An Experiment in Voting and Attitude Change." In *Public Opinion and Propaganda*, ed. Daniel Katz, Dorwin Cartwright, Samuel J. Eldersveld, and Alfred McClung Lee. New York: Dryden, 532–542.

Gavin, Jennifer. 1990. "Senate Committee Advances Presidential Primary Bill." *The Denver Post*, February 8.

Gerber, Alan S., and Donald P. Green. 2000. "The Effects of Canvassing, Telephone Calls, and Direct Mail on Voter Turnout: A Field Experiment." *American Political Science Review* 94(3): 653–663.

———. 2005. "Correction to Gerber and Green (2000), Replication of Disputed Findings, and Reply to Imai." *American Political Science Review* 99(2): 301–313.

Gosnell, Harold Foote. 1927. *Getting out the Vote*. Chicago: University of Chicago Press.

Green, Joshua. 2008. "The Front-Runner's Fall." *The Atlantic* (September).

Hennessey, Kathleen, and Stephen Ohlemacher. 2008. "When Winning the Delegates Isn't Enough." *Associated Press*, February 23.

Hersh, Eitan. 2010. "Primary Voters vs. Caucus Goers and the Peripheral Motivations of Political Participation." Paper presented at the annual conference of the Midwest Political Science Association, April 7, Chicago.

Hillygus, D. Sunshine. 2005. "Campaign Effects and the Dynamics of Turnout Intention in Election 2000." *Journal of Politics* 66(1): 50–68.

Hubbard, Burt. 2009. "Colorado Population Grew at Fourth-Highest Rate in U.S." *The Denver Post*, December 24.

Imai, Kosuke. 2005. "Do Get-out-the-Vote Calls Reduce Turnout? The Importance of Statistical Methods for Field Experiments." *American Political Science Review* 99(2): 283–300.

Jarmin, Gary. 2008. "Keys to Obama Victory." *The Washington Times*, November 7, A18.

Karlin, Mark. 2008. "In Praise of the Iowa Caucuses: Transparent Democracy at Its Best." *Buzzflash*. Available at http://blog.buzzflash.com/editorblog/026. Accessed October 1, 2010.

Kramer, Gerald. 1970. "The Effects of Precinct-Level Canvassing on Voter Behavior." *Public Opinion Quarterly* 34: 560–572.

Loevy, Robert D. 2009. "Colorado: Is a Red State Turning Blue?" Paper presented at the annual conference of the Southwest Political Science Association, April 11, Denver.

Magleby, David B., J. Quin Monson, and Kelly D. Patterson. 2007. *Dancing without Partners: How Candidates, Parties, and Interest Groups Interact in the Presidential Campaign.* Lanham, MD: Rowman and Littlefield.

Marshall, Joshua. 2008. "About Those 'Caucus' Delegates" [cited March 11]. Available at http://www.talkingpointsmemo.com/archives/182722.php. Accessed October 1, 2010.

Marshall, Thomas R. 1978. "Turnout and Representation: Caucuses versus Primaries." *American Journal of Political Science* 22(1): 169–182.

Masket, Seth E. 2009a. "Did Obama's Ground Game Matter? The Influence of Local Field Offices during the 2008 Presidential Election." *Public Opinion Quarterly* 73(4): 1023–1039.

———. 2009b. "Painting the High Plains Blue: Musgrave vs. Markey in Colorado's 4th Congressional District." In *Cases in Congressional Campaigns: Incumbents Playing Defense*, ed. Randall Adkins and David Dulio, 93–108. New York: Routledge.

———. 2010. "The New Style: How Colorado's Democratic Party Survived and Thrived Amidst Reform." Paper presented at the annual State Politics and Policy Conference, June 4, Springfield, IL.

Monson, J. Quin. 2004. "Get on Television versus Get on the Van: G.O.T.V. and the Ground War in 2002." In *The Last Hurrah? Soft Money and Issue Advocacy in the 2002 Congressional Elections*, ed. David B. Magleby and J. Quin Monson. Washington, DC: Brookings Institution, 90–116.

Montero, David. 2008. "Obama Campaign to Open Five More Offices in Colorado." *The Rocky Mountain News*, January 26, 25.

Nickerson, David W., Ryan D. Friedrichs, and David C. King. 2006. "Partisan Mobilization Campaigns in the Field: Results from a Statewide Turnout Experiment in Michigan." *Political Research Quarterly* 59(1): 85–97.

Pearson, Kathryn. 2008. "Caucuses Are the Voices of the Few." *The Minneapolis Star-Tribune*, February 10.

Perry, Marc J. 2003. *State-to-State Migration Flows: 1995 to 2000.* Washington, DC: US Census Bureau.

Purdum, Todd. 2004. "Outside Campaigners Flood Iowa, Sharing Their Candidates' Styles." *The New York Times*, January 13, 1.

Riccardi, Nicholas. 2007. "Democrats to Hold 2008 Convention in Rockies." *The Los Angeles Times*, January 11.

Riley, Michael. 2008. "Both Parties Hit with Caucus Crunch." *The Denver Post*, February 6, 5–6.

Rosenstone, Steven J., and John Mark Hansen. 1993. *Mobilization, Participation, and Democracy in America.* New York: Macmillan.

Schrager, Adam, and Rob Witwer. 2010. *The Blueprint: How Democrats Won the West (and Why Republicans Should Care).* Golden, CO: Fulcrum.

Sherry, Allison. 2008. "Ground Game Licked G.O.P." *The Denver Post*, November 5, A–07.

Sides, John. 2008. "The Hunt for Campaign Effects in 2008" [weblog; cited November 8]. Available at http://www.themonkeycage.org/2008/11/the_hunt_for_campaign_effects.html. Accessed October 1, 2010.

Silver, Nate. 2008. "The Contact Gap: Proof of the Importance of the Ground Game?" [weblog; cited November 8]. Available at http://www.fivethirtyeight.com/2008/11/contact-gap-proof-of-importance-of.html. Accessed October 1, 2010.

Trish, Barbara. 1999. "Does Organization Matter? A Critical-Case Analysis from Recent Presidential Nomination Politics." *Presidential Studies Quarterly* 29(4): 873–895.

Vavreck, Lynn, Constantine J. Spiliotes, and Linda L. Fowler. 2002. "The Effects of Retail Politics in the New Hampshire Primary." *American Journal of Political Science* 46(3): 595–610.

Verba, Sidney, Kay Lehman Schlozman, and Henry E. Brady. 1995. *Voice and Equality: Civic Volunteerism in American Politics*. Cambridge: Harvard University Press.

CHAPTER FOUR

Impact of Direct Democracy on Colorado State Politics

Daniel A. Smith

Colorado has a rich history of direct democracy. The most widely used form of direct democracy—the so-called citizen initiative—allows individuals and groups to circulate petitions in an effort to qualify a statutory or constitutional measure on the ballot for a statewide vote.[1] For nearly a century, the initiative has shaped the political landscape of Colorado. As we have seen in earlier chapters, many Coloradans consider direct democracy the bane of the state's existence, allowing disjointed and destabilizing policies to become embedded into the state constitution. Others, though, view the initiative process as the state's salvation, rightfully returning the policymaking process to the people. Regardless of which extreme depiction is a more accurate portrayal of the initiative process, voting on ballot measures has become a permanent fixture in the Centennial State. In the 1990s, Colorado pollster and political analyst Floyd Ciruli (1996) referred to the initiative process as the state's "New Growth Industry." That description is still apt today. At times over the past century, the process of direct democracy has managed to share equal billing with the traditional institutions of representative democracy, leading some scholars to refer to such a blend in some US states as "hybrid democracy" (Garrett 2005; Kousser and McCubbins 2005).

Colorado's experience with the institution of the initiative, adopted during the Progressive Era, is neither unique nor without controversy. As we shall see, Colorado is a high-use initiative state. Immediately following the adoption of direct democracy in 1910, wealthy individuals and economic interests were frequently able to co-opt the plebiscitary mechanism. The irony is rich, as the initiative process in particular was originally advanced by populist and progressive political forces intent on wrestling power from a slate of entrenched interests and the elected officials who did their bidding (Cain and Miller 2001; Goebel 2002). To be sure, since that time citizen groups have placed dozens of liberal and conservative initiatives on the statewide ballot. Voters have cast ballots on initiatives dealing with abortion restrictions, parental rights, hunting and trapping regulations, education vouchers, the expansion of water rights, restrictions on hog farming, the legalization of medical marijuana, the banning of gay marriage, tax and spending limitations, and legislative term limits. Colorful defenders of the initiative process itself—led perhaps most prominently by Douglas Bruce, the author of the notorious 1992 Taxpayer's Bill of Rights (TABOR)—have helped animate the process over the years. Using populist tropes, they have rather successfully used the language of "us" versus "them" to cast the initiative process as a mechanism for "the people" to keep the state legislature in check and more responsive to citizen demands (Citrin 1996; Smith 1998).

After detailing the adoption and early use of direct democracy in Colorado, I trace the recent rise in the number of initiatives on the ballot and the role of money in ballot measure campaigns. In doing so, I highlight some of the more captivating initiative campaigns over the past century and briefly profile the efforts of Douglas Bruce and other initiative proponents. I then assess the impact of increasingly partisan ballot initiatives on minority populations, including racial, ethnic, and sexual-orientation minorities as well as the state's rural residents. Finally, after acknowledging lawmakers' bipartisan attack on the initiative process in recent years, I conclude with normative considerations of the practice of direct democracy in Colorado. As Fred Brown, one of the state's most sage political observers, wrote nearly two decades ago, many see the citizen initiative as "needed as a safety valve, but not as a replacement for the legislative process"; further, election day lawmaking "wouldn't be a problem if we actually had some real deliberation during the initiative process . . . but [instead] we have 30-second sound bites on some very complicated questions" (quoted in Smith 1998: 2–3).

ADOPTION OF DIRECT DEMOCRACY IN COLORADO

The movement for direct democracy in Colorado grew out of the doctrines put forth by the Populist (People's) Party in the late nineteenth century. During the 1890s, Populist Party officials, most notably Dr. Persifor Cooke of Denver, advocated the adoption of the initiative and popular referendum (Cronin 1989; Schmidt 1989). The initiative process was especially prized by reformers as a populist device that could be used directly or indirectly to clean up the spoils of a highly partisan, corrupt state legislature. Reformers claimed, with considerable veracity, that state legislators were being unduly swayed by big business, most notably the railroads and mining interests in the state. They argued that the initiative process could serve as an institutional check on unresponsive state legislatures, which were often under the thumb of corrosive special interests and party bosses (Cronin 1989; Smith and Tolbert 2004). As political scientist Delos Wilcox (1912: 10) commented, the "pure" and unmediated procedures of direct democracy would incite "a great forward movement toward stability, justice, and public spirit in American political institutions."

In 1896 Cooke helped establish the Colorado chapter of the Direct Legislation League (DLL), a national advocacy organization that pressured state legislatures to adopt plebiscitary mechanisms (Piott 2003). In Colorado the DLL was composed of members of the Progressive Party, the Trades and Labor Assembly of Denver, the State Federation of Labor, several women's organizations, and a few maverick members of the Democratic and Republican Parties. The DLL was aided considerably by the persistence, eloquence, and energy of progressive reformer Benjamin B. Lindsey, a nationally recognized juvenile court judge in Denver. After he became head of the DLL, Lindsey saw the push for direct democracy as his "ten year program to make Denver and Colorado the most complete democracy in the nation" (quoted in Smith and Lubinski 2002: 353).

Lindsey's efforts were aided greatly by Democratic governor John Shafroth, a reformer who in the 1908 campaign had pledged that, if elected, he would push the legislature to consider placing the mechanisms of direct democracy on the ballot (Smith and Fridkin 2008). Despite vociferous opposition from the state's business community, Shafroth—with the popular backing of Lindsey, former president Theodore Roosevelt, and other state progressive forces—convened a special legislative session in August 1910 to consider the reforms. After three weeks of debate, the legislature passed a bill that would add the initiative and popular referendum to the state constitution, contingent upon statewide voter approval in the November election. Commenting on the populist zeal for the reforms, reporter George Creel of *The Denver Post* stated, "The people are not viewing this extra session through political glasses. For them the division is not Democratic or Republican, but Corporations and the People" (quoted in Smith and Lubinski 2002: 354). With a resounding statewide vote of 75.4 percent, Coloradans in all but one county voted by wide margins to adopt the constitutional amendment adding the initiative and popular referendum to the state constitution (Martin and Gomez 1976; Piott 2003).[2]

The 1910 election ushered in a new era of plebiscitary politics in Colorado. The state's mechanisms of direct democracy have been in place—and relatively unchanged—for a century. Article V of the Colorado state constitution still includes the original language of the 1910 popular vote (Colo. Const. Art. V, §1, cl. 1):

> The legislative power of the state shall be vested in the general assembly consisting of a senate and house of representatives, both to be elected by the people, *but the people reserve to themselves the power to propose laws and amendments to the constitution and to enact or reject the same at the polls independent of the general assembly and also reserve power at their own option to approve or reject at the polls any act or item, section, or part of any act of the general assembly.* (emphasis added)

Petitioning and qualification requirements for ballot initiatives remain fairly similar to the original provisions crafted in 1910. Ballot initiative proponents need to collect just 5 percent of the total vote for secretary of state in the previous election to qualify an initiative. Following the 2000 election, proponents needed to gather roughly 63,000 valid signatures. As a result of the combination of population growth and high turnout for the 2010 election, proponents currently need slightly more than 85,000 valid signatures to qualify either a statute or an amendment to the constitution. Signature gatherers have six months to circulate petitions once the Title Setting Board—made up of the secretary of state, the attorney general, and the director of the Office of Legislative Legal Services—approves the ballot language, including the ballot title and summary that goes directly before the voters.[3] Ballot measures must also conform to a single-subject requirement, which voters approved for all initiatives and popular referendums in a 1996 legislative referendum (Campbell 2001). Compared to other states that permit direct democracy, the requirements to qualify ballot measures in Colorado are remarkably lax (Bowler and Donovan 2004).

EARLY BALLOT MEASURE CAMPAIGNS

In the inaugural 1912 direct democracy election, progressive forces led by Judge Lindsey and the DLL quickly turned to the initiative to push their wide-ranging social and economic agenda. As table 4.1 details, ballot measure proponents qualified twenty statewide initiatives and six popular referendums on the November general election ballot, a record number that still stands (Smith and Lubinski 2002). State lawmakers added an additional six legislative referendums. As we shall see, however, not all of the measures that appeared on the ballot were "progressive," and not all Coloradans seemed to embrace their newfangled plebiscitary powers.

It is apparent when examining the voting patterns for the thirty-two measures on the 1912 ballot that many Coloradans were not particularly enthusiastic about

TABLE **4.1.** 1912 ballot measure election results

Measure	Subject	Type	"Yes" Votes	"No" Votes	Total Votes	Percent "Yes"
1	Statewide prohibition	Constitutional amendment initiative	75,877	116,774	192,651	39.39
2	Enforcement of prohibition laws	Statutory initiative	64,616	79,190	143,806	44.93
3	Women's eight-hour workday	Statutory initiative	108,959	32,019	140,978	77.29
4	Regulation of public utilities	Statutory initiative	30,347	64,138	94,485	32.12
5	Establishment of a state fair	Statutory initiative	49,102	52,462	101,564	48.35
6	Creation of a State Immigration Bureau	Constitutional amendment initiative	30,359	54,272	84,631	35.87
7	Publishing initiatives and referendums in newspapers	Statutory initiative	39,551	50,635	90,186	43.85
8	Granting home rule to cities and towns	Constitutional amendment initiative	49,596	44,778	94,374	52.55
9	Providing recall from office	Constitutional amendment initiative	53,620	39,564	93,184	57.54
10	Publishing ballot pamphlet	Statutory initiative	37,616	38,537	76,153	49.40
11	Providing special elections for initiatives and referendums	Constitutional amendment initiative	33,413	40,634	74,047	45.12
12	Defining contempt of court and providing for trial by jury	Constitutional amendment initiative	31,850	41,855	73,705	43.21
13	Regulation of public utilities	Constitutional amendment initiative	27,534	51,820	79,354	34.70
14	Amending election laws and providing for a "headless ballot"	Statutory initiative	43,390	39,504	82,894	52.34
15	Providing for wider control of public schools	Constitutional amendment initiative	38,318	55,691	94,009	40.76
16	Overrule supreme court decisions and create juvenile courts	Constitutional amendment initiative	55,416	40,891	96,307	57.54
17	Mothers' compensation and aid to dependent children	Statutory initiative	82,337	37,870	120,207	68.50
18	Regulating civil service	Statutory initiative	38,426	35,282	73,708	52.13

continued on next page

TABLE 4.1—continued

Measure	Subject	Type	"Yes" Votes	"No" Votes	Total Votes	Percent "Yes"
19	Eight-hour workday for miners	Statutory initiative	52,525	48,777	101,302	51.85
20	Funds for state highways	Statutory initiative	44,568	45,101	89,669	49.70
21	Eight-hour workday for miners	Popular referendum	69,489	30,992	100,481	69.16
22	Regulating branding and marking of livestock	Popular referendum	37,387	37,740	75,127	49.77
23	Custody and management of public funds	Popular referendum	20,968	44,322	65,290	32.12
24	Establishing teachers' summer normal schools	Popular referendum	23,521	63,266	86,787	27.10
25	Examinations of teachers	Popular referendum	25,369	54,086	79,455	31.93
26	Concerning water rights and irrigation	Popular referendum	22,931	47,614	70,545	32.51
27	Designating mining and smelting business as in public interest	Constitutional amendment Legislative referendum	35,997	37,953	73,950	48.68
28	Creating a State Tax Commission	Constitutional amendment Legislative referendum	32,548	40,012	72,560	44.86
29	Linking fees and salaries of local officials	Constitutional amendment Legislative referendum	28,889	41,622	70,511	40.97
30	Raising limitation on county debts	Constitutional amendment Legislative referendum	29,741	47,284	77,025	38.61
31	Authorizing a bonded indebtedness for public highways	Constitutional amendment Legislative referendum	36,636	53,327	89,963	40.72
32	Construction of tunnel through James Peak	Statutory legislative referendum	45,800	93,183	138,983	32.95

Source: Daniel A. Smith and Joseph Lubinski. 2002. "Direct Democracy during the Progressive Era: A Crack in the Populist Veneer?" *Journal of Policy History* 14: 349–383.

becoming citizen lawmakers. There is also evidence that their voting intentions were not necessarily clear. Although official records on turnout are no longer available for the 1912 general election, on average, only 38 percent of those who cast a ballot for a presidential candidate voted on the twenty initiatives on the ballot; even fewer voted "yes" or "no" on the six popular and six legislative referendums (Smith and Lubinski 2002). The ballot initiative with by far the most popular appeal was Measure 1, which called for statewide prohibition; nearly 200,000 voters cast ballots on the initiative, although only two in five supported banning the sale of alcohol in the state.[4] Other measures received less than half the total votes Measure 1 obtained, indicating substantial ballot roll-off among some voters. Overall, voters shot down all six of the legislative referrals, and a majority of voters supported only eight of the twenty initiatives on the ballot. In contrast, voters overturned five (of six) laws recently approved by the state legislature by rejecting them at the polls after the laws were petitioned onto the ballot through the popular referendum process. Three of the eight successful initiatives—including the ban on the sale of alcohol—amended the state constitution, while the five others created new statutory language.

Among the successful initiatives were several advanced by Judge Lindsey's DLL. The reformers persuaded voters to adopt an eight-hour workday for women (Measure 3), the Australian "headless ballot" (Measure 14), and a law establishing compensation for mothers with dependent or neglected children (Measure 17). Voters also approved the DLL's constitutional amendment allowing citizens to recall elected officials from office (Measure 9),[5] as well as a constitutional amendment creating a juvenile court system—a pet project of Judge Lindsey's. Voters, however, rejected the several other initiatives the DLL had placed on the ballot, including measures to allow initiated and referred laws to be placed on ballots of special elections (Measure 11), trial by jury for charges of contempt in certain cases (Measure 12), a public utilities court with the power to fix and enforce the rates of public monopolies (Measure 13), and expanded use of public schools when not in session (Measure 15).

Nonetheless, the DLL's record of success was impressive considering that its measures challenged the dominant economic interests of the day and were frequently the target of smear campaigns by the corporate-controlled media. *The Denver Republican*, for example, editorialized that the leaders of the DLL were a bunch of "professional reformers and agitators," and a coalition of public schoolteachers strongly condemned the DLL's public school measure as "reckless" (Smith and Lubinski 2002). There was likely some truth to the charges. The following year, for example, the DLL went so far as to circulate an initiative petition intended to dissolve the state senate. The DLL failed to qualify the measure for the 1914 ballot.

One of the greatest ironies of the first direct democracy campaigns in Colorado is that the same corporate interests that were unsuccessful in preventing the adoption of the plebiscitary mechanisms in 1910 quickly realized that they could use the initiative and popular referendum to advance their own agendas. Of the initial twenty initiatives to make it onto the ballot, no fewer than five were sponsored by millionaires or vested corporations—the same interests the process was intended to eliminate. Amendment 5 sought to "establish" a state fair in Pueblo. In actuality, a state fair had existed for many years, but the powerful agricultural interests that operated the event wanted the legislature to fully fund future state fairs and pay off their accumulated debts. Amendment 7, which proponents contended would lower the state's costs to publish sample ballots in newspapers prior to elections, was secretly sponsored by newspaper publishers who wanted to secure their monopoly to publish the protracted texts of ballot measures in their papers. Not surprisingly, the initiative received little negative press in the state's dailies. Another measure, Amendment 19, was a specious eight-hour workday for miners funded by industrialists George Jay Gould and John D. Rockefeller. Their initiative aimed to reverse a progressive eight-hour law passed by the legislature in 1911.

As Daniel Smith and Joseph Lubinski (2002) recount, perhaps the most egregious example of corporate interests using the initiative process occurred in 1912 when Colorado businesses colluded to thwart Measure 13, the DLL's effort to regulate public utility companies. Judge Lindsey's initiative would have staunchly regulated public utility companies (water, sewer, gas, electric, phone, rail, and tramway) that typically charged consumers extortionate rates. There is considerable evidence that many voters became confused about DLL's issue because of a counterproposition placed on the ballot—Measure 4—an intentionally opaque initiative that would have established a toothless regulatory Public Utilities Commission controlled by the public utilities themselves. Measure 4 was secretly drafted and financed by several businessmen with huge financial stakes in the public utilities, including William G. Evans, the son of Colorado's first territorial governor and the major tramway operator in Denver. The backers went so far as to secure union leaders as the public face of the initiative and paid unwitting signature gatherers to qualify the measure. Most voters, however, were not aware of this fact, as the complicit media failed to expose the sham. The resulting confusion concerning the two competing measures led to high ballot roll-off on the two measures and may have led voters to reject both proposals.[6]

The failure of Amendment 13, as well as some of the other progressive measures placed on the ballot, left some proponents of direct democracy less than enamored with the process. Despite being a leading advocate for the adoption of direct democracy reforms, the Western Federation of Labor panned voters' ability in the 1912 election to make well-reasoned choices on the admittedly

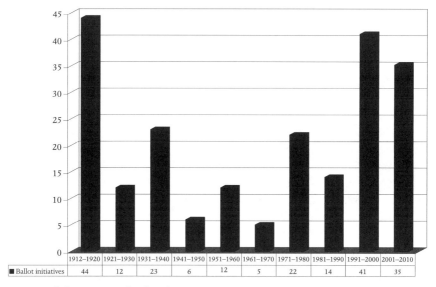

Ballot initiatives	1912–1920	1921–1930	1931–1940	1941–1950	1951–1960	1961–1970	1971–1980	1981–1990	1991–2000	2001–2010
	44	12	23	6	12	5	22	14	41	35

4.1. Use of the initiative, by decade, 1912–2010

complicated ballot measures, especially those advanced surreptitiously by vested special interests. "The initiative and referendum is but a tool in the hands of the voter, useless to him [*sic*] who does not know how to use it and [who is not] thoroughly acquainted with the issues that are to be decided by his ballot," the union regretfully concluded. "Our greatest foe is ignorance, knowledge is the only emancipator" (Smith and Lubinski 2002: 369). The lament of voter ignorance on ballot measures continues today for many critics of the process. It is one of detractors' many concerns about ballot measures.

THE RISE OF INITIATIVE USE IN COLORADO

Colorado trails only Oregon and California in the total number of citizen-initiated measures placed on statewide ballots for voters to accept or reject since the inception of the process. Beginning with the inaugural use of direct democracy in 1912, Coloradans have voted on 214 initiatives, a biennial average of 4.2 measures on the ballot. Citizens have proved rather skeptical about initiatives, approving just 72 of the 214 measures—a passage rate of 33.6 percent. As figure 4.1 reveals, the use of the initiative process during the past century has fluctuated over the decades. Beginning with a flourish of initiative activity in the 1910s, ballot propositions slowed, bottoming out in the 1960s. Still, since 1912 there has been at least one statewide initiative on the ballot in every even-numbered year.

The use of the initiative picked up rapidly in the 1990s, with proponents qualifying more than forty initiatives for the ballot in that decade alone. Most recently, Coloradans faced seven initiatives in 2006; two years later voters were asked to consider ten more measures, the most initiatives on the ballot since 1992. This resurgence was fueled largely by the anti-tax efforts of a single person, Douglas Bruce, although tax-related ballot measures long preceded the passage of TABOR in 1992. Unlike citizens in most states, since 1993 and the implementation of TABOR, Coloradans have been able to qualify statewide ballot measures that deal with fiscal issues in odd-year elections. Between 1993 and 2009, voters faced eleven odd-year statewide initiatives, but they approved only two—a 2001 open-space acquisition measure and Referendum C in 2005, which temporarily rolled back some of the fiscal limits of TABOR.

Since the first usage of direct democracy in 1912, Coloradans have been asked to vote on ballot measures concerning taxes and government spending more than any other issue. Nearly one-fifth of all ballot measures have directly tried to change the state's tax system. Perhaps somewhat surprisingly considering all the attention placed on TABOR, voters have been fairly reluctant to change the tax code through the initiative process. Only ten of the fifty-four tax-related initiatives placed on the ballot by fellow citizens have been approved, and several of them actually raised taxes. In 1920 voters approved a one-mill-levy increase to pay for state education institutions, and in 1922 voters authorized a $1.5 million bond issue for the construction of public highways. During the Great Depression Coloradans approved a popular referendum that overturned a $.05/pound tax increase on oleomargarine the legislature had approved earlier that year. In 1934 a majority of voters supported placing a license fee on national chain stores doing business in the Centennial State, and two years later they approved raising taxes to increase per-month outlays for old-age pensions. More recently, in 2000, 53 percent of voters approved Amendment 23, which increased state funding for public schools; four years later more than 60 percent supported raising taxes on tobacco products to pay for health-related programs.

Voters have also been asked to consider numerous growth-related issues over the years. Since 1912, voters have considered more than a dozen ballot measures dealing with the financing of road-related projects. During the 1970s, when the state witnessed a slight up-tick in the number of initiatives that reached the statewide ballot, ballot measures aimed at controlling the state's growth had broad appeal. A little-known state lawmaker, Dick Lamm, led a grassroots movement that opposed Denver hosting the 1976 Winter Olympics. His 1972 anti-growth initiative, Amendment 8, was approved by nearly 60 percent of the voters. It altered the state constitution to prohibit the state from levying taxes or raising revenue to bring the 1976 Winter Olympic Games to Colorado. Also in the 1970s, suburban activist Freda Poundstone authored a 1974 initiative—dubbed the Poundstone Amendment—that took aim at Denver's expansive growth in an effort to protect suburban political independence, tax bases, and school district identity. Six years after approving her first measure, voters statewide overwhelmingly approved Amendment 3, known as Poundstone Two, an initiative requiring a popular vote on any annexation of an unincorporated area by a municipality. Proponents convinced voters that generous municipal annexation powers were being manipulated by developers and complicit local officials, contrary to the residents' will. Still actively pushing ballot measures today, Poundstone's efforts at the ballot box more than a quarter of a century ago continue to affect local government growth management in Colorado.

Several other ballot initiatives have dealt with growth issues in the state. In 1992, voters approved a constitutional amendment with 58 percent of the vote that created the Great Outdoors Colorado program, which dedicated state lottery proceeds for the purchase and maintenance of public spaces. In doing so, voters closed a loophole in the original lottery bill that allowed the legislature to divert parks and open-space funds to prisons and other capital construction. Since its adoption, the program has spent millions to preserve, protect, and enhance open space in the state. Four years later, in 1996, voters approved Amendment 16 by a slim margin. The initiative amended the state constitution regarding the management of state assets related to the state's public lands held in trust. However, in 2000 voters soundly rejected Amendment 24, a proposed constitutional amendment that would have required voter approval for any changes in local governments' plans for growth and development (Smith 2001a).

MONEY IN BALLOT INITIATIVE CAMPAIGNS

One of the persistent charges against the initiative process is that special interests are able to utilize the process for their own ends (Broder 2000; Ellis 2002; Sabato, Larson, and Ernst 2001; Smith 1998). In Colorado, as in other initiative states, there is ample evidence that special interests have been involved in promoting ballot measures since the Progressive Era. Of course, whether ballot measures are more susceptible to the influence of money than is the traditional representative system of government remains an open question. Nevertheless, wealthy and organized interests in Colorado and other states have little difficulty qualifying measures for the ballot (Garrett and Gerber 2001), and money will likely continue to dominate the initiative process in the future (Smith 2009).

For some scholars, the establishment of an "Initiative Industrial Complex" (Magleby and Patterson 1998) appears to be a fairly recent phenomenon, but the role of money in ballot campaigns has deep roots in Colorado. The professionalization of the inaptly named "citizen" initiative in Colorado and other states is not recent. As far back as the 1910s, proponents of ballot initiatives hired legal talent to draft the wording of petitions and pay petitioners to collect signatures to qualify measures for the ballot (Donovan and Smith 2008). By 1926, signature gatherers in Colorado were paid the princely sum of $0.03 a signature, and some were contracted with a flat sum of $1,000 to collect the requisite number of signatures to qualify a statewide measure. That year, for example, proponents and opponents spent nearly $25,000 on a single statutory initiative calling for dentists licensed in other states to be able to practice in Colorado without taking an examination. The measure failed (Smith 2001b).

The growth of the Initiative Industrial Complex has been exponential in recent years. In contrast to races for public office that have strict regulations on how much money candidates can raise and from what sources (not surprising, as a result of limits imposed by Amendment 27, a ballot initiative passed by voters in 2002), besides disclosure, there are no restrictions on contributions or expenditures for a ballot issue. In 1978, citing First Amendment protections, the US Supreme Court decision *First National Bank of Boston v. Bellotti* struck down a Massachusetts state statute that banned corporate expenditures in initiative and referendum campaigns. Three years later, in its 1981 ruling *Citizens against Rent Control v. City of Berkeley*, the court found contribution limitations to ballot issue committees unconstitutional. In both cases the court found no compelling reason for the state to regulate the amount of money raised or spent on issues, as it deemed there was no possibility of quid pro quo corruption with measures on the ballot (Smith 2009).

Regardless of whether it is tied to the high court's opinions, the amount spent on ballot measures in Colorado has risen steadily over the years. Expenditures on ballot issues increased more than threefold in the 1990s compared with the 1980s, rising to $29.8 million versus $9.2 million. Over $11 million was spent on eight ballot campaigns in 1998 alone, nearly doubling the total spending on all statewide races—including the race for governor. Between 1976 and 2000, the amount spent for or against a ballot measure was a strong predictor of whether that measure would pass or fail. Voters approved only one-third of the sixty initiatives on the ballot during that period. With each of the seven measures on which proponents were outspent by opponents by $500,000 or more, voters defeated the initiative; when backers were outspent by more than $200,000, voters approved only three of the seventeen measures. Proponents of a 1994 initiative to raise the sale tax on tobacco products (including the American Cancer Society) found this out the hard way. After proponents had raised more than $200,000 to qualify and promote their ballot measure, tobacco companies contributed more than $8 million to defeat the measure—by far the most one side has spent on a ballot measure to date (Smith 2001c). In 1994, spending on ballot measures in Colorado exceeded spending on all races for political office (including a hotly contested race for governor).

Spending on ballot measures in Colorado has continued to escalate, with campaigns becoming increasingly expensive. According to campaign finance data collected and coded by the National Institute on Money in State Politics,[7] total contributions made to ballot issue committees during three of the most recent election cycles (2004, 2006, and 2008) have escalated. Over those cycles, ballot issue committees raised nearly $125 million, including $73 million in the 2008 election cycle alone. In the 2006 election cycle, issue committees raised close to $28 million, and in the previous cycle they brought in nearly $24 million. In these three election cycles, total contributions to ballot issue committees averaged more than $41.5 million; by comparison, total contributions to state candidates and political party committees averaged just $13.9 million per cycle during the same time period.

A variety of interest groups, along with well-heeled individuals, contribute financially to promote and oppose measures on the ballot. An array of industries—agriculture, construction, communications and electronics, energy and natural resources, finance, insurance, real estate, general business, health, lawyers and lobbyists, and transportation—are typically the largest contributors to ballot issue committees. In the 2004, 2006, and 2008 election cycles, these industries contributed nearly $19 million per election cycle to ballot issue committees. In the 2008 election cycle alone, industry contributions to ballot issue committees exceeded $27.6 million. For comparison, corporate and business contributions to state candidates and political party committees during the same three election cycles totaled $3.6 million. In an effort to defend its turf, organized labor in Colorado has responded forcefully to the increased corporate spending on ballot measures. In response to a flurry of ballot measures intent on diminishing its political clout, in the 2008 election cycle organized labor contributed more than $25 million to various ballot measures, listed in table 4.2. In the two previous cycles, labor unions had spent a fraction of that amount on ballot measures (a total of $2.51 million). Finally, ideological groups and their members also contribute substantial amounts to ballot issue committees. Between 2003 and 2008, ideological groups contributed more than $29.6 million to such committees. In the 2008 election cycle, in which several controversial socially conservative initiatives were on the ballot—including the Colorado Civil Rights Initiative (Amendment 46) and the Colorado Definition of Person Amendment (Amendment 48)—ideological groups and individuals contributed $13.9 million to ballot issue committees.

Although Colorado state law requires ballot issue committees to regularly file their contributors and expenses publicly with the Office of the Secretary of State, a considerable amount of money flows from nonprofit organizations that are able to conceal their donors. Groups with notable industry ties—including Colorado at Its Best, Coloradans for Economic Growth, Colorado Citizens for

TABLE **4.2.** 2008 ballot initiatives and titles

Amendment 46, Discrimination and Preferential Treatment by Governments
Amendment 47, Prohibition on Mandatory Labor Union Membership and Dues
Amendment 48, Definition of Person
Amendment 49, Allowable Government Paycheck Deductions
Amendment 50, Limited Gaming in Central City, Black Hawk, and Cripple Creek
Amendment 51, State Sales Tax Increase for Services for People with Developmental Disabilities
Amendment 52, Use of Severance Tax Revenue for Highways
Amendment 53, Criminal Accountability of Business Executives (withdrawn on October 1)
Amendment 54, Campaign Contributions from Certain Government Contractors
Amendment 55, Allowable Reasons for Employee Discharge or Suspension (withdrawn on October 1)
Amendment 56, Employer Responsibility for Health Insurance (withdrawn on October 1)
Amendment 57, Additional Remedies for Injured Employees (withdrawn on October 1)
Amendment 58, Severance Taxes on the Oil and Natural Gas Industry
Amendment 59, Education Funding and TABOR Rebates

Source: National Institute on Money in State Politics. 2009. "Advanced Search." Available at http://www.follow themoney.org/database/advancedsearch.phtml. Accessed December 2, 2009.

Change, Protect Colorado Jobs, and New Leadership Colorado—funneled well over $4 million to ballot issue committees in the 2008 election cycle, keeping their donors' identities anonymous.[8]

Because it is permissible in Colorado for ballot issue committees to make expenditures on multiple ballot measures, it is impossible to determine precisely how much each committee spends for or against a specific ballot measure in a given election.[9] Yet as table 4.3 documents, industry, labor, and ideological groups receive significant contributions from a wide array of sources. In the 2008 election cycle, the ballot issue committee Protect Colorado's Future, a coalition led by organized labor, received over 1,000 contributions and raised nearly $17 million in its effort to oppose three initiatives—Amendments 47, 49, and 54. Another labor-backed ballot issue committee, Coloradans for Middle Class Relief, funded by a coalition of labor unions to oppose Amendment 47, raised nearly $7.95 million from six national unions and their local chapters. Several ballot issue committees were funded principally by corporate interests, most notably Colorado for a Stable Economy, the primary issue committee that opposed Amendment 58. Colorado for a Stable Economy received nearly $12 million in contributions from roughly two dozen sources, nearly all oil and natural gas corporations. Nine corporations—Anadarko Petroleum Corporation, BP Corporation North America, Chevron Corporation, ConocoPhillips, Encana Oil

TABLE **4.3.** Total contributions received by select ballot issue committees, by major funder, 2008 election cycle

Ballot Measure (and major funder stance)	Ballot Issue Committee	Total Contributions Received
Ballot Issue Committees Funded Principally by Organized Labor		
53 (yes), 55 (yes), 56 (yes), 57 (yes), 47 (no), 49 (no), 54 (no)	Protect Colorado's Future	$16,982,972
47 (no)	Coloradans for Middle Class Relief	$7,948,965
47 (no)	Committee for Fair Wages Benefits	$2,444,297
Ballot Issue Committees Funded Principally by Corporations and Business Groups		
58 (no)	Colorado for a Stable Economy	$11,967,500
53 (no), 55 (no), 56 (no), 57 (no)	Coloradans for Responsible Reform	$3,236,718
47 (yes)	Defend Our Economy	$1,482,929
47 (yes)	A Better Colorado	$3,789,530
47 (yes)	Colorado Right-to-Work Committee	$346,148
47 (no), 49 (no), 54 (no)	Colorado Businesses for Sensible Solutions	$2,413,410
Ballot Issue Committees Funded Principally by Ideological/Single-Issue Groups		
58 (yes)	A Smarter Colorado	$5,056,433
49 (yes), 54 (yes)	Clean Government Colorado	$1,838,287
58 (yes), 59 (yes)	Responsible Colorado	$138,776

Source: National Institute on Money in State Politics. 2009. "Advanced Search." Available at http://www.followthemoney.org/database/advancedsearch.phtml. Accessed December 2, 2009.

and Gas, Exxon Mobil, Noble Energy, Pioneer Natural Resources, and Williams Companies—all chipped in $1 million or more to oppose the liberal ballot initiative. Another ballot issue committee, Coloradans for Responsible Reform, was composed of a coalition of businesses led by the Denver Metro Chamber of Commerce. Coloradans for Responsible Reform raised $3.2 million in its successful effort to broker a compromise among competing labor and corporate interests to have four initiatives—Amendments 53, 55, 56, and 57—withdrawn from the 2008 ballot. The corporate-backed ballot issue committee Colorado Businesses for Sensible Solutions raised more than $2.4 million in the election cycle, including contributions of at least $100,000 from seven businesses: the Colorado Bankers Association, Dish Network, 4334 LLC, Lockheed Martin, ProLogis Management, Vail Resorts, and Western Plains Capital.

Several of the ballot issue committees that received the bulk of their contributions from ideological groups acted like Veiled Political Actors (Garrett and Smith 2005). Clean Government Colorado, the sponsoring ballot issue committee for Amendment 54, received a total of $1,838,287, with 99.9 percent ($1,836,000) of its contributions coming from Colorado at Its Best—a nonprofit organization based in Golden, Colorado, run by Dennis Polhill (a longtime affiliate of the Independence Institute) and with strong ties to another nonprofit, Americans for Limited Government, based in Fairfax, Virginia. It is ironic that a ballot issue committee named Clean Government Colorado—which funneled its contributions through Colorado at Its Best in support of Amendment 54—assiduously avoided the state's law mandating campaign finance disclosure so as not to reveal its true financial sources (Rosa 2008).

Based on the past practices of these and similar nonprofit organizations in Colorado and elsewhere, the nonprofits were likely created intentionally to serve as flow-through entities, acting as fronts for business interests that wanted to conceal their contributions to ballot issue committees (Garrett and Smith 2005). Indeed, Colorado ballot issue committees' practice of keeping donors anonymous is nothing new. These committees have long utilized nonprofit organizations as cleansing operations, hiding from voters and the media the true source of their financial backing.

In 1998, for example, the Independence Institute—a 501(c)(3)—was the tax-deductible vehicle of choice for individuals who wanted to financially support a school choice tax credit program. Steve Schuck, chair of the Independence Institute, concurrently served as the director of Coloradans for School Choice . . . for All Kids, the ballot issue committee that sponsored Amendment 17. Between September 1997 and August 1998, under Schuck's instructions, the Independence Institute was the sole contributor to the issue committee, contributing $84,000. "The early part of the campaign," Schuck admitted to a reporter, "was funded entirely by donations made by the institute," adding that "there was an enormous amount of informal communication at the institute." At the time, he freely admitted that he informed potential contributors to the issue committee that they could make tax-deductible donations to the Independence Institute, which would then be redirected to the issue committee sponsoring Amendment 17. "I've put my own money into this," Schuck said. "So have a lot of other people." According to Schuck, his scheme had real benefits: "The contributor gets the advantage of passing the money through a tax-deductible organization" with good name recognition, and the donor remains "anonymous" (quoted in Smith 2001b: 68).

Two years earlier, in 1996, a nonprofit organization headquartered in Virginia with the benign-sounding name Of the People contributed the bulk of the amount raised by a Colorado issue committee sponsoring a "parental rights" amendment (Amendment 17) to the state constitution (Smith and Herrington 2000). Although voters ended up defeating the initiative at the polls, Of the

People raised $362,900 (82 percent) of the $444,609 contributed to Coalition for Parental Responsibility, the official sponsor of the ballot issue. Much of Of the People's proceeds likely flowed from Amway and members of the DeVos family, although because it is a nonprofit, it is impossible to know for certain (Garrett and Smith 2005).

Over the years, an impressive number of wealthy individuals have contributed vast amounts to promote ballot initiatives. In 1998 Gary Boyce and his Stockman Water Company contributed more than $1 million to qualify a pair of ballot measures dealing with water rights on the state's western slope, and oil and telecom mogul Philip Anschutz spent more than $400,000 of his own money to successfully regulate corporate hog farms through a ballot initiative. In 2002 three millionaires—Coloradans Rutt Bridges and Jared Polis and Californian Ron Unz—collectively contributed $1.4 million to qualify four separate initiatives on the ballot. Bridges, who contributed over $550,000 to qualify initiatives expanding voting by mail and requiring candidates to petition to be placed on primary ballots, was the sole contributor to the ballot issue committees sponsoring the measures—doling out over $550,000, including more than $210,000 for paid signature-gathering efforts. Polis, now a US congressman representing the Boulder area, was the sole underwriter of an election day registration constitutional amendment. Funneling nearly half of his contributions through the eponymous Jared Polis Foundation, Polis contributed roughly $400,000 to his issue committee, Colorado Voters, to qualify the measure. A handful of other individuals contributed less than $100 each to his issue committee. Unz, an entrepreneur from Silicon Valley, lent his issue committee, English for the Children in Colorado, $450,000 to qualify the measure; no one else contributed a dime to the committee.

To be sure, there is nothing illegal about wealthy individuals using the initiative process to shape public policy, and it is difficult to qualify a ballot initiative without enlisting paid signature gatherers. The days of grassroots, volunteer initiative campaigns are long gone (if they ever existed in the first place). Furthermore, there is no guarantee that a majority of voters will support fat cats' often whimsical initiatives at the polls. But the question remains, has the process of direct democracy become captured by special interests and wealthy individuals? Activists like Douglas Bruce would surely disagree.

DOUGLAS BRUCE AND TABOR

In 1992 Douglas Bruce, an erstwhile attorney from California and an apartment building owner, placed the Taxpayer's Bill of Rights on Colorado's November ballot. After two of his similar tax and spending limitation measures had failed at the polls in 1988 and 1990, voters approved Bruce's 1992 Amendment 1 with

53.6 percent of the vote (Smith 1996). Ever the faux populist, Bruce has been one of the state's most vociferous defenders of direct democracy. In the mid-1990s, when critics claimed that the initiative process was running amok, Bruce replied: "If you're saying we have too many (amendments), you're saying we have too many choices . . . I think our opponents long for [the] good old days when there was no Baskin-Robbins. You could only have vanilla, and you could have any car—so long as it was painted black" (quoted in Smith 1998: 3).

With respect to the myriad policy outcomes of TABOR, many were not foreseen in 1992 when a majority of voters approved the measure (Young 2006). As has been discussed in previous chapters, TABOR turned out to have several unintended consequences that have affected Colorado's state and local governments. Bruce designed the constitutional amendment to severely restrict the taxing and spending powers of all state and local government entities, hailing the measure as "the single most important political event in Colorado since statehood" (quoted in Smith 1998: 128). He effectively marketed the complex, 1,703-word amendment as a way to curb "runaway taxes" and downsize the state's "bureaucratic Big Brother" (quoted in Smith 1998: 128). Specifically, the measure required that a public vote be held on any new or increased tax or government debt and limited future government spending to a set formula based on population growth and the Consumer Price Index for the Denver-Boulder-Greeley metropolitan area. Furthermore, TABOR mandated that if a given governmental unit's total annual revenue exceeded its total annual spending, the unit had to refund the difference to taxpayers or hold an election to retain the surplus (Smith 1996).

The passage of Amendment 1 set off an explosion of tax-related ballot measures at the state and local levels, including more attempts to cut taxes and spending, efforts to reverse cuts to social programs resulting from TABOR, and a slew of "de-Brucing" efforts by state and local governments eager to retain any surplus revenue (Smith and Golich 1998). Bruce sponsored several other ballot measures in the 1990s, but voters rebuffed him each time at the polls. In 2000, after personally filing 165 statewide ballot initiatives with the Title Setting Board, Bruce qualified Amendment 21. He spent nearly $500,000 of his own money promoting the measure that, according to its ballot summary, would cut a panoply of basic state and local services by $25 per year "in perpetuity or until the tax and the services paid for by the tax are eliminated or until the services are paid for in some other way" (CFPI 2000). Voters defeated the measure by a two-to-one margin. But the legacy of TABOR lives on. As noted previously, under TABOR, state and local governments are required to ask voters for their permission to spend any surplus revenue; if permission is not granted, governments must refund the surplus back to the citizens. Immediately following the implementation of TABOR—between 1994 and 1996—1,274 special districts, more than 50 school districts, over 180 municipalities, and a handful of counties held de-Brucing elections (Smith and Golich 1998). The practice continues in earnest today.

DIRECT DEMOCRACY, MINORITY RIGHTS, AND PARTISANSHIP

Ballot entrepreneurs such as Bruce often use "faux populist" anti-government tropes to tap into Coloradans' collective consciousness (Smith 1998). Sometimes these populist appeals have policy consequences that negatively affect minority populations (Bell 1978). Axiomatically, direct democracy *is* a majoritarian system of representation, as a ballot measure requires a simple majority of voters to support a particular policy. By definition, then, the minority is disadvantaged under the process of direct democracy (Matsusaka 2004).

Much has been written about ballot initiatives in Colorado that have targeted racial and ethnic minorities, gays and lesbians, and even linguistic minorities. Scholars have engaged in a robust discussion of whether minorities are systematically disadvantaged under a system of direct democracy.[10] Perhaps the most famous example of an initiative trampling on the rights of a minority population in the state was the passage of Amendment 2 in 1992, a constitutional amendment that prohibited any level of government from adopting or enforcing any protections for gays and lesbians. Placed on the ballot by Colorado for Family Values, an evangelical group based in Colorado Springs and financed by Focus on the Family, the passage of Amendment 2 surprised many pundits and political observers. Amendment 2 was overturned by the US Supreme Court in 1996. In its decision, *Romer v. Evans*, the court ruled that Amendment 2 was an unconstitutional abridgment of equal protection under the law (Gerstmann 1999; Miller 2009). More recently, in 2006 a majority of Coloradans again voted against the interests of homosexuals, this time by supporting a ban on same-sex marriage. The vote in favor of Amendment 43—with 55 percent of the electorate supporting the ban—was considerably closer than the outcomes in most of the twenty-six other states that have adopted a ban on gay marriage through the initiative or legislative referendum. Nevertheless, the Colorado Constitution now defines marriage "as only a union between one man and one woman" (Colo. Const. Art. II, §31, cl. 1).

With respect to voting on ballot measures that deal with racial and ethnic issues, Colorado stands in stark contrast to other states. Citizens in several states have voted to repeal affirmative action protections; voters in California, Michigan, Washington, and Nebraska have ended affirmative action in their states through the ballot box. In 2008, however, Colorado voters bucked the trend and narrowly defeated Amendment 46, an anti–affirmative action initiative. In addition, as discussed previously, in 2002 Coloradans rallied against Ron Unz's initiative (Amendment 31) that would have ended bilingual education in the state. As is the case in other states, then, the impact of direct democracy on minority interests in Colorado is a mixed bag.

One other "minority" negatively affected by ballot initiatives that has received little attention is composed of residents who live in rural parts of the state. Demographically, Colorado has long been divided along urban and rural lines. This bifurcation is visible in many statewide votes on ballot measures. There is considerable evidence that, even after controlling for a range of factors, Colorado's rural voters tend to vote significantly differently than their urban counterparts on ballot issues. Occasionally, they end up on the short end of the stick when battling the state's population center along the Front Range. Between 1990 and 2006, for instance, a majority of voters living in the state's fifty-three predominantly rural counties were substantially less supportive of the fifty-six initiatives on the ballot than were the majorities living in the state's urban counties. On nine of the fifty-six measures, the mean preferences of voters in rural counties were trumped by those in the Front Range counties. In each case, statewide majorities approved the initiatives, even though average support for the measures in the state's fifty-three rural counties was below 50 percent. In contrast to the statewide majority, rural voters systematically opposed three legislative term-limit initiatives, two anti-hunting initiatives, an initiative legalizing marijuana for medical purposes, an initiative requiring background checks at gun shows, and an initiative increasing K–12 education funding. The bias against rural interests raises questions about how the initiative process might systematically render minority spatial communities more vulnerable to majority tyranny (Smith 2007).

Because these anti-minority ballot initiatives—successful and unsuccessful ones alike—are inherently divisive, they often create partisan divisions among political elites as well as within the electorate. Political elites and party leaders, as strategic actors, increasingly see ballot initiatives as a way to promote voter turnout for their candidates running for elected office. They also try to use ballot issues as partisan wedges in an effort to split off some traditional supporters of the opposing political party. Because of restrictive campaign contribution limits on candidates running for state and local offices in Colorado, some political elites have even tried to use ballot initiatives to generate unlimited spending on issues that can be tied to a specific candidate or that might be in sync ideologically with their preferred candidates (Smith 2005; Smith and Tolbert 2001). All of these efforts to use ballot measures for their "educative effects" (Smith and Tolbert 2004) may have a polarizing effect, as voting on ballot initiatives in Colorado has become increasingly partisan. With few exceptions, voting patterns on ballot initiatives fall largely along Republican and Democratic lines. Directly but even more so indirectly, political parties are fairly engaged in ballot initiative campaigns in Colorado; as a result, party identification is one of the strongest predictors of vote choice on ballot measures.

CONCLUSION

Colorado politics can aptly be described as a "hybrid democracy," as direct democracy has shaped the state's politics and policies. One cannot understand Colorado politics without an appreciation of initiative politics. The influence of citizen-lawmakers in the Centennial State dates to the Progressive Era, but for many Coloradans the legacy of direct participation by citizens in the policymaking process has come to a head in recent years.

Because of the influence of the initiative process on the state's politics and policies, legislators have understandably felt threatened by direct democracy. The backlash against direct democracy is nothing new; since the 1910s, elected officials have seen the use of the initiative as weakening their own institutional powers. In the 1980s the state legislature passed a law banning paid signature gatherers, but the US Supreme Court, in its 1988 decision *Meyer v. Grant*, struck down the Colorado law. In 1999 the court ruled against another effort by the state legislature to regulate the initiative process. In its decision *Buckley v. American Constitutional Law Foundation*, the court ruled that several Colorado laws were unconstitutional because they infringed on the circulator's political expression, including requirements that petitioners be registered voters and wear a badge identifying their employer. Despite being overturned by the high court, the bipartisan legislative effort to crack down on direct democracy persists. Between 2000 and 2009, members of the state legislature filed forty bills intent on regulating the initiative process, passing thirteen of them.

While most of the proposed bills involved minimal changes to the plebiscitary process, some were more draconian. In 2001 the legislature passed a law requiring that a fiscal impact statement and pro and con arguments for all ballot measures be published in the state's information booklet, known as the "Blue Book." Most notably, the legislature voted in 2008 to place a constitutional amendment (Referendum O) on the November ballot that would have lowered the signature threshold for statutory initiatives from 5 percent to 4 percent of the previous total votes cast for governor and restricted the ability of the state legislature to amend, repeal, or supersede a law passed by initiative. However, it would also have increased to 6 percent the signature requirement for constitutional amendments, and initiatives qualifying for the ballot would first be considered by the state legislature. Referendum O would also have added a geographic distribution provision, requiring that 8 percent of total signatures required to be gathered come from each of the state's congressional districts. In the 2008 general election, Coloradans narrowly defeated the measure, which garnered 47.6 percent support. In 2008, as the number of initiatives on the ballot was escalating, the legislature passed a law that would have prohibited convicted felons from being circulators and required paid signature gatherers to be residents of the state. Governor Bill Ritter vetoed the bill. However, in 2009 Governor Ritter signed into law a bill requiring all issue committees that accept contributions or make expenditures greater than $200 to register with the Office of the Secretary of State within ten days of such transactions.

This chapter began by assessing the origins of this populist, citizen-driven sentiment in Colorado. From a normative perspective, many of the same criticisms leveled at the process today—that special interests dominate the process and that citizens are not fully informed about the issues on which they are asked to decide at the polls—are not new and have actually been floated by skeptics for the past 100 years. But is direct democracy—in particular, the citizen initiative—a good or bad political institution?

Clearly, direct democracy has both positive and negative aspects. As we have seen, direct democracy as practiced in Colorado is not without flaws. Ballot measures are often poorly worded or confusing, making it difficult for citizens to vote their true preferences and creating the potential for implementation and coordination problems. Vested special interests often drive the initiative process. As a purely majoritarian system, the initiative can lead to majority tyranny, as some argue has been the case in issues dealing with homosexuality. The process has few checks and balances, which often discourages substantive debate and iterative policymaking and arguably has contributed to increased partisan polarization in the state. But examples too numerous to recount demonstrate how concerned citizens can use the process to bypass an intransigent or inactive legislature, thereby bringing issues directly to the citizenry (Gerber 1999). Even when they are not successful at the polls, ballot measures can raise awareness of an issue and indirectly pressure elected officials to address the issue. Initiatives in Colorado and in other states also have an "educative effect" (Smith and Tolbert 2004), increasing citizen participation and providing a sense of efficacy to ordinary people who, as citizen lawmakers, become policymakers for a day (Donovan, Tolbert, and Smith 2009). Finally, the use of direct democracy generates public debate and raises public awareness about issues and can even shape the political agenda and affect voters' perceptions of candidates (Donovan, Tolbert, and Smith 2008; Nicholson 2005).

Normatively, then, we should appreciate direct democracy for what it is—an imperfect plebiscitary process that allows for expression by the median voter. It is not a perfect process, but direct democracy in Colorado is not going away any time soon. Colorado is likely to be a hybrid state for years to come.

NOTES

1. In addition to the initiative, direct democracy is composed of the popular referendum and the recall. The popular referendum permits citizens to challenge a statute passed by the state legislature by collecting signatures to place the law on the statewide ballot for a popular vote. The recall, adopted through the initiative process in 1912, per-

mits citizens to remove from office any officer of the state of Colorado at any time, provided petitioners submit valid signatures equaling 25 percent of the total vote in the last election for the official being recalled.

2. Two years later, in 1912, voters approved a citizen initiative adding to the state constitution the popular recall of any state official.

3. Prior to 1919, the titles and summaries of ballot measures were formulated solely by the proponents of the measures—which, not surprisingly, led to several intentionally misleading ballot titles and sizable voter confusion.

4. Voters would end up casting ballots on five separate measures relating to prohibition between 1912 and 1932.

5. Ironically, Judge Lindsey, the principal author of the recall initiative, was subsequently nearly recalled in one of the first uses of the recall (Smith and Lubinski 2002).

6. Only 94,485 voters (of the more than 263,000 who voted for president) cast ballots on Measure 13, and just 79,354 voted on Measure 4. There is also considerable evidence of voter confusion on the two competing ballot measures dealing with the regulation of public utilities. Although there is compelling evidence today that voters are able to use cues to inform their decision-making on ballot measures (Bowler and Donovan 1998; Lupia 1994), Smith and Lubinski's (2002) county-level analysis of the results of the two ballot measures reveals that voters in the state's sixty-two counties did not vote as consistently on the opposing measures as might be expected. Voters in counties that broadly supported the DLL's Measure 13 might have been expected not to support the utility companies' Measure 4. Yet the bivariate correlation between the percentage of the county "yes" votes for both measures is positively related ($r = .600$) and significant ($p < .01$, 2-tailed, $n = 62$), indicating that there may have been considerable voter confusion.

7. All of the subsequent contribution data (various years) were accessed through the National Institute on Money in State Politics online database, available at http://www.followthemoney.org/database/IndustryTotals.phtml.

8. For example, Colorado Citizens for Change was created by Jonathan Coors, director of government relations for Golden-based ceramics maker CoorsTek; see Vuong (2008a). A HealthOne spokesperson for the for-profit hospital in Denver acknowledged that the corporation contributed money in the spring of 2008 to help place Amendment 47, a right-to-work initiative, on the ballot. Yet Fair Campaign Practices Act (FCPA) records indicate no direct contributions from HealthOne to the Colorado Right-to-Work Committee, the ballot issue committee collecting signatures for the initiative, at this time. For more information about HealthOne's involvement with Protect Colorado Jobs, see Vuong (2008b); for more information about the nonprofit organization Protect Colorado Jobs, see Rosa (2008).

9. To determine which ballot issue committees were engaged in which issues on the ballot, I conducted searches on each ballot measure using the National Institute on Money in State Politics online database, available at http://www.followthemoney.org/database/StateGlance/state_ballot_measures.phtml?s=CO&y=2008. I then downloaded the Colorado secretary of state FCPA contribution database and searched for these ballot issue committees to determine their contributions for each quarterly report, then summed the four quarterly reports to determine the total contributions each issue committee received in a given year. The Colorado FCPA contribution database is available at http://www.elections.colorado.gov/DDefault.aspx?tid=498.

Daniel A. Smith

10. See, for example, Chavez (1998); Gamble (1997); Haider-Markel, Querze, and Lindaman (2007); Hero and Tolbert (1996).

REFERENCES

Bell, Derrick. 1978. "The Referendum: Democracy's Barrier to Racial Equality." *Washington Law Review* 54: 1–29.

Bowler, Shaun, and Todd Donovan. 1998. *Demanding Choices: Opinion and Voting in Direct Democracy.* Ann Arbor: University of Michigan Press.

———. 2004. "Measuring the Effects of Direct Democracy on State Policy." *State Politics and Policy Quarterly* 4: 345–363.

Broder, David. 2000. *Democracy Derailed: Initiative Campaigns and the Power of Money.* New York: Harcourt Brace.

Cain, Bruce, and Kenneth Miller. 2001. "The Populist Legacy: Initiatives and the Undermining of Representative Government." In *Dangerous Democracy? The Battle over Ballot Initiatives in America,* ed. Larry Sabato, Bruce Larson, and Howard Ernst, 33–62. Lanham, MD: Rowman and Littlefield.

Campbell, Anne. 2001. "In the Eye of the Beholder: The Single Subject Rule for Ballot Initiatives." In *The Battle over Citizen Lawmaking,* ed. M. Dane Waters, 131–164. Durham, NC: Carolina Academic Press.

Chavez, Lydia. 1998. *The Color Bind: California's Battle to End Affirmative Action.* Berkeley: University of California Press.

Ciruli, Floyd. 1996. "Direct Democracy: Colorado's New Growth Industry." *The Variable* (Winter). Available at http://www.circuli.com/variables/variable-0196.htm. Accessed May 17, 2011.

Citrin, Jack. 1996. "Who's the Boss? Direct Democracy and Popular Control of Government." In *Broken Contract,* ed. Stephen Craig. Boulder: Westview, 268–294.

Colorado Fiscal Policy Institute (CFPI). 2000. "TABOR Trouble 2000: Tax Cuts Proposed on November Ballot." *Issue Brief* 00–03 (Summer). Available at http://www.cclponline.org/uploads/files/Issue00–03.pdf. Accessed December 10, 2009.

Cronin, Thomas. 1989. *Direct Democracy: The Politics of Initiative, Referendum, and Recall* Cambridge: Harvard University Press.

Donovan, Todd, and Daniel A. Smith. 2008. "Identifying and Preventing Signature Fraud on Ballot Measure Petitions." In *Election Fraud: Detecting and Deterring Electoral Manipulation,* ed. Michael Alvarez, Thad E. Hall, and Susan D. Hyde, 130–145. Washington, DC: Brookings Institution.

Donovan, Todd, Caroline J. Tolbert, and Daniel A. Smith. 2008. "Priming Presidential Votes with Direct Democracy." *Journal of Politics* 70(4): 1217–1231.

———. 2009. "Political Engagement, Mobilization, and Direct Democracy." *Public Opinion Quarterly* 73: 98–118.

Ellis, Richard. 2002. *Democratic Delusions: The Initiative Process in America.* Lawrence: University Press of Kansas, 2002.

Gamble, Barbara. 1997. "Putting Civil Rights to a Popular Vote." *American Journal of Political Science* 41: 245–269.

Garrett, Elizabeth. 2005. "Hybrid Democracy." *George Washington Law Review* 73:1096–1130.

Garrett, Elizabeth, and Elisabeth Gerber. 2001. "Money in the Initiative and Referendum Process: Evidence of Its Effects and Prospects for Reform." In *The Battle over Citizen Lawmaking*, ed. M. Dane Waters. Durham, NC: Carolina Academic Press, 73–89.

Garrett, Elizabeth, and Daniel A. Smith. 2005. "Veiled Political Actors and Campaign Disclosure Laws in Direct Democracy." *Election Law Journal* 4: 295–328.

Gerber, Elisabeth. 1999. *The Populist Paradox: Interest Group Influence and the Promise of Direct Legislation*. Princeton, NJ: Princeton University Press.

Gerstmann, Evan. 1999. *The Constitutional Underclass: Gays, Lesbians, and the Failure of Class-Based Equal Protection*. Chicago: University of Chicago Press.

Goebel, Thomas. 2002. *A Government by the People: Direct Democracy in America, 1890–1940*. Chapel Hill: University of North Carolina Press.

Haider-Markel, Donald, Alana Querze, and Kara Lindaman. 2007. " 'Win, Lose or Draw?' A Reexamination of Direct Democracy and Minority Rights." *Political Research Quarterly* 60: 304–314.

Hero, Rodney, and Caroline Tolbert. 1996. "A Racial/Ethnic Diversity Interpretation of Politics and Policy in the States of the U.S." *American Journal of Political Science* 40: 851–871.

Kousser, Thad, and Mathew McCubbins. 2005. "Social Choice, Crypto-Initiatives, and Policymaking by Direct Democracy." *Southern California Law Review* 78: 949–984.

Lupia, Arthur. 1994. "Shortcuts versus Encyclopedias: Information and Voting Behavior in California Insurance Reform Elections." *American Political Science Review* 88: 63–76.

Magleby, David. 1984. *Direct Legislation: Voting on Ballot Propositions in the United States*. Baltimore: Johns Hopkins University Press.

Magleby, David, and Kelly Patterson. 1998. "Consultants and Direct Democracy." *PS: Political Science and Politics* 31: 160–169.

Martin, Curtis, and Rudolph Gomez. 1976. *Colorado Government and Politics*, 4th ed. Boulder: Pruett.

Matsusaka, John. 2004. *For the Many or the Few: The Initiative, Public Policy, and American Democracy*. Chicago: University of Chicago Press.

Miller, Kenneth P. 2009. *Direct Democracy and the Courts*. New York: Cambridge University Press.

National Institute on Money in State Politics. 2009. "Advanced Search." Available at http://www.followthemoney.org/database/advancedsearch.phtml. Accessed December 2, 2009.

Nicholson, Steven. 2005. *Voting the Agenda: Candidates, Elections, and Ballot Propositions*. Princeton, NJ: Princeton University Press.

Piott, Steven. 2003. *Giving Voters a Voice: The Origins of the Initiative and Referendum in America*. Columbia: University of Missouri Press.

Rosa, Erin. 2008. "Unions, Businesses Are Top Donors in 'Right-to-Work' Campaign." *Colorado Confidential*, May 12. Available at http://coloradoconfidential.com/. Accessed December 10, 2009.

Sabato, Larry, Bruce Larson, and Howard Ernst, eds. 2001. *Dangerous Democracy? The Battle over Ballot Initiatives in America*. Lanham, MD: Rowman and Littlefield.

Schmidt, David. 1989. *Citizen Lawmakers: The Ballot Initiative Revolution*. Philadelphia: Temple University Press.

Smith, Daniel A. 1996. "Populist Entrepreneur: Douglas Bruce and the Tax and Government Limitation Moment in Colorado, 1986–1992." *Great Plains Research* 6: 269–294.

———. 1998. *Tax Crusaders and the Politics of Direct Democracy*. New York: Routledge.

———. 2001a. "Growth and Transportation Ballot Measures in Colorado." In *Moving Visions: Next Steps Toward Growing Smart* (June). Available at http://www.sixandsix.net/sampleart/movingvisions.pdf. Accessed December 9, 2009.

———. 2001b. "Special Interests and Direct Democracy: An Historical Glance." In *The Battle over Citizen Lawmaking*, ed. M. Dane Waters. Durham, NC: Carolina Academic Press, 59–71.

———. 2001c. "Campaign Financing of Ballot Initiatives in the American States." In *Dangerous Democracy? The Battle over Ballot Initiatives in America*, ed. Larry Sabato, Bruce Larson, and Howard Ernst. Lanham, MD: Rowman and Littlefield, 71–90.

———. 2005. "The Initiative to Party: The Role of Parties in State Ballot Initiatives." In *Initiative-Centered Politics*, ed. David McCuan and Stephen Stambough. Durham, NC: Carolina Academic Press, 97–117.

———. 2007. "Representation and the Spatial Bias of Direct Democracy." *University of Colorado Law Review* 78(4): 1395–1434.

———. 2009. "Financing Ballot Measures in the U.S." In *Financing Referendum Campaigns,* ed. Karin Gilland-Lutz and Simon Hug. New York: Palgrave, 39–61.

Smith, Daniel A., and Dustin Fridkin. 2008. "Delegating Direct Democracy: Interparty Legislative Competition and the Adoption of the Initiative in the American States." *American Political Science Review* 102: 333–350.

Smith, Daniel A., and Nathaniel Golich. 1998. "Some Unintended Consequences of TABOR." *Comparative State Politics* 19: 33–40.

Smith, Daniel A., and Robert Herrington. 2000. "The Process of Direct Democracy: Colorado's 1996 Parental Rights Amendment." *Social Science Journal* 37: 179–194.

Smith, Daniel A., and Joseph Lubinski. 2002. "Direct Democracy during the Progressive Era: A Crack in the Populist Veneer?" *Journal of Policy History* 14: 349–383.

Smith, Daniel A., and Caroline Tolbert. 2001. "The Initiative to Party: Partisanship and Ballot Initiatives in California." *Party Politics* 7: 739–57.

———. 2004. *Educated by Initiative: The Effects of Direct Democracy on Citizens and Political Organizations in the American States*. Ann Arbor: University of Michigan Press.

Vuong, Andy. 2008a. "Union Issue Draws Funds: Backers of a Right-to-Work Initiative Gain Support from a Builders Group in Raising $355,000 in the Latest Period." *The Denver Post*, September 9. Available at http://www.denverpost.com/business/ci_9821739. Accessed December 8, 2009.

———. 2008b. "Two Firms Back Right-to-Work Effort." *The Denver Post*, April 18. Available at http://www.denverpost.com/business/ci_8965005. Accessed December 8, 2009.

Wilcox, Delos. 1912. *Government by All the People (or the Initiative, the Referendum and the Recall as Instruments of Democracy)*. New York: Macmillan.

Young, Bradley J. 2006. *TABOR and Direct Democracy: An Essay on the End of the Republic*. Golden, CO: Fulcrum.

This chapter examines multiple changes in Colorado's election procedures in recent decades and their subsequent impacts. One major change, arguably the most innovative electoral development in the past century, has been the development of vote centers that have replaced precinct voting in a growing number of Colorado jurisdictions. Another significant change is the widespread use of permanent mail balloting that has recently correlated closely with increased voter participation.

Still other changes have resulted from the increasingly complex mix of new federal and state election laws that have often created challenging and costly problems for the county officials who must implement the laws and conduct the elections. Certainly, the Help America Vote Act of 2002 (HAVA), enacted by the US Congress following the 2000 electoral debacle in Florida, triggered significant election process changes. Beyond this, both the political parties' self-interest and the activities of political "hobbyists," who often suspect dark motives in the use of new electronic voting equipment, have continued to tax the time and patience of state legislators, secretaries of state, and—perhaps most pointedly—local officials.

US ELECTIONS: LEGAL AND ORGANIZATIONAL CONTEXT

Elections in the United States are legally and organizationally complex. Elections are state enterprises administered by counties, which are legally political subdivisions of the state. Election oversight is the responsibility of the states' executive branches, usually the secretary of state. Most of Colorado's election laws are embedded in statutes written by state legislators and further detailed in volumes of rules written by secretary of state officials. In addition, a patchwork of federal government statutes and constitutional provisions, plus a century and a half of US Supreme Court rulings, create legal parameters for everything the states and their counties do.

The US Constitution contains a number of amendments that provide a legal context for US elections. The Fourteenth Amendment, ratified in 1868 following the Civil War, requires states to provide equal protection of the law to all citizens and is the basis for the concept "one person one vote." The Fifteenth Amendment (1870) prohibits states from denying anyone the right to vote on the basis of race, and the Nineteenth Amendment (1920) does the same with respect to sex. The Twenty-Fourth Amendment (1964) bans the use of poll taxes that had been employed to keep the poor—often southern blacks—from voting, and the Twenty-Sixth Amendment (1971) allows eighteen-year-olds to vote.

Over the years the US Congress has adopted a string of measures to enforce these constitutional provisions and thus has affected the electoral process in additional ways. The 1965 Voting Rights Act, as well as amendments adopted in 1975 and 1982 and a host of related court decisions, have placed strict requirements on state and local units in their treatment of minority racial and ethnic groups in elections. Whether in the process of decennial redistricting, the establishment of precinct boundaries, or voter registration procedures, states and their political subdivisions must operate within strict legal parameters with respect to minority groups and the electoral process.

Congressional acts have impacted state and local election administration in other ways as well. The 1993 "motor voter" legislation prompted states to enable citizens to register to vote in locations other than the County Courthouse, which was formerly the only place to do so. The Help America Vote Act now impacts states and localities with respect to voting sites, accessibility and equipment for disabled voters, and statewide voter registration systems.

Within this national legal context, election law is the business of the states. State legislatures govern the political parties and their nomination processes, write the laws counties must follow as they register voters, and decide whether county clerks are allowed to conduct elections by mail and whether voters can cast ballots prior to the traditional November election date. The state decides if local elections are to be conducted in April or May or if they are to be tacked onto November ballots. The secretary of state oversees the process to ensure that state law is followed when county officials actually conduct elections at the ground level.

But the majority of the actual work "on the ground" in the US electoral system is the responsibility of individual counties. County officials arrange for election sites, print the ballots and secure the machinery, and recruit and train election workers and elections judges. County officials gather the ballots, count them, and report the results to the state. When elections run late, county workers are up all night, and they are on the receiving end of discontent when lines become long or procedures go awry. It is also at the county level where the most recent and highly consequential election innovation—vote centers—took root.

VOTE CENTERS

BACKGROUND

Throughout most of US electoral history, citizens traveled to their neighborhood precinct locations to vote on election day, except for those few who had legitimate reasons to vote absentee by mail. If a person lived on the north end of town but worked on the south end, he or she would likely vote on the way to or from work. This proved inconvenient and often led to de facto disenfranchisement. In addition, with hundreds of precinct locations in a typical community, it proved costly to provide the personnel to oversee the process.

US election processes were developed over 200 years ago, at a time when the use of neighborhood precincts allowed poll workers to know everyone in a given locale and voters to walk to the voting booth. But the America of the twenty-first century is radically different, both sociologically and technologically, than it was in the past. Most Americans live and work in different places, and associations and daily routines extend far beyond the neighborhood. Further, modern electronic technology has made data transmission rapid and fairly secure. In spite of these changes over two-plus centuries, until recently, alternatives to the neighborhood precinct had not been attempted.

Beginning in 2003, officials in Larimer County, Colorado, changed all that. The 2000 presidential election helped establish an atmosphere amenable to new ideas and electoral processes. Larimer County's clerk and recorder, newly elected (2002) and with a business rather than a political background, wondered why citizens could convenience shop for food, drink, and hardware supplies at any one of a number of community locations but could not do likewise when voting. As reported in the National Association of Counties "County News Online,"

Larimer County's clerk stated: "I didn't have a clue how elections ran when I came out of industry four years ago to be the deputy, and I had always wondered why you could go to a Super WalMart and get whatever you wanted, but you couldn't vote where you wanted to. So when my predecessor was term-limited, I thought here was an opportunity to try to do something good" (Moretti 2004).

In a culture where workplace, residence, and recreational locations may be distributed across a metropolitan area and extensive commuting is the norm, it seemed reasonable to the new clerk and his staff to do what smart retailers had done for decades and provide multiple voting locations where the modern and mobile American could drop in at his or her convenience. The notion of converting from precinct to vote center balloting thus took root.

Vote Center: What Is It?

A vote center is a voting location capable of accommodating high voter traffic on election day. Voters may show up at any one of a number of centers, selecting the location that best suits their election day routine. They can vote on their way to work, en route to picking up their children, or on the way to lunch. Once a person votes, this information is communicated to a central registry, and that person is technically and legally unable to vote again.

Vote centers were first used in Larimer County in the 2003 election. Colorado law at the time did not allow non-precinct voting in even-year November general elections but did permit the combining of precincts in off-year elections, such as 2003. The vote center experiment was such a success that the Colorado legislature adopted Senate Bill 04–153, which extended the authority to use vote centers in general elections as well for any Colorado county that wanted to employ them.

Getting Ready: Educating Voters

The shift from large numbers of neighborhood precincts to a system based on a smaller number of large vote centers (a decrease from 153 precincts to 25 or 30 vote centers for an even-year November election), where voters had a wide range of locations from which to choose, clearly required an effective public relations and voter education effort. Not unexpectedly, the most frequently asked questions in the conversion from precinct to vote center were, what is a vote center, and how does it work? In Larimer County, a carefully devised public information campaign sought to anticipate these questions and provide answers through every possible medium.

As an additional strategy to dispense information and simplify the election process, the Larimer County clerk's office included absentee ballot requests in an early vote center informational mailer and signature cards in a second mailing sent just a week before election day. Colorado law permits the use of permanent mail ballots, and early voting is allowed two weeks prior to the general election. The Larimer County clerk mailers were intended to educate voters about vote centers and encourage them to vote by mail or to vote early at one of a number of early voting sites that had been established.

Logistics: Vote Center Design

The large reduction in the number of voting locations in Larimer County made the design of the vote centers a complicated matter. With the number of voting locations greatly reduced, the centers had to be placed and spaced to relate appropriately to the distribution of the county's population. Centers in the mountain and ranch areas were smaller but still sufficiently large to accommodate the expected turnout. In heavily populated areas, the centers were designed to process 5,000 voters in each election. In addition to the size, layout, and location factors, it was critical to ensure that ballot supplies and technical equipment were adequate in each center. Finally, the facilities had to comply with the Americans with Disabilities Act and be user-friendly for voters with disabilities.

Results and Reaction

Judging from voter turnout, citizen reaction, cost savings, and the growing use of vote centers both in Colorado and across the nation, vote centers have been a blockbuster success. Since their inception in 2003, Larimer County's clerk and recorder has been asked to explain vote centers in dozens of cities and states as well as overseas, and many jurisdictions have begun the transfer from precincts to vote centers. Officials from the United Kingdom and Russia have traveled to Fort Collins to study the process. The concept has been a major agenda item at a host of professional meetings and academic conferences. *The Washington Post* carried a piece in 2005 that opened: "The nation's election administrators say it's time to restructure elections to reflect the way Americans live, scrapping neighborhood precincts and Election Day for large, customer-oriented 'vote centers' where people could cast ballots over a period of weeks" (Tanner 2005).

More than twenty Colorado counties have begun conducting their elections with vote centers. Texas held a successful vote center pilot election in 2006, and Henderson, Nevada, held its first municipal election with vote centers in May 2007. The state of Indiana has moved forward with the model as well, and the secretary of state was sufficiently pleased that he made Larimer County's clerk, Scott Doyle, Indiana's "Honorary Secretary of State" in 2005.

From both a financial and an administrative standpoint, vote centers are a success because they require half as many election judges as were needed under the old system, thereby reducing the cost of elections and easing the increasingly difficult process of recruiting enough judges. While there are startup costs for the procurement of proper equipment and the assembly of central county poll books and communication networks, once these are in place the costs are reduced as a result of less manpower and lower transportation expenses.

By all accounts, voters prefer vote centers to precinct voting. A distinct advantage is that there is no wrong place to vote. No longer will a voter be turned away for showing up at the wrong precinct. In addition, media reaction has been positive. Following the 2004 election, the Fort Collins *Coloradoan* editorialized: "Larimer County voters appeared to roundly endorse the voting center concept on Election Day. The model in Larimer County is based on making voting and counting ballots more efficient, cost-effective and more secure than using dozens of precinct locations" (*The Fort Collins Coloradoan* 2004).

The editorial went on to note that "a phenomenal 93.5 percent [of county voters] cast ballots" (*The Fort Collins Coloradoan* 2004). This high number represented a significant increase in participation and is in part the product of vote center convenience because turnout numbers have grown since the initial use of the centers. Early voting and no-excuse absentee balloting were in place before the invention of vote centers, however, so it is difficult to disentangle the multiple factors that may have pushed participation upward. In recent years the parties, candidates, and outside groups have all waged more sophisticated and intense mobilization efforts. Closely contested elections might also have contributed to increased turnout, and the historic nature of Barack Obama's 2008 candidacy may have played a role as well.

Limited negative assessments have been made by some members of the two major political parties, who were concerned initially about the absence of precinct-specific voting results, and by the American Civil Liberties Union, which worried about increased transportation needs for senior citizens. Political operatives have long used precinct data to plot their election strategy. The Larimer County clerk eventually developed a way to provide such data, but, in any case, political strategists' claimed needs were not destined to trump citizen convenience and public treasury cost savings.

While vote centers have been successful and increasingly popular beyond their place of origin in Larimer County, their increased use has not been problem-free. Perhaps the most notable examples of problems occurred in Denver and Douglas Counties in 2006. The 2006 election featured one of the longest and most complex ballots in state history, and the combination of ballot length/complexity, the first-ever use of vote centers, and both technical and planning glitches caused some fairly serious problems. One technical problem in Denver was created when judges were unable to verify voter registration and residency quickly. In Douglas County there was too little equipment and too few voting locations. These problems, however, can be avoided with extensive planning and increased experience with the new systems.

These problems aside, vote centers have worked well, are growing in popularity, and are likely here to stay. Along with their simplicity, popularity, and financial advantages, the centers have eased the task of meeting requirements put in place when the US Congress enacted the Help America Vote Act in 2002.

EARLY VOTING, MAIL BALLOTS, AND VOTE CENTERS

While vote centers represent the major change in the conduct of elections in Larimer County and other jurisdictions where they have been adopted, other significant electoral changes have occurred as well. These include an expansion of the availability and use of early voting and provisional balloting. In combination, these factors have had a major impact on both electoral participation and voter behavior. Indeed, according to one study, 79 percent of Colorado voters voted early in 2008, compared to 47 percent in 2004 (McDonald and Schaller 2010).

Beginning in 1992, Colorado law allowed any registered voter to vote early or by absentee mail ballot. Voters could submit their ballots in person prior to election day at a designated polling place and could vote early until the close of business the Friday before the election (CRS 1-1.5-104).

Several modifications were made to early and absentee voting provisions in subsequent years. Voters may now request to receive mail ballots on a permanent basis rather than having to ask for them in advance of each election, and one or more early voter polling places must be available on election day to receive personally delivered mail-in ballots. Numerous statutory changes enacted over the past two decades have had the effect of both expanding mail balloting and tightening signature requirements.

The combination of early voting, mail balloting, and vote centers has provided voters with a variety of options and places to vote. County clerks can and do send ballots to all voters who request them. Voters can then mail their ballots to the clerk's office, deliver them in person to the courthouse or to any one of the established service centers, or bring them to any vote center or the courthouse on election day. Essentially, what for decades was an "absentee" ballot process had by 2008 become a county clerk "mail-out" ballot process, with the time and place of ballot return essentially left up to the voter. Simply put, voting has become much more convenient.

It is difficult to disentangle the impact of vote centers, early voting, and mail balloting on voter turnout. For example, turnout in 2008 in Jefferson County, which did not employ vote centers, exceeded that in Larimer County, which did.

In Denver County, which used vote centers in 2006 but not in 2008, the early and mail voting proportion was similar to that in Larimer County (Colorado Secretary of State 2008). Research conducted by Professors Robert Stein and Greg Vonnahme of Rice University concluded, however, that vote centers have indeed boosted voter participation. Their work involved comparing voter turnout in Larimer and adjacent Weld Counties—Larimer with vote centers and Weld without them—and comparing voting by individual voters in the two counties, paired by age, gender, and voting history (Stein and Vonnahme 2006).

Stein and Vonnahme drew two conclusions. First, vote centers likely account for an increase in turnout ranging from 2.5 percent to 7.1 percent (Stein and Vonnahme 2006: 13). They stated, "There is evidence at the individual level that Election Day Vote Centers [EDVC] have led to higher turnout in elections in Larimer County than would have otherwise been the case" (Stein and Vonnahme 2006: 9). Second, Stein and Vonnahme suggest that the impact is uneven across the electorate. Again, in their words, "Younger and more intermittent voters are more likely to vote with Election Day Vote Centers. The effect might be greater with less regular voters" (Stein and Vonnahme 2006: 12). In an undated document they stated, "Voter turnout among voters using vote centers increased significantly over turnout among precinct voters controlling for age, gender, party affiliation and prior voting history, " and the "effect of EDVC [was] strongest among infrequent voters" (Stein and Vonnahme undated).

Despite assumptions that early voting will increase voter turnout, the evidence is less than conclusive. Indeed, Joseph Giammo and Brian Brox (2010) argue that early voting by itself seems to produce a short-lived increase in turnout that fades by the second presidential election in which it is available. Their study of 500 randomly selected counties across the United States confirms earlier findings by Jeffrey Karp and Susan Banducci (2001) and Grant Neeley and Lilliard Richardson (2001), who argued that counties that offer in-person early voting have shown no long-term increase in turnout.

Other research into early voting has shown that individuals with high levels of political interest, strong partisan attachments, and strong ideological affiliations are more likely to vote early (Berinsky, Burns, and Traugott 2001). Similarly, J. Eric Oliver (1996) showed that liberalizing absentee voting requirements resulted in an increase in absentee voting but not in overall turnout. But Oliver also found that turnout levels did increase when liberalized absentee requirements were combined with party efforts to encourage absentee voting. This may help explain the Colorado case—the state has been host to several competitive races in recent years, so both parties have devoted considerable time and effort to early vote campaigns.

It is clear, though, that in combination, vote centers, early voting, and mail balloting have dramatically altered the patterns by which voters cast their bal-

TABLE **5.1.** Balloting methods and voter turnout

Year	Early Voting	Absentee/Mail Voting	Early plus Mail Voting	Vote Center/ Precinct	Percent Vote Center/Precinct	Total	Percent Vote Center/Precinct	Percent of Active Registered Voters
2008	32,326	106,652	138,978	26,155	15.0	167,292	83.1	92.0
2006	25,362	46,010	71,372	42,203	37.8	114,827	62.2	74.3
2004	45,718	47,116	92,833	52,481	35.7	147,112	63.1	94.6
2002	8,325	37,235	45,560	48,919	51.3	95,276	47.8	66.8
2000	13,769	47,633	61,402	57,582	48.5	119,201	55.5	62.4
1998	10,969	19,401	30,370	56,484	65.0	86,875	40.0	52.1
1996	11,103	17,534	28,637	71,278	71.3	99,992	28.6	69.9
1994	5,990	16,692	22,682	52,981	71.0	745,92	30.4	57.5
1992	20,102	—	20,105	80,650	80.0	100,755	20.0	82.3

Source: Larimer County Clerk and Recorder, Fort Collins, CO.

lots. Over the course of just a few recent election cycles, election day voting at neighborhood precincts has become a relic of the past in many Colorado jurisdictions and in a growing number of other locations as well. Precincts are gone, and the proportion of citizens who vote on election day is shrinking.

As table 5.1 shows, the shift in the method of balloting over a decade and a half has been dramatic. In the November 1992 election, 80 percent of active registered voters in Larimer County voted in their neighborhood precinct on election day. The number remained above 70 percent in both 1994 and 1998. But by the 2008 election, just under 15 percent of voters cast their ballot on election day, and those who did voted at vote centers rather than at neighborhood precincts.

One of the most striking consequences of the combination of vote centers, early voting, and mail ballots is the way they have skewed election expenditures and their potential to dramatically reduce costs. In the 2008 general election in Larimer County, 85 percent of the electorate cast ballots early or by mail. Nevertheless, with the need to operate vote centers and early voting locations, the price tag for that election was $1.2 million. Had the election been conducted through mail balloting alone, the price would have been approximately $327,000 (Doyle analysis 2009). The expansion of the law permitting mail balloting, its increased use by voters, and the obvious cost savings involved suggest that, in time, vote centers may disappear and be replaced by multiple service centers where ballots can be dropped off, resulting in an "all-mail-for-all-elections" world.

The growing use of early and mail balloting has altered campaign strategies too, as election day get out the vote (GOTV) efforts, candidate monitoring of what were previously low numbers of absentee ballots, and final-week advertising blitzes are now less effective. Early and mail voting have extended the election season and require campaigns to do a better job of managing their databases. Campaign operatives must now monitor the inflow of ballots almost continuously, update their voter contact lists, and eliminate those who have already voted. Early voting also forces campaigns to make strategic decisions as to which voters to target for early voting efforts (McDonald and Schaller 2010). Mail and media advertising must cover extended periods of time. When the vast majority of ballots are "in the vault" a week or more before election day, an election may be decided before the polls open on the first Tuesday after the first Monday in November.

In Colorado in 2008, both presidential campaigns timed rallies to coincide with the onset of early voting. Vice presidential candidates Joe Biden and Sarah Palin visited the state at the start of early voting (Corsaro 2008). At a Biden rally in Commerce City, supporters who had voted early were given the best seats (McDonald and Schaller 2010). Barack Obama held two large rallies in Denver and Fort Collins on Sunday, October 26; Obama urged the estimated 100,000 who attended the Denver rally and the 40,000 in Fort Collins to vote early (Boniface 2008). Campaign volunteers at these events provided information to voters about early voting. The city of Denver took the unusual step of opening its vote centers on a Sunday to accommodate the expected crowd of voters.

The Obama campaign made registering new voters and turning out early voters priorities in 2008. According to Jon Carson, Obama's national field director, those efforts paid off. In a conference call with reporters, Carson said, "There are 234,000 Democrats who've never cast a vote in a general election before, and 43 percent of them have already requested a mail-in ballot. Compare that to 196,000 new Republicans, of which only 36 percent have requested a mail-in ballot." Moreover, Carson continued, "20 percent of all the Democrats voting by mail in Colorado so far this year have never before voted in a general election" (quoted in Boniface 2008). In the end, Democrats did a far better job with early voting that they had in previous elections and were able to neutralize a traditional Republican advantage in that area. Obama's Campaign for Change conducted considerable outreach to Latino and black voters in Colorado, holding many early vote rallies—often adjacent to early vote centers (Waak 2008).

In many ways, the Obama effort in 2008 was the culmination of years of attention to early voting by Colorado Democrats. As a case in point, Colorado Victory, the party's coordinated campaign in 2006, carried out a major absentee and early voting GOTV program. Centered in the open-seat race in the competitive Seventh Congressional District, which pit Democrat Ed Perlmutter against Republican Rick O'Donnell, the Democratic effort employed a variety of techniques to boost early voting. The effort included numerous rallies in parks in targeted neighborhoods, door-to-door canvasses, phone calls, and more. Absentee ballot applications were distributed at every event, and campaign staffers noted who received them and tracked them to see who had returned them. Those who had not sent in their ballots were contacted by the campaign. The early vote efforts worked—nearly 67 percent of Democrats voted early in the race (Saunders and Duffy 2008).

HELP AMERICA VOTE ACT

If vote centers constitute one of the significant innovations in the conduct of elections at the local level, the Help America Vote Act of 2002 is arguably the most far-reaching piece of national election legislation since the 1965 Voting Rights Act. As mentioned earlier, HAVA was put in place in the aftermath of the troubled 2000 presidential election, which featured an almost comical—if not tragic—string of foul-ups in Florida, Ohio, and a number of other jurisdictions. Problems ranged from bad machinery, problematic ballots, voter confusion, and questionable processes to outright fraud.

HAVA impacts virtually every element of the election process. The overall objective of the law is to avoid the repetition of past mistakes and ensure that nothing impedes a citizen's ability to vote, whether as a result of purposeful obstruction or record-keeping errors. As the actual conduct of US elections falls to the states and especially to local officials, HAVA has forced major changes and significant costs on the states and counties. HAVA has placed more of the administration of elections under the authority of the Office of the Secretary of State rather than with local election officials. It addresses several areas in the election process, including provisional voting, military and overseas citizen voting, statewide voter registration systems, voting system requirements, training, and accessibility—all of which affect the state's administration and the county's planning and implementation of elections.

Perhaps most significant, HAVA requires states to compile statewide voter registration lists, which reduce data collection costs for parties and enable them to create a national voter registration list (McDonald and Schaller 2010: 97). Until 2008, Republicans had benefited from superior voter lists, but the Obama campaign's financial and technological superiority allowed Democrats to neutralize that advantage. As noted in chapter 2, with improved voter lists, Democrats were able to make major gains in voter registration, targeting, and mobilization.

WHERE ARE WE GOING?

Since 2002, numerous changes have been implemented in Colorado to comply with HAVA. The secretary of state, along with the election administration authority, has made significant staffing and training changes to try and meet HAVA requirements and to assist counties with HAVA compliance. The secretary has implemented numerous rule changes and continues to make them, albeit not always to the satisfaction of local officials. The implementation of the mandated statewide voter registration system continues to experience numerous growing pains. The system is functioning well within counties, but numerous software patches and workarounds have been required for counties to adequately use the system for daily processes and procedures.

A major task currently being worked through is the consolidation of voter registration records for voters with duplicate records. Steps have been taken to make sure there is only one active voter record per voter, but numerous cancelled and inactive records remain to be consolidated with an active record. This project was begun in 2009, but it will likely be several years until the Colorado database is entirely compliant with the HAVA requirement of one record per voter. Once this project is complete, the database will more accurately reflect the current voting population in Colorado.

In summary, then, the 2002 Help America Vote Act has required states and counties to purchase new election equipment. The state now requires machinery that produces verifiable paper records of voter choices for review should questions arise later. The law requires provisional ballots for use when questions arise as to voters' identity, residence, or registration status. A citizen is allowed to vote, with eligibility determined later. In addition, HAVA requires equipment and procedures that allow citizens to change their votes and to review ballots prior to submission.

HAVA requires the use of polling stations that accommodate the needs of persons with disabilities, including the blind, handicapped, and quadriplegic. Prior legislation requires that ballots be available in Spanish as well as English in certain jurisdictions, albeit not in Larimer County.

Under HAVA, states are required to have in place single interactive voter registration systems that communicate electronically with registration records in the counties. This allows instant polling place checks on a voter's registration status and keeps the data instantly up to date. This instantaneous communication prevents a person from voting twice or voting when not registered. Some smaller Colorado counties still use paper poll books, but, over time, electronic books will replace them.

COUNTY CLERKS: THE BOTTOM OF THE INTERGOVERNMENTAL FOOD CHAIN

The complex modern US intergovernmental system requires that both elective and appointed public officials at multiple levels of government work together in every policy area, from social services and transportation to education. It is no different with elections. Among the common features of such interactions are political conflict and the propensity of one level of government to seek to use other levels to do its bidding and then claim credit while shifting the associated costs. Local government officials often refer to this practice as "shift and shaft"—shift responsibility to others, and shaft them by failing to provide the resources needed to get the job done. Describing the same phenomenon, state officials complain about nationally "unfunded mandates."

So it is with county clerks. The US Congress writes many of the election rules, such as the Voting Rights Act and HAVA. State legislators write the state statutes that tell local officials what they can do, must do, and cannot do—what types of voting equipment to use, for example. Secretaries of state follow up on state statutes with a host of rules and regulations. Then it is up to the clerks to conduct elections and figure out how to pay the bills. At the same time, an assortment of citizen groups and self-appointed watchdogs of the public interest, along with the modern media, are quick to publicize election system problems when they arise, often pointing the finger at local officials.

When the Larimer County vote center system was initiated, three complaints were raised. The first came from elected state officials, Democrats and Republicans alike, who worried that with the elimination of precinct voting, precinct-specific voting data would not be available. Sure, convenience and potential cost savings mattered, but for some of those officials what really mattered was the potential absence of information they and their political operatives needed for political strategy and political survival. As it turned out, Larimer officials were able to tack on to the vote-counting procedure a method to generate the desired precinct information, at some added expense, but there is continuing interest in some quarters in banning the use of vote centers for precisely this reason.

A second, purely political objection to the use of vote centers came from elected officials who worried that the increased convenience would drive up participation in areas where the opposition party might be numerically superior—on a college campus, for example. Similarly, and for precisely the same reason, concerns were raised about promoting expanded use of mail ballots—doing so might alter turnout and shift the political advantage.

The third concern was that with the election season extended by mail and early voting, campaign costs in terms of both money and time would increase, given the difficulty of determining who had and who had not voted at any particular point in time. This, some candidates said, made the timing of political mailings and calls urging non-voters to cast their ballots more difficult and expensive because some of their efforts would be wasted targeting those who had already voted. Of course, careful historical tracking of the pace of early voting and mail-in ballot submissions by neighborhood could obviate this alleged problem and perhaps make targeted mailings and voter contact even more effective.

The combination of new national and state laws requiring accommodation of the needs of the disabled and advances in election machinery has made county clerks' job more complicated. All polling places must meet the requirements of the Americans with Disabilities Act, which requires an assortment of accommodations for persons with mobility and vision challenges. Every polling location, for example, must be equipped with at least one electronic voting device, and all polling places must be structured to accommodate the challenged voter. For clerks and their staffs, these requirements are not objectionable, but they do result in added costs—borne largely by the counties—and often in complaints and the threat of lawsuits from those whose perspective regarding the adequacy of the accommodations differs from that of the election officials. Indeed, the state has established a hotline to field complaints, plus processes for dealing with them.

Some citizens worry that modern electronic vote-counting equipment is subject to misuse and fraud by tech wizards; therefore, they demand the use of paper ballots exclusively. Others worry that some new machines work well but that some do not; thus they remain suspicious of equipment certification processes. Still others fear that the use of mail ballots will allow family bullies to manipulate the choices of others in the household or that the mentally impaired might vote. Thus when election issues are discussed at the state capitol or with the secretary of state, county clerks often find themselves across the table from non-elected but self-described "guardians of the public interest" and their lawyers. Some consider themselves spokespersons for the public and view elected clerks as "mere functionaries." When the worriers bring their concerns to state lawmakers, they often get a hearing that may trigger more legislation.

Then there is the matter of cost. Whether it is a question of legislative requirements for new election equipment or more personnel, additional laws and rules can drive up election costs. Rarely do new laws and rules come with more funding. Rather, the local clerks must make them work. County commissioners dictate county budgets, and they, too, are partisan elected officials, sensitive to citizen concerns—which almost always include a desire for low-cost government. Clerks thus often find themselves squeezed between costly national and state rules and miserly budgeters in their own courthouses.

Thus in addition to functioning as partisan elected officials and local election administrators, county clerks must be lobbyists as well. What happens in the state capitol lands on their plates. When those who are chronically suspicious of election chicanery pester elected lawmakers, the clerks must head to the capitol to defend the reliability and integrity of equipment and procedures. They must endlessly explain to those less familiar with on-the-ground election operations the consequences and costs of new ideas that are never in short supply. When political hobbyists turn their eyes to elections, they often end up in the clerk's office. When politicians who are seeking an edge demand data, they join the hobbyists in the courthouse.

As this chapter is being written, Colorado's legislators and secretary of state continue to consider even more ideas for electoral change, the implementation of which will fall to the clerks. There are discussions about more mail balloting—maybe universal, maybe permanent, maybe mandatory. There is a push for changes in voter registration, perhaps allowing registration up to election day. Questions of security, equipment, and equipment certification are still on the agenda. From the viewpoint of the clerks, the number-one election issue should be "who pays for all this," but they do not control the agenda. Yet in the conduct of US elections for the thousands of national, state, and local offices and issues, the clerks are the ones for whom the proverbial "rubber meets the road."

REFERENCES

Berinsky, Adam J., Nancy Burns, and Michael W. Traugott. 2001. "Who Votes By Mail? A Dynamic Model of the Individual-Level Consequences of Voting-by-Mail Systems." *Public Opinion Quarterly* 65: 178–197.

Boniface, Dan. 2008. "Obama Bringing Confidence to Fort Collins." Available at http://www.9news.com/rss/article.aspx?storyid=102599. Accessed May 26, 2010.

Colorado Revised Statutes, Title I (CRS 1–1.5–104), Uniform Election Code of 1992.

Colorado Secretary of State. 2008. "Abstract of Votes Cast."

Corsaro, Ryan. 2008. "Biden Tries to Keep Colorado out of the Red." Available at http://www.cbsnews.com/8301-502443_162-4538033-502443.html. Accessed May 26, 2010.

The Fort Collins Coloradoan. 2004. "Voting Centers Receive Endorsement." Editorial, January 5.

Giammo, Joseph G., and Brian J. Brox. 2010. "Reducing the Costs of Participation: Are States Getting a Return on Early Voting?" *Political Research Quarterly* 63: 295–303.

Karp, Jeffrey A., and Susan A. Banducci. 2001. "Absentee Voting, Mobilization, and Participation." *American Politics Research* 29: 183–195.

Larimer County Clerk and Recorder Office files, Fort Collins, CO.

McDonald, Michael P., and Thomas Schaller. 2010. "Voter Mobilization in the 2008 Presidential Election." In *The Change Election: Money, Mobilization, and Persuasion in the 2008 Federal Elections,* ed. David B. Magleby. Provo, UT: Center for the Study of Elections and Democracy, 89–108.

Moretti, M. Mindy. 2004. "Voting Made Easy in Larimer County, Colo." *County News Online.* Available at http://www.naco.org/CountyNewsTemplate.ctm?template=/CenterManagement/Content. Accessed November 7, 2004.

Neeley, Grant W., and Lilliard E. Richardson Jr. 2001. "Who Is Early Voting? An Individual Level Examination." *Social Science Journal* 38: 381–392.

Oliver, J. Eric. 1996. "The Effects of Eligibility Restrictions and Party Activity on Absentee Voting and Overall Turnout." *American Journal of Political Science* 40: 498–513.

Saunders, Kyle L., and Robert J. Duffy. 2008. "Volatility and Volition: The Pendulum Swings High and Hard in Colorado's Seventh District." In *The Battle for Congress: Iraq, Scandal, and Campaign Finance in the 2006 Election*, ed. David B. Magleby and Kelly D. Patterson, 62–81. Boulder: Paradigm.

State of Colorado. 2007. "Help America Vote Act, Revised State Plan." March 12. Available at http://www.elections.colorado.gov. Accessed May 23, 2010.

Stein, Robert, and Greg Vonnahme. 2006. "Election Day Vote Centers and Voter Turnout." Paper presented at the Annual Meeting of the Midwest Political Science Association, April 20–23, Chicago.

———. N.d. "An Assessment of Election Day Vote Centers." Presentation in outline form.

Tanner, Robert. 2005. "Election Administrators Want Restructure." *The Associated Press*, June 7. Available at Washingtonpost.com. Accessed June 9, 2005.

Waak, Pat. 2008. Chair, Colorado Democratic Party. Interview with Robert Duffy, Denver, CO, November 14.

CHAPTER SIX

The Colorado General Assembly:
It Ain't What It Used to Be

John A. Straayer

FROM REPRESENTATIVE GOVERNMENT
TO SOMETHING ELSE

The "Old Days"

What a difference a few decades and shifts in political winds can make. The Colorado General Assembly in the early 1980s—under the control of a Republican Party with comfortable house and senate majorities—featured strong leadership, a dominating House Rules Committee run by an experienced and strategic veteran speaker, experienced committee chairs, and a senate with a similarly experienced president and committee chairs. Both chambers had considerable election-to-election turnover but were shaped by the long-term tenure of a small number of veteran members. For example, Speaker of the House Carl "Bev" Bledsoe served nineteen years in the house, ten as speaker. Committee chairs similarly logged lengthy tenures in both the house and the senate.

Then came the late 1980s and early 1990s, a period characterized by political dissatisfaction in Colorado and the United States more broadly. The political winds blew in a conservative and anti-government direction. In 1978 California voters adopted Proposition 13 to limit property taxes; other states soon followed, with measures limiting revenues, spending, or both. In this environment and following the tax and spending limits, voters found term limits for elected officials to be similarly attractive. What happened nationally and in many other states happened in Colorado as well and affected the legislature in major ways. The Colorado General Assembly today is a very different institution than it used to be.

FAST-FORWARD TO THE GENERAL ASSEMBLY TODAY

In the aftermath of the years of voter discontent, Colorado's legislature changed greatly. In 2004 Democrats took control of both legislative chambers; as of 2010 they enjoyed margins of 21–14 in the senate and 38–27 in the house. Term limits have shortened members' tenure and weakened leadership. Since the first year of the term-limit impact (1998), the house has had five speakers, with four serving just two years each. The senate had five presidents during the 1998–2010 span. The formerly powerful House Rules Committee is gone, a victim of a 1988 "reform" measure passed by voters. Term limits have produced inexperienced committee chairs in the House of Representatives. With political careers legally wounded by term limits, a growing number of members now leave to pursue other political opportunities before their terms expire.

Whether the result of term limits or general changes in the US and Colorado political environments, the internal operations of the General Assembly have changed. There are fewer cross-party coalitions such as bipartisan women legislator groups, which often coalesced to develop compromises on such issues as education and health care. Increasingly, the podium in the "well" at the front of the chamber is a place for speech making and political point scoring. New and inexperienced members are increasingly less timid about pushing themselves into the middle of contentious debates. Both parties now employ an enlarged cadre of political staffers who track opponents' voting records, issue a steady flow of political spin, and help plot strategy.

Then there is the impact of direct democracy. Beginning with what is called the Gallagher Amendment in 1982 and running through voter adoption of the Taxpayer's Bill of Rights (TABOR) (1992); Amendment 23, which drives K–12 school funding (2000); Great Outdoors Colorado (2000); and some of the legislators' own actions, the institution's fiscal authority has been severely limited. It is not unreasonable to assert that Colorado's legislature has been so weakened by direct democracy that it no longer qualifies as a representative government.

What follows in this chapter is an examination in some detail of several of the major factors that have changed Colorado's General Assembly and the institution's role in the governance of the state. Many of these changes are what can be termed institutional, as with voter approval of citizen-initiated term limits and Give a Vote to Every Legislator (GAVEL), as well as fiscal measures including TABOR, Amendment 23, and the General Assembly's own multiple tax cuts in 1999 and 2000. Others, including the deep divisions that emerged within the long-dominant Republican Party and the Democrat's ascendancy to majority status, are more clearly political in nature.

INSTITUTIONAL CHANGES

TERM LIMITS

One of the most consequential institutional changes in Colorado governance has been the imposition of term limits on state lawmakers, adopted by voters in 1990. Colorado's senators and representatives are limited to eight consecutive years in their chamber, although they may then immediately run for a seat in the other house if they choose to do so or sit out for four years and run again for a seat in the same chamber.

Along with California and Oklahoma, Colorado was among the first states to adopt term limits. Colorado state senator Terry Considine, who had US Senate ambitions, and Dennis Polhill, a political activist associated with the conservative Independence Institute, led the way in securing a sufficient number of voter signatures to place the measure on the ballot. Term-limit advocates sold their "reform" as an antidote for several alleged governmental ills. They argued that political careerism, coupled with noncompetitive elections, created a permanent political class that was insufficiently responsive to the citizens. Term limits would end lengthy stays in elective bodies, increase competition, and recreate the nostalgic "citizen" legislature of olden days (Tabarrok 1994).

Term-limit promoters also saw their proposal as a way to reduce the influence of lobbyists and staff members and to diversify legislative membership in terms of gender and ethnicity (Carroll and Jenkins 2001). These claims were attractive to many citizens, who viewed lobbyists as hired guns whose clout should be reduced and staffers as unelected insiders who enjoyed excessive influence over the members they were hired to serve. In addition, term limits were attractive to some women and minority groups, which saw lengthy tenures as barriers to the entry of a more diversified pool of candidates.

THE CONSEQUENCES

In Colorado, none of the term-limit proponents' promised changes have come to fruition; instead, many of the opponents' concerns have proven accurate (Straayer 2003; Straayer and Bowser 2004). Election-to-election turnover remains what it had been for years prior to the limits, and there has been no increase in the number of women or minority members. On the other side of the coin, the limits have weakened leadership, sapped the General Assembly of much of its collective experience and policy history, heightened partisanship, and—irony of ironies—increased political careerism.

In the decades prior to term limits, the 100-member General Assembly (sixty-five representatives, thirty-five senators) typically contained one or two dozen long-term experienced members, and it was common for those in top leadership slots and committee chairs to stay in their positions for many years. The legislature was populated by a mix of newcomers and veterans. Members knew that from election to election, they were likely to return to work under the same leaders. This provided incentives to "follow the leader," precluded constant campaigning for leadership positions, and increased the experience and political savvy of those in leadership. But with the onset of the limits in 1998, that changed: the members with long tenure and long memories began to disappear.

Table 6.1 depicts the impact of term limits on General Assembly leadership beginning in 1998. In the twelve years between 1998 and 2010, the house had five speakers and the senate six presidents. With a single exception in each chamber, it has been two years and out for those in the top two positions of power and responsibility. Members know from the moment of leadership selection that those at the top are immediate lame ducks with relatively little legislative experience. Incentives to General Assembly members have shifted from working with the leaders and following their cues to moving strategically as candidates for the next round of leadership selection.

A similar pattern is evident in committee chairmanships. During the 1981–1982 sessions, for example, the Senate Education Committee was chaired by Republican Al Mieklejohn who had served in that chamber for twenty years, including fourteen as Education Committee chair. Ted Strickland, in addition to his ten years as president, served twenty-six years in the chamber and chaired committees for over two dozen of those years. Senator Tillman Bishop served twenty-eight years and chaired the Agriculture Committee for ten years and the Transportation Committee for four years. Les Fowler chaired the Senate Finance Committee for sixteen of his twenty-two years in the chamber.

This pattern was replicated in the House of Representatives. Paul Schauer spent twenty years in the house, ten of them as chair of the Finance Committee and seven chairing the Business Affairs and Labor Committee. During his fourteen years in the house, John Hamlin chaired four committees and spent eight years on the powerful Rules Committee.

That was in the 1980s. With committees, as with leadership, the sessions today are a different world. In the house, the eight-year term limit means no

TABLE **6.1.** House speaker and senate president tenure, 1975–2010

House Speaker	Senate President
Ruben Valdez 1975–1976 (2)	Fred Anderson 1975–1982 (8)
Ron Strahle 1977–1978 (2)	Ted Strickland 1983–1992 (10)
Bob Bufford 1979–1980 (2)	Tom Norton 1993–1998 (6)
Carl "Bev" Bledsoe 1981–1990 (10)	Ray Powers 1999–2000 (2)
Chuck Berry 1991–1998 (8)	Stan Matsunaka 2001–2002 (2)
Russ George 1999–2000 (2)	John Andrews 2003–2004 (2)
Doug Dean 2001–2002 (2)	Joan Fitz-Gerald 2005–2007 (3)
Lola Spradley 2003–2004 (2)	Peter Groff 2008–2009 (2)
Andrew Romanoff 2005–2008 (4)	Brandon Shaffer 2010 (1)
Terrance Carroll 2009–2010 (2)	

Source: Legislative Council records, various years. The numbers in parentheses are the numbers of years the person held the position.

committee chair can take the position following an election with more than six years' experience, and even that brief tenure is uncommon. Members often leave after one, two, or three terms to seek other elective offices or for other reasons. In 2004, when the Democrats captured the house majority for the first time in four decades, every committee chair was new to the position, if not to the committee itself.

The 2009 session is also illustrative. The chairs of the nine committees of reference, plus that of the Appropriations Committee, averaged just 4.2 years of legislative experience at the start of the session. Only four of the ten had ever chaired a committee.

The 1981 versus 2009 experience differential in the senate was somewhat different. In recent years a majority of senators have previously served in the house. While they may be short on chairmanship experience, they are much more familiar with institutional procedures and policy content than are their house counterparts. Entering the 2009 session, eight of the ten senate committee chairs had at least some prior experience in the position and averaged 7.2 years of legislative experience. Still, the picture of committees in Colorado's General Assembly today contrasts starkly with that of the years and decades that predated term limits.

What difference does this make? Again, committee chairs who have logged a decade or more in the legislature come to their positions having seen thousands of bills and having heard testimony from scores of interest groups on all sides of the issues, and they have come to know and understand the content of existing statutes. They have very likely witnessed the unanticipated and unwanted consequences of what at one time seemed to be good legislation. These experienced lawmakers are in a position to help bring new members up to speed with respect to current law and the interest group lineup, to give new members reliable information, and to help them hone their questioning skills as committees examine bills and query witnesses.

There is little reason to believe legislators today are less intelligent, less public spirited, or less interested in making good public policy than were their earlier counterparts. But experience and knowledge matter as well. Now, more so than before term limits, one observes committee chairs who are unfamiliar with procedure, who get "rolled" by the other party, and who allow their committees to lose focus. Unlike earlier years, some committee members move motions to amend so they can insert into bills provisions that are already in statute. Respondents in a major study of term-limit impacts reported more passing on votes as members searched for cues, less procedural control by chairs, higher bill passage rates, and a decline in civility (Straayer and Bowser 2004).

An associated consequence is the propensity of inexperienced members to prematurely commit their support for bills to lobbyists or colleagues. This places them in the awkward position of having to renege or seek release from their pledge when they learn more about what is at stake. Similarly, inexperience can leave members unequipped to ask probing questions before pledging support for a bill or an amendment. This occurred less frequently in the past.

Table 6.2 displays both experience differentials between the 1997 pre–term-limit session and the 2009 session and the extent to which the pre– and post–term-limit gap is much greater in the house than in the senate. Whether regarding leaders, committee chairs, or the members as a whole, the experience-draining impact of term limits is clear.

Another striking result of term limits has been an increase in political ambition rather than the decrease term-limit champions had promised. By forcing out longtime members, the limits have indeed opened more seats, and thus the political door, for newcomers. But rather than serving a term or two and going home, as was supposed to be the case with "citizen" legislators, the influx of newcomers has meant an enlarged supply of those who want to stay—if not in the General Assembly, at least in the political world. One term-limit study respondent noted that "the new members are more anxious, in a hurry, and looking to their next political move" (Straayer and Bowser 2004: 25). Insightful veteran lobbyist Lynn Young quipped, "Once these guys get here under that gold dome, they never want to go home" (Straayer conversation with Young, March 2003).

The numbers support her observation. As table 6.3 demonstrates, since term limits first took effect in 1998, the proportion of members who seek another elective office after leaving the General Assembly has gone up, not down, and the proportion of those who retire from politics following their legislative careers has declined. Further, the post–term-limit members who leave before the end of

TABLE **6.2.** Years legislative experience at the start of the session, 1997 and 2009

Group	1997	2009
Average HR committee chair	9.3	4.2
Average Senate committee chair	8.7	7.2
HR chair 10-plus years	5	0
Senate chair 10-plus years	6	5
Joint Budget Committee member 10+ years	4	2
Leaders (top 3 H/S) 10+ years	4	0
HR grand total years	269	154
Senate grand total years	294	222

Source: Legislative Directories, 1997 and 2009.

TABLE **6.3.** Legislative departures (initial post–General Assembly move), 1990–2008

	1990–1998 Pre–Term Limits (n=97)	1998–2008 Term Limit Departures (n=105)	1998–2008 Non–Term Limit Departures (n=78)
Sought another elective office	29.0%	44.8%	56.4%
Lost reelection	24.0%	NA	23.1%
Executive branch appointment	3.0%	11.4%	3.8%
Became lobbyist	1.0%	10.5%	0%
Other political involvement	0%	7.7%	1.3%
Retired from politics	43.0%	26.7%	14.1%

Source: Tracked and calculated by author.

their allowed tenure are the most inclined to seek further elective office and the least likely to exit the political world. Both the numbers and direct observation tell us that the 100-member General Assembly contains a large supply of politicos watching for opportunities to make their next political moves.

The voluntary departure of members as they move on to other political roles has led to a growth in the number who begin their legislative career selected not by voters but by small political party vacancy committees. During the 2010 session, for example, 20 percent of the house members first came to office in this fashion.

While doing little to advance the objectives of term-limits advocates, the reform has changed the General Assembly in other ways. The three major nonpartisan staffing units—the Legislative Council, Legislative Legal Services, and the Joint Budget Committee—look much as they did twenty or thirty years ago. Now, as then, they work hard and successfully to stay out of the partisan political fray. But perhaps more now than before, they influence both process and policy by having to fill informational voids created by the absence of what for decades was the small cadre of veteran lawmakers. The General Assembly has long been heavily dependent on the expertise of its nonpartisan staff members, but it is even more dependent in this post–term-limit era. More than ever, it is the staff members who know the most about both policy and process and the institution's history and traditions (Straayer 2007). A striking example is the 2011–2012 Joint Budget Committee, whose six members began with a total of three years' experience on the committee. This contrasts with the 1998 committee, whose six members had an aggregate thirty-three years on the committee.

A change in legislative staffing that has had political consequences is the growth in the number and role of partisan staff members. All four party caucuses, the Democrats more than Republicans, have increased the number of their partisan helpers. Party staff members publicize their members' work and keep track of the other party's foibles. They are often in the middle of party strategy and play an instrumental role in building support for legislation and in making sure the press and the public are fed an adequate diet of mistakes and ethics problems regarding the other side of the political aisle. As leaders' tenure and experience have decreased in the wake of term limits, the presence of partisan staffers has increased.

GAVEL

GAVEL is an acronym for "give a vote to every legislator." It is a constitutional measure placed on the ballot through the initiative process and passed overwhelmingly by voters in 1988. GAVEL is treated in some detail in chapter 7 of this book, but the measure altered the legislature's procedural rules and thus will be discussed briefly here. Before GAVEL, after bills were referred to committee, the committee chair enjoyed the discretion to move bills forward for hearings and votes or to hold them and let them die, a tactic known as the "pocket veto." Further, the majority party caucuses would take votes to establish the party position on bills, the most important of which was the "long" budget bill. When a sufficient number of caucus members voted for a position, caucus rules required that all caucus members support that position when the measure came to the floor. It was simply a mechanism to shut out the minority party—to negate the effect of minority party member floor votes entirely.

The initiative that placed GAVEL on the state ballot was the work of a consortium of "reform," or "good government," groups, such as the League of Women Voters. It was supported by the Democratic Party, which, as the minority party, suffered from the use of the committee pocket veto and the majority party binding caucus technique. GAVEL weakened the majority party and its leadership and opened the door for more cross-party voting.

AMENDMENT 41

Amendment 41 was another "good government" reform measure, placed on the 2006 statewide ballot through the work of Common Cause. It passed comfortably, with 66 percent of the popular vote. Amendment 41 was designed to curtail the influence of interest groups and their lobbyists by severely limiting their ability to offer gifts to public officials. It banned any legislator from accepting even a cup of coffee from a lobbyist and restricted gifts to public officials and their families to fifty dollars per year.

Amendment 41, entitled "Standards of Conduct in Government," turned out to have consequences far beyond those its sponsors intended. The amendment raised questions as to whether children of public employees, from professors to janitors, could accept gifts in the form of higher education scholarships. It made legislator acceptance of a meal at an industry conference questionable. The amendment wiped out a decades-old tradition of interest groups' provision of a light breakfast in the capitol each morning, at which legislators, staffers, and interns were invited to pick up a cup of coffee, a donut, or some other morsel of food. In addition, Amendment 41 essentially put an end to evening social events such as hockey games, concerts, and cocktails at which members of both chambers and parties mixed.

Similar to term limits, Amendment 41 reduced the propensity of members to become long-term colleagues and friends. It altered behavior patterns in which personal connections were often developed, connections that could soften partisan edges.

FISCAL POLICY AND BUDGETING

Thanks largely to citizen-initiated constitutional measures, Colorado's fiscal policy and budgeting process have undergone dramatic and highly consequential changes in recent decades. Both usage of the citizen initiative and fiscal policy are treated in detail in other chapters. Here, it is sufficient to note that these changes in policy and process have both complicated budgeting and restricted the legislature's taxing and spending authority. Indeed, when combined with the impacts of term limits, these changes have made it increasingly difficult for legislators to fully comprehend the state's budget and for the institution as a whole to engage in forward-looking policy development.

CUMULATIVE IMPACT

Wrapped together, the measures discussed here have changed the character of Colorado's legislature in major ways. Today, leadership is weaker and leaders, committee chairs, and members alike are policy and process novices compared

TABLE **6.4.** Knowledgeable observers' perceptions of legislators, 2003 vs. a decade earlier

Questions	Percent Agreeing
1. Less knowledgeable about statewide issues	84
2. Less knowledgeable about legislative operations	84
3. Less knowledgeable about issues in committee	70
4. Less likely to follow floor leaders	62
5. Less collegial and courteous in committee	84
6. Less collegial and courteous on the floor	78
7. More partisan legislature	84
8. Leaders more focused on campaigns	91
9. Members more aggressive in fundraising	82
10. Plan path to leadership earlier	77
11. Less apt to use established leadership ladder	72
12. Legislators have lost power to lobbyists	72
13. Legislature have lost power to governor	73
14. Legislators less supportive of institution	70

Source: Mail questionnaire sent by National Conference of State Legislatures to selected knowledgeable persons who had observed legislators for a minimum of ten years, 2003. Number of persons surveyed: 128; response rate: 30 percent.

with their counterparts of just two or three decades ago. Members know less about the issues and focus more on their campaigns, fundraising, and partisan jousting on the chamber floors. The lobby corps has changed, featuring more women and younger members, and it is no less influential. Nonpartisan staffers have more influence on process, albeit not purposefully, and the size and role of the partisan staff have increased. Partisanship is up, and civility is down. The collective institutional and policy memory of the General Assembly has suffered.

A survey of "knowledgeables"—including lobbyists, staff members, former legislators, and media personnel closely familiar with the legislature—captures much of what has changed. Their perceptions of the changes are shown in table 6.4. For those who watch the General Assembly closely, it has changed in important and, by and large, unfortunate ways.

DIFFERENT POLITICS AND THE
REPUBLICAN QUEST FOR MINORITY STATUS

As much as Colorado's General Assembly has changed institutionally, it is a different place politically as well. By 2004 two major shifts, causally intertwined, had turned the Republican Party—which had enjoyed four decades of almost uninterrupted dominance—into an unhappy minority. As late as the 2002 ses-

TABLE 6.5. Party control, 1982–2008

Time Period	House		Senate		Combined	
	R	*D*	*R*	*D*	*R*	*D*
1982–2002	R	D	R	D	R	D
Average number of members	39.55	25.45	21.0	14.0	60.45	39.45
2004–2008	R	D	R	D	R	D
Average number of members	27.33	37.67	15.33	19.67	42.67	57.33

Source: Legislative Directories, various years.

sion, both chambers were under Republican control. In 2004 Republicans lost their majorities in both chambers, and in 2010 the Democrats enjoyed a very comfortable majority in both the house (37–27–1) and the senate (21–14). As table 6.5 shows, the GOP surrendered decades of comfortable party control in 2004, in rather dramatic fashion.

It is difficult to separate the misfortunes of the Republican Party from the successes of the Democrats. Over a three-decade span the Republicans moved slowly but surely to the political right, found themselves deeply divided ideologically in one election after another, and failed to address the state's serious fiscal trauma. The Democrats—long a hapless minority—benefited from the Republican dysfunctions, became aggressive in running qualified candidates in most legislative districts, and came to enjoy the largesse of a group of four deep-pocket political benefactors.

House "Crazies" and the Early Years

The Republican shift to the political right began in the 1970s with the election of a group of self-designated House "crazies." Four notables among them were Anne Gorsuch, Tom Tancredo, Steve Durham, and Cliff Dodge. They were largely fiscal conservatives and not notably concerned with the social and cultural issues much of their party later embraced.

In the legislature, these "crazies" were often an influential thorn in the side of their own party as when, for example, they engineered the ouster of Speaker Ron Strahle and replaced him with the more conservative western slope rancher Bob Bufford. On the 1977–1978 Colorado Conservative Union legislative scorecard, they held the top four "most conservative" spots.

The Republican Party's slide to the political right continued through the 1980s, but a substantial moderate contingent remained including Paul Schauer, Bob Kirscht, Betty Neale, Jeannie Faatz, Al Mieklejohn, Martha Ezzard, Lewis Entz, Dottie Wham, Jack Fenlon, and David Wattenberg. Hard-core conservatives included Maynard Yost and Elwood Gillis from rural Colorado; Phil Pankey, Ruth Pendergast, Jim Lee, and Sam Zakhem from suburban Denver districts; Mary Anne Tebedo from El Paso County; and Steve Erickson and Wayne Allard from Larimer County. Others included Bill Owens, Don Mielke, and Richard Mutzebaugh. As a party, the majority Republicans were moving more and more to the political right but were still balanced to some degree and emphasized fiscal rather than social-cultural conservatism.

Going into the 1991–1992 legislative sessions, Republicans controlled Colorado's house of representatives 38–27 and the senate with a whopping 23–12 margin. As the 1990s progressed, a number of Republican moderates retired from legislative service and were replaced by conservatives, some of whom were fiscal conservatives and others who were social-cultural conservatives. By mid-decade the trend had accelerated, augmented by term limits that pushed out even more moderate Republicans and made room for more of what were then called the new House "crazies."

The slide continued through the 1990s, and by 2000 a large contingent of moderate marquee-name Republicans who had held critical leadership slots were gone. The positions vacated by these moderates included the senate president and majority leader and chairs of three critical committees, including the Joint Budget Committee. On the house side they included the speaker, committee chairs, and a Joint Budget Committee member.

The replacements for these departed majority party moderates brought an altered brand of conservatism, one that melded fiscal libertarianism and the social-cultural agenda. By 2009–2010 the new brand of Republicanism dominated both chambers. Following the 2008 election, the only house Republican members who resembled the GOP of 1998 were Don Marostica, Tom Massey, and Ellen Roberts. In the senate the lone moderates were Al White, Ken Kester, and sometimes Nancy Spence.

In the 2000 election Democrats displaced Republicans as the majority party in the senate, but they gave it back in 2002. Then in 2004 Democrats took control of both chambers. In 2006 they increased both their house and senate margins, dominating the 100-member General Assembly 60 to 40—a striking contrast to 1998 when Republicans held a similar advantage. In 2008 Democrats again controlled both chambers, having lost a net of just one seat in that election.

Clearly, a number of factors led to Democrats replacing Republicans as the majority party in the General Assembly, including shifts in the political winds nationwide, improved Democratic candidate recruitment, the launch of challenges in most districts, and the impact of deep-pocket supporters and independent expenditures. But the political environment that came to favor Democrats was created in major ways by the Republicans themselves. Their transformation from a secular moderate-to-conservative party to one farther to the right and with a pronounced social-cultural component made the party less attractive to voters, rendered Colorado's GOP incapable of responding to growing fiscal problems, and led to deep divisions within the party.

Gifts to Democrats: Republican Family Feuds and Cannibalism

As the moderate-conservative divide within the Republican Party grew, it began to manifest itself in nomination contests. In 2004 Republican US senator Ben Nighthorse Campbell retired from office. Colorado Republicans lined up and chose sides between Bob Schaffer and Pete Coors for their nominee. Governor Bill Owens sided with Coors. Longtime party godfather and former US senator Bill Armstrong backed Schaffer and ran attack ads accusing Coors of supporting the "homosexual agenda." Before it was over, well-known political consultant Walt Kline commented that he had "never seen a Republican primary in the state that had taken a nasty turn like this in a major race with major candidates" (quoted in Harsanyi 2004; *The Economist* 2004). Coors won but then lost to Democrat Ken Salazar in the general election. A US Senate seat thus flipped from Republicans to Democrats.

Party divisions exposed during the Coors-Schaffer contest reemerged in the 2005 battle over Referendum C. With TABOR constitutionally limiting state revenues, revenues coming in over the TABOR limit, and the state unable to spend to repair budget-cutting damage done by the 2001 economic recession, Colorado faced the prospect of further cuts to higher education, transportation, and health care programs and at the same time having to push hundreds of millions of dollars in revenue out the door in the form of tax refunds. The coming crisis was evident even to the casual observer, but the Republican-controlled legislature did nothing about it.

In this environment, a cross-party coalition developed to place on the ballot a legislatively referred measure to suspend the TABOR revenue lid for five years and eliminate a "ratchet" provision that pegged allowable revenues in any given year as the starting point when calculating the revenue cap for the following year. This provision was replaced by one that made any previous high-revenue year the starting point. Governor Owens and many moderates in his party teamed with Democrats to put the proposal on the ballot and campaigned in its favor. Other important political supporters included Democratic house speaker Andrew Romanoff, Republican senate assistant minority leader Steve Johnson, former Republican US senator Hank Brown, and past GOP Party chair Bruce Benson.

Opposing Referendum C were Republican senate president John Andrews and a majority of General Assembly Republicans. TABOR author Douglas Bruce, the conservative Independence Institute, and a host of interests outside the state—including Grover Norquist and Dick Armey, leaders of national anti-tax, minimal-government organizations—also got in the game as opponents of the referendum. House minority leader Joe Stengel worked hard to kill the measure, commenting that "now, with the governor standing shoulder to shoulder with his Democratic friends, I think we are probably going to have a tough time regaining the House and the Senate" (quoted in Couch and Hughes 2005). Once again, the party was split along virtually the same lines as it had been during the Coors-Schaffer contest.

The 2006 gubernatorial election came on the heels of the Referendum C campaign, and again Republicans suffered some self-inflicted wounds. Their two prime candidates were Marc Holtzman and Bob Beauprez. The campaign was both bitter and comical and featured a two-man race to the political right, each seeking to outdo the other as "the" fiscal conservative. Holtzman attacked Beauprez, labeling him "Both Ways Bob" for being insufficiently vigorous in opposing Referendum C. The line stuck. Beauprez became the standard bearer for the GOP, but the label hurt him in his race against Democrat Bill Ritter.

In the end, Holtzman, the favorite of many conservatives in the party, failed to gain the requisite 30 percent of the delegate votes in the nominating assembly. He then tried to petition his way onto the primary ballot, only to fail to collect enough signatures. Beauprez enjoyed the support of the Republican establishment but ran an often unorganized campaign and lost to Ritter, having been politically wounded by the struggle against Holtzman.

The divisive campaigns for US Senate and governor and the battle over Referendum C were statewide and high-profile, but the Republicans managed to tear at each other in more localized contests as well. Contests in 2006 for the Republican nomination in state Senate Districts 13 in Weld County and 22 in Jefferson County reflected deep intra-party divisions and may have set new standards for attack-and-destroy politics. In District 13, term-limited representative and Joint Budget Committee member Dale Hall sought to take the seat vacated by term-limited senator Dave Owen. Hall was conservative, experienced, and a likely successor to Owen. In District 22, Kiki Traylor was finishing a one-year stint in the senate as a vacancy committee replacement for longtime veteran Norma Anderson, and she sought the nomination to run for a full four-year term. Traylor was a familiar name in Republican political circles, as both her father-in-law and her mother-in-law had served in the General Assembly on the Republican side.

What in some other era might have been logical and easy campaigns for a veteran such as Hall and a known name such as Traylor proved to be anything but easy. Both were opposed by challengers who were political novices and darlings of the Republican Party's right wing. Hall lost to Scott Renfroe, who, according to Hall, announced his intention to run at a party organization meeting with the comment that "it's about time a Christian ran" (Straayer 2006a). Throughout the campaign Renfroe noted that he was "motivated by faith" (quoted in Boyle 2006). Traylor lost her primary run to Mike Kopp, who had a bachelor's degree in ministry from a "Christ-centered Pentecostal school." During the campaign Kopp's wife described him as having "an incredibly strong set of core values that came from his strong faith from extensive [*sic*] life-experiences" (K. Kopp 2006).

Both campaigns featured repeated attacks on Hall and Traylor by a trio of groups—the Christian Coalition, the Rocky Mountain Gun Owners PAC, and Colorado Alliance for a Secure America (CASA,). The religious-right blog "Mt. Virtus" also opposed both Hall and Traylor. The lineup of supporters in both races reflected the party divisions seen in the statewide races. Hall and Traylor backers included Governor Bill Owens; past party chair, Referendum C leader, and now University of Colorado president Bruce Benson; and a number of more moderate past and present Republican lawmakers, including Ron Teck, Dave Owen, Nancy Spence, Lewis Entz, Steve Johnson, Sally Hopper, Bill Schroeder, and Norma Anderson. On the Renfroe and Kopp side were former US senator Bill Armstrong, John Andrews, David Schultheis, Kevin Lundberg, Ted Harvey, Rob Fairbank, Mark Paschall, and Pam Rhodes—all current or past legislators from the party's most right-leaning wing.

The campaigns against Hall and Traylor were brutal. The gun lobby accused Hall of siding with "gun-hating Denver liberals," and the Christian Coalition accused him of advancing the cause of the "abortion-on-demand lobby." CASA attacked Hall, stating that he was trying to "weasel out of his own voting record," trying to "manipulate the judicial system," and engaging in "legal terrorism" (CASA 2006a). Hall—an anti-abortion Catholic and known in the capitol as very conservative and a vocal critic of illegal immigration—commented after the race that he considered his attackers to be political "terrorists," that he would never again enter the political arena, and that, in his judgment, the right-leaning attack-oriented wing of the Republican Party was "driving sane folks out" (Straayer 2006a).

A pediatrician and a graduate of Stanford and the University of Colorado medical school, Traylor was on the receiving end of a Christian Coalition piece asserting that she "marched arm-in-arm with the abortion lobby and cast her vote to commend the organization that kills children and gives away abortion drugs" (Christian Coalition 2006). In the 2006 legislative special session on immigration, Traylor had sponsored one of the party's anti-immigration bills. But for CASA she was "possibly the worst Republican on immigration" (CASA 2006b). The gun lobby also blasted her in one of its Kopp endorsements, saying that "given Traylor's occupation . . . and her association with leftist Republicans, Mike Kopp is the easy choice" (Rocky Mountain Gun Owners 2006).

Traylor agreed with Dale Hall's comment about the right-leaning wing driving folks out of the party. When gubernatorial candidate Bob Beauprez asked her to "bury the hatchet" and endorse Kopp, she replied, "The Republican women I talk to do not believe that Mike Kopp represents them" and added, "you can't tear people apart, lie about them and then turn around and ask for their support" (Straayer 2006b; also Bartels 2006).

Party divisions that were manifest in these and other electoral contests were not the only factors to weaken the formerly dominant Republican Party. As the state reeled from successive economic and fiscal problems, first in 2000–2001 and again in 2004–2005, majority Republicans did little to seek to avert fiscal disaster until their governor and some moderates teamed with Democrats and an assortment of statewide groups to push Referendum C. Indeed, 2004–2005 Senate president John Andrews made sure that no remedies made it out of the General Assembly. As the party in power, the GOP was the party to blame for the fiscal woes. Further, Colorado Republicans, like their comrades nationally, suffered politically under the cloud of President Bush's Iraq War and his seeming unwillingness to draw the line on spending by his own Republican Congress.

NEW CENTURY, NEW GENERAL ASSEMBLY

The multi-decade rightward movement of the Republican Party and the severe internal divisions it produced, as well as growing party problems on the national level and the term-limit–induced exodus of Republican moderates from the General Assembly, merged with more vigorous Democratic challenges and financial help from deep-pocket political supporters to end four decades of Republican legislative control. While a solid Democratic Party strategy and money were a major part of the change, Republicans had opened the door for them.

Perhaps the most striking picture of the change in party control is seen in table 6.6. Not only did the Republicans cease to be the comfortably dominant party in both legislative chambers, the party's internal demographics also changed dramatically. For years, Republican women had been numerous and had constituted much of the moderate wing of the party; by 2008, however, they were virtually gone. As chapter 8 shows, the slow but sure erosion of party toleration of moderates, which disproportionately meant female Republicans, took a major toll.

DISTRICT-BY-DISTRICT DEMOCRATIC GAINS: SUBURBS AND BEYOND

While the tide that moved in the Democratic direction came as a result of party switches in districts across the state, the switches were concentrated in the Denver suburbs, where the demographics had been changing for some time. In addition, there were several Republican losses in districts where the religious right harmed the party. In the 2000 election, Democrats picked up one house seat in Larimer County and another in Jefferson County and gained three seats in the senate—one when term-limited representative Ken Gordon captured a

TABLE **6.6.** Member count by party and gender, 1998 and 2008

	1998	2008
House Republicans	41	25
House female Republicans	15	4
House Democrats	24	40
House female Democrats	10	20
Senate Republicans	20	15
Senate female Republicans	5	1
Senate Democrats	15	20
Senate female Democrats	5	11

Source: Legislative Directories, 1998 and 2008.

core city of Denver seat vacated by term-limited, moderate Republican senator Dottie Wham and two others in western Denver suburbs. The 2002 election produced just two changes; Democrat Buffie McFayden won in the southern Colorado district of Republican Ken Kester, who moved to the senate, and Republican Steve Johnson took over the Larimer County seat left open because Senate president Stan Matsunaka, a Democrat, was term-limited.

The 2004 presidential-year election produced huge Democratic gains: seven seats in the house and one in the senate. In western slope House District 55, the candidacy of religious right Republican Sherry Bjorklund, who had challenged her own party's Gayle Berry two years earlier, led to a victory for Democrat Bernie Buescher in a district where the numbers favored Republicans by more than two to one. Republicans recaptured the seat in 2008 with a more moderate candidate. Weld County District 50 winner Jim Riesberg benefited from the Republicans' internal spat, and in Jefferson County, Ramey Johnson lost to Democrat Gwen Green after having been wounded by a mailer from far-right fellow Republicans accusing her of inadequately supporting charter schools. Two open seats in rural Colorado, one in the southeast and another in the west, went Democratic. The other two Democratic gains were in Adams and Jefferson Counties. Just one senate seat changed as term-limited Representative Suzanne Williams unseated the religious right's Bruce Carins, but it was enough to produce an eighteen-to-seventeen Democratic majority.

Democratic gains continued through the 2006 election, in which their margin in both chambers grew to a combined count of 60 of the 100 General Assembly seats. Two house seats in Jefferson County went to the Democrats, as did one in Larimer County and one in the far southeastern corner of the state. In Arapahoe County, Republican Debbie Stafford later switched to the Democratic side. In the senate, Republican Ed Jones lost an El Paso County seat to John

TABLE **6.7.** Party control over time, house, senate, and combined, 1969–2010

Time Frame	Republicans	Democrats	Republicans	Democrats	Republicans	Democrats
1969–2004 average	38	27	21	14	59	41
1997–1998	41	24	20	15	61	39
1999–2000	40	25	20	15	60	40
2001–2002	38	27	17	18	55	45
2003–2004	37	28	18	17	55	45
2005–2006	30	35	17	18	47	53
2007–2008	25	40	15	20	40	60
2009–2010	27	38	14	21	41	59

Source: Legislative Directories, various years.

Morse, and longtime lawmaker Lewis Entz lost to Gail Schwartz. Jones had been one of the senate's more right-leaning members, while Entz was one of the remaining GOP moderates.

The 2008 election changed the makeup of the General Assembly very little. Democrats gave back two house seats but gained another in the senate. The most notable house loss was in the heavily Republican western slope District 55, where presumptive 2009–2010 Speaker Bernie Buescher lost to Laura Bradford. Another house loss occurred in party-switcher Debbie Stafford's District 40 and the other in an Adams County district in which the Democratic candidate failed to run a robust campaign.

Table 6.7 shows the two parties' almost complete reversal of fortunes, from the four decades of Republican control to more recent Democratic dominance. The trajectory of the Democratic gains, and hence the Republicans' misfortunes, are evident in voting patterns over the past several electoral cycles. Increases in Democratic margins in several senate and house seats serve to illustrate.

In Senate District 16, Democrat Joan Fitz-Gerald's winning margin increased from 54.2 percent in 2002 to 61.2 percent in 2006. For Democrat Moe Keller in District 20, the margin grew from 50.4 percent to 56.4 percent for the same period. In 2002 Republican Norma Anderson, District 22, prevailed with 65.2 percent of the vote, but in 2006 Republican nominee Mike Kopp won with just 52.9 percent in the same district. Three other 2002 Republican districts produced Republican winners again in 2006 but with reduced margins: declines of 8.1 percent for Ted Harvey in District 43, 14.2 percent for David Schultheis in District 14, and 23.6 percent in Scott Renfroe's District 13. During the 2009–2010 legislative sessions, six senate seats from districts with Republican registration advantages were held by Democrats; three others held by Democrats showed a Democratic registration edge of 51 percent or less (figures from the Colorado secretary of state).

The house was no different. In the highly competitive suburban House District 29, Democrat Debbie Benefield lost to Republican Bob Briggs in 2002 in a very close contest, but she prevailed in 2004 with 51 percent of the vote and in 2006 with 52.7 percent. In 2008 she captured 58.4 percent of the vote. In District 52, Republican Bob McCluskey ousted Bryan Jameson in 2002 in a close race, narrowly defeated Democrat John Kefalas in 2004, but then lost to Kefalas in both 2006 and 2008. Kefalas's 2008 margin was nearly 60–40 percent. There are numerous additional examples of Democrats capturing seats and increasing their margins of victory in potential swing districts (figures from the Colorado secretary of state).

In some areas such as Arapahoe and Jefferson Counties, Democratic gains can be attributed to demographic trends, as formerly white, middle-class neighborhoods have become progressively more diversified in terms of ethnicity, occupations, and family makeup. Indeed, these changes are reflected in party registration trends that show a progressive erosion of the long-term Republican advantage to the extent that by November 2008 the statewide party numbers were virtually identical, with Republican losses most severe in the close-in Denver metro-area suburbs. Further, some of the increases in Democratic winning margins can likely be traced to the advantage of incumbency.

DEEP-POCKET HELP

Beyond these factors, deep-pocket Democratic benefactor spending has made a difference. In advance of the 2004 election, four wealthy donors joined forces to fund independent group efforts to help Democratic candidates in targeted competitive districts. Known as the "Gang of Four," they were billionaire Pat Stryker and millionaires Tim Gill, Rutt Bridges, and Jared Polis.

In the 2004 campaign the "Gang of Four" reportedly spent $2 million—twice the amount spent by counterpart Republican groups—on hard-hitting negative mailings. According to widely respected Denver pollster Floyd Ciruli, "They all came together and they had a profound effect. But for them, the Democrats wouldn't have won" (quoted in Frank 2007). Ciruli's perspective was shared by former house Republican Rob Witwer, who, in an article in the conservative journal *National Review*, described the "Gang's" spending and strategy and characterized the 2004 Democratic success as "one of the most stunning reversals of fortune in American political history" (Witwer 2009).

While the help of their rich supporters in 2004 and again in 2006 and 2008 surely contributed to the Democrats' successes, Ciruli and Witwer are likely exaggerating the impact of the deep-pocket money. The reversal in fortunes came in the context of over two decades of Republican Party movement further and further toward the social-cultural agenda of the political right, the party's strident opposition to fixing the state's troubled fiscal system, and the resulting internal party wars. A past state Republican Party chair may have said it best: "Winning in competitive, independent-minded Colorado is more than just winning the Republican primary" (Wadhams 2011).

SUMMARY AND PROJECTION

Although Republicans rebounded in 2010 to recapture the house of representatives by a one-vote margin, over the past several decades Colorado's General Assembly had morphed from a representative body dominated by the Republican Party to an institution dominated by the Democrats but denuded of much of its authority. As of 2011 the state is mired in a deep fiscal crisis, and voters are restless. Republicans show precious little interest in fixing the fiscal policy morass that is responsible in part for the problem. Democrats have chipped away at the crisis with some patchwork fiscal changes but nothing more. As the party in power, Democrats have taken a pounding for their patchwork efforts to balance the state budget. They may, as a result, pay a price at the polls, and the door may open for the renewed election of Republican majorities.

Republicans set the stage for their own descent into minority status through several decades of movement to the political right and their embrace of social and cultural issues. The party went from moderately conservative to libertarian to hard right. Along the way, fiscal problems emerged; as Republicans did little to address them, the voting public shifted toward the Democrats. This set the stage for Democratic successes, which were fueled further by the recruitment of able candidates and campaign spending by deep-pocket benefactors.

Today, the legislative leadership is weak, and new members come into office without the mentoring of longtime veteran colleagues. Committees lack chairs who can lead by sharing a deep knowledge of policy history. Term limits have opened the door for newcomers who quickly drink the Kool-aid of political ambition. One observer noted that term limits "drive the agenda, careful consideration of issues has regressed and the new norm seems to be 'I'll carry what gets me elected.'" Another individual expressed a fairly widely held view to the effect that "behavior is less civil, more partisan, more 'true believers v. enemies'" (quoted in Straayer and Bowser 2004).

It is not unreasonable to ask whether representative government even exists in Colorado. Fiscal policy, it seems, is increasingly beyond the reach of Colorado's duly elected representatives. Along with the rest of the nation, Colorado has suffered through two fiscal downturns since 1999, and in a major way these events have created severe policy problems for the state. But so have self-imposed institutional and political changes.

Politically and institutionally, Colorado's government in 2011 is very unlike the Colorado government of 1970 or even 1980, and this is especially the case with its General Assembly. Three decades back it would have been difficult to predict this major transformation, and it is hard to know what lies ahead.

REFERENCES

Bartels, Lynn. 2006. "Outgoing Senator Won't Back Primary Foe. *The Rocky Mountain News*, October 25.

Boyle, Rebecca. 2006. "Family-Oriented Man Is Driven by His Faith." *The Greeley Tribune*, July 30.

Carroll, Susan J., and Krista Jenkins. 2001. "Increasing Diversity or More of the Same? Term Limits and the Representation of Women, Minorities and Minority Women in State Legislatures." Paper presented at the Annual Meeting of the American Political Science Association. San Francisco, CA, August 20–September 2.

Christian Coalition of Colorado. 2006. Campaign mailer, July 6. PO Box 8317, Denver, CO 80201; http://www.CCCO.org. Fugitive campaign materials in author's files.

Coach, Mark, and John Hughes. 2005. "Referendum Recriminations Fly." *The Denver Post*, November 3.

Colorado Alliance for a Secure America (CASA). 2006a. Dear Republican Friend campaign mailer, June 29. PO Box 8766, Denver, CO 80201; http://www.casapac.com. Fugitive campaign materials in author's files.

———. 2006b. Dear Republican Friend campaign mailer, dated "Thursday morning." PO Box 8766, Denver, CO 80201; http://www.casapac.com. Fugitive campaign materials in author's files.

Colorado Secretary of State. Elections information website, http://www.sos.state.co.us. Accessed April 30, 2011.

The Economist. 2004. "Beer Today, Gone Tomorrow." April 12. Available at http://www.economist.com/node/3092935. Accessed April 30, 2011.

Frank, Robert. 2007. " 'Gang of Four' Helped Democrats Win in '04." Perspectives section of *The Denver Post*, September 15. Available at http://www.denverpost.com/opinion/ci_6896086%22. Accessed April 30, 2011.

Harsanyi, David. 2004. "Republican Infighting Tars Primary." *Free Republic*. August 8. Available at http://209.157.64.201/focus/F-news/1188252/posts. Accessed November 6, 2006.

Kopp, Kimberly. 2006. Handwritten campaign letter. Unpublished document, July.

Rocky Mountain Gun Owners. 2006. "Vote Pro-Gun in the Primary Elections." Available at http://www.rmgo.org/alert/2006-news/vote-pro-gun-in-the-primary-elections. Accessed March 25, 2011.

Straayer, John. 2003. "Colorado's Term Limits: Consequences, Yes, But Were They Intended?" *Spectrum: The Journal of State Government* 77(4): 34–37.

———. 2006a. Conversation with Representative Dale Hall, Greeley, October 6.

———. 2006b. Conversation with Senator Kiki Traylor, Denver, September 22.

————. 2007. "Direct Democracy's Disaster." *State Legislatures* (March): 30–31.

Straayer, John, and Jenny Bowser. 2004. *Colorado's Legislative Term Limits.* Joint Project on Term Limits. Denver: National Conference of State Legislatures, Council of State Governments, and State Legislative Leaders Foundation. Available at http://www.nasl.org/Portals/1/documents/JP+L/casestudies/Coloradov2.pdf. Accessed April 30, 2011.

Tabarrok, Alexander. 1994. "A Survey, Critique and New Defense of Term Limits." *The Cato Journal* 14(2) (Fall). Available at http://www.cato.org/pubs/journal/CVJ14m2-9.html. Accessed April 30, 2011.

Wadhams, Dick. 2011. "More Than Just a GOP Primary." *The Denver Post,* March 26. Available at http://www.denverpost.com/opinion/ci_17702594. Accessed April 30, 2011.

Witwer, Rob. 2009. "Rocky Ride: The Republican Fall from Power in Colorado and How the Democrats Hope to Replicate It." *The National Review*, March 23. Available at http://nrd.nationalreview.com/article/?q=ODJmYWRIMDkkMzXxMzM1NTY3YmMwZDc1Mz. Accessed April 30, 2011.

CHAPTER SEVEN

How GAVEL Changed Party Politics
in Colorado's General Assembly

Mike Binder, Vladimir Kogan, and Thad Kousser

On November 8, 1988, an overwhelming 72 percent to 28 percent majority of Coloradans voted for a democratic experiment that remains unique in US political history. They approved an initiative, put on the ballot by a coalition of twenty-three government reformers and civic groups, that promised to "Give a Vote to Every Legislator" (GAVEL). This initiative resulted in a reorganization of the state legislature, the Colorado General Assembly, and played an important role as one catalyst for the broader transformation taking place in Colorado politics. The changes it brought were especially acute in the Colorado House of Representatives and were felt most strongly in the initiative's immediate wake. By changing the internal workings of the state's General Assembly, the GAVEL Amendment succeeded—at least during a short but critical time period—in altering patterns of political alliances, the types of laws coming out of the statehouse, and, ultimately, the way Colorado government translates public sentiment into policy.

GAVEL originated from a failed rebellion within the legislature by members frustrated with the firm grasp majority party leaders held over its policymaking apparatus. Prior to GAVEL, Colorado operated much like the US House of Representatives. Committee chairs wielded great influence and were able to kill bills without a hearing, and a Rules Committee controlled the flow of legislation to the floor. The initiative stripped away these powers, promising a hearing for every bill and a spot on the floor agenda for every bill passed out of committee (Straayer 2000). Although its passage did not succeed in bringing about all of these results, GAVEL did systematically alter the process of lawmaking in Colorado. This chapter examines the results of the experiment voters endorsed in 1988 and analyzes every roll call vote cast on the floor of Colorado's house in the sessions held just before and after GAVEL's passage. In addition, it examines accounts of later adaptations to the rule changes GAVEL imposed and presents eyewitness accounts of the initiative's passage and implementation.

This unprecedented initiative provides a unique opportunity to study the ways voting coalitions and party alignments shift when legislative rules change. GAVEL was designed to curb the power of the speaker of the house, improve the representation of voters, and empower moderate legislators in both the minority and majority caucuses. These moderates were often trapped by powerful leaders, unable to show their centrist stripes because many of the bills they favored most were bottled up in committees. When GAVEL opened the flow of legislation to the floor, it freed moderates in both parties to form occasional coalitions of the center. At least in the short term, this changed the types of policies the legislature considered and slightly altered the ideological map of Colorado politics. In this way, the story of GAVEL yields larger lessons.

One is that much of the power of a legislative party lies in its control of the agenda (Cox and McCubbins 2005). When it loses that power, as the Republican leadership of the General Assembly did in 1988, it loses some of its ability to keep rebellious members in line and to protect its policy turf. Republican leaders and the party's most conservative members lost on more of their bills after GAVEL, as the GOP's moderate faction made temporary alliances with Democrats on some bills. More policies moved to the left in the 1989–1990 session than had been the case before, and an ideological snapshot of the legislature showed that it appeared less polarized as a result (our interviews reveal that these changes were much more pronounced in the house than in the senate, which was less dominated by leaders and the chair before the passage of GAVEL). A second lesson from these changes is that the internal rule changes imposed by GAVEL had broader consequences for Colorado politics, helping expose rifts within the Republican Party that widened in later years and ultimately opened a path for the Democratic takeover. GAVEL did not cause this transformation, but it illuminated divisions in the old political order and, along with other major institutional changes such as the Taxpayer's Bill of Rights (TABOR) and term limits, created an opportunity for new alliances that led to the creation of the new Colorado politics.

This chapter tells the story of GAVEL—beginning with its inception—to record the goals of its backers, the fears of its detractors, and the regional patterns of voter support for the initiative. The chapter then looks at roll call voting patterns—analyzed in greater depth in a technical article by Gary Cox, Thad Kousser, and Matthew McCubbins (2010)—to gauge its immediate impact on legislative alliances, policy shifts, and ideological positions within Colorado's house. As leaders became used to operating under GAVEL, they began to adapt to its structures, an evolution traced in the next section. The chapter concludes by considering the initiative's impact on larger trends in Colorado politics.

GENESIS OF LEGISLATIVE REFORM

Formal rules in place at the Colorado General Assembly until the late 1980s endowed the leaders of the majority party—except for one small interruption, always the Republicans—with near-total control over the flow and content of legislation. The power of the speaker in the house and of the majority leader of the senate was derived from their role in determining the membership of policy committees—charged with reviewing proposed bills before they were considered on the floor—and their influence over the party caucuses. For decades, Republican leadership in the house had used both venues to effectively kill bills the party opposed before they ever reached a floor vote and to build an impenetrable majority bloc that allowed the Republicans to pass their preferred legislation without a single Democratic vote being needed and thus without any concessions to the minority party.

The Colorado senate operated somewhat differently. Senate rules were more open, caucuses were transparent, there was no Rules Committee or Calendar Committee, and committee chairs exerted their power over the agenda rarely, if at all (Strickland 2009). When senate Republicans did caucus, mostly during the budgeting process, they made conscious efforts to include some of the Democrats' key issue concerns (Schroeder 2009). In fact, senate president Ted Strickland quipped about Governor Roy Romer, who defeated him in his race for governor, "there were times when Roy spent more time up in my office on the second floor than in his own down on the first floor" (Strickland 2009). This is not to say that senate Republicans were the picture of bipartisan virtue, but the institutional rules and leadership in place did encourage more openness and inclusivity in the upper house of Colorado's General Assembly.

Before an introduced bill became law in the house, it had to travel down a tortuous path in the legislative process. At each fork in the road, the majority leadership could exercise indirect influence to stop it in its tracks. For example, bills introduced by lawmakers first had to survive at least one policy committee, known as the committee of reference. Committee chairs could kill a bill by exercising the pocket veto—failing to schedule it for a committee vote. Even if a vote was held, a majority of the committee could choose not to send the legislation to a full floor vote. Because majority party leaders decided where the bills were sent and appointed both the chairs and their party's committee members, they could effectively block legislation they opposed without risking an uncertain vote in the full house. Ignoring their leaders' wishes often proved costly for other Republican members. As one scholar noted, "Veteran lawmakers, it is said, have been denied reappointment to committees on which they had served because they pursued excessively independent courses of action or a political philosophy too divergent from that of the leadership" (Straayer 1990: 93).

If an undesired bill somehow survived the committee of reference in the house, it could also be killed in the Rules Committee, which was chaired by the speaker and included other top leaders among its membership. Although formally tasked with managing the house schedule, the Rules Committee served as a graveyard for unwanted—primarily Democratic—bills. Spending bills required dual assignment, to a committee of original jurisdiction and the Appropriations Committee, which could serve as another barrier for bills not favored by the majority. With non-spending bills, the State Affairs Committee had a reputation for advancing the majority party's agenda by quickly voting down unpopular bills and passing bills favored by the Republican majority.

While committees helped Republican leaders block unwanted bills, the party caucus in each house was the place to make deals among party members to ensure that the Republicans' preferred legislation sailed smoothly through its final floor vote. Meeting in caucus, Republicans would negotiate to reach the magic number of votes—thirty-three in the house, eighteen in the senate—needed to ensure that the legislation could survive a floor vote without attracting a single Democratic "yes" vote. The caucus votes were binding in that members were expected to vote the same way on the floor as they had in the caucus, although party rules did not spell out the punishment for those who experienced a change of heart.[1] As house speaker Carl "Bev" Bledsoe noted, "At the start of each session, I would give the same speech: in this business, in order to be effective, you have to keep your word. You don't have to give it, but you have to keep it. I was very insistent that if you give your word, you've got to keep it. And it worked" (Bledsoe 2009). The caucus was especially important to assure a drama-free passage of each year's budget.

The Democratic minority complained that leaders used their influence over the flow of legislation and the party caucuses to exclude them from the legislative process. Controversial Democratic bills never made it out of committee, and the floor votes on Republican bills were a mere formality since a solid majority had already been assembled in the caucus. Democrats also charged that such pro-majority rules resulted in legislation that was far more conservative than that preferred by moderate Republicans and Democrats, who easily made up the majority of each house (Cronin and Loevy 1993: 188; Straayer 1990: 157–158). The Republican Party in particular was deeply divided between its moderate and extremely conservative factions (Cronin and Loevy 1993: 18–20). However, leaders in the house—and, to a much smaller extent, the senate—used the rules to kill bills that threatened to split their party before they could reach the floor and relied on caucus votes to present a united agenda.

While Republicans leaders had exercised these powers for decades, a series of public controversies in the late 1980s involving Speaker Bledsoe laid the groundwork for the Democrat-led campaign to fundamentally overhaul the rules of the General Assembly through a constitutional amendment. Elected to his post in 1980, Bledsoe skillfully used the formal and informal powers of the speaker to amass great power and pursue a markedly conservative agenda. In 1987 and 1988, however, Democrats were joined by a growing chorus of good government groups, such as the League of Women of Voters and Common Cause, which argued that Bledsoe and the rest of the Republican leadership were abusing their influence to thwart the democratic process.

In the spring of 1987, rather than present a full budget to the Republican caucus, as was the usual practice, the leadership convinced the party to accept a "conceptual" budget that left many details unfinished. When the final document cut funding to several popular programs, many Republicans, who were already committed to support it on the floor, expressed great dissatisfaction (Straayer 1990: 95). In another alleged abuse, Bledsoe, a rancher, sent a popular bill to move Colorado to yearlong daylight saving time to the House Agriculture Committee, where it was sure to face an imminent death at the hands of agriculture interests opposed to the change (Paige 1988). For months, Republican leaders stalled another bill to build a new convention center in Denver (Roberts 1988a).

In 1988 Republicans also blocked or greatly watered down two key initiatives proposed by Democratic governor Roy Romer. The majority opposed the governor's plan to stimulate the state's economy by spending more than $700 million on the construction of new highways because it called for tax increases. After much wrangling, they approved the Romer-backed legislation to provide increased funding for the state's most disadvantaged schools, although not before stripping out tax increases necessary to pay for most of the changes. Romer, who enjoyed record approval even among Republican voters, complained of the Republicans' "crazy antics" and "excessively partisan" approach to governing (quoted in Dias 1989).

In its defense, the majority party argued that the GOP only flexed its muscle to ensure an efficient pace in the legislative process. As a part-time legislature, the General Assembly usually met only in the winter and spring, so powerful committees were a necessary evil to weed out defective bills and preserve scarce floor time for meaningful legislation. The powerful Rules Committee, Bledsoe argued, "saved a lot of time, and it made for a much smoother process for all of the members. It was also a lot cheaper for those who were paying for it" (Bledsoe 2009). Senators faced a similar time crunch, but without the Rules Committee to manage traffic, bills that came to the floor at the end of the session often never received a vote.

THE CAMPAIGN FOR GAVEL

Capitalizing on the media coverage of Bledsoe and the tension between the legislature and Romer, Democratic state representative Wayne Knox, a veteran from Denver, introduced a constitutional amendment that promised to ensure a committee vote on every bill. In interviews, Knox charged that "there is no question that the Republican leadership in the House is oppressing the Democrats. Under Speaker Bledsoe there has been a steady accumulation of tactics and decisions limiting the role of the minority" (quoted in Cronin and Loevy 1993: 182). Calling his bill "Give a Vote to Every Legislator," Knox borrowed heavily from ideas that emerged from the 1987 Model Constitutional Convention organized by the University of Colorado. His bill promised to amend the state constitution to ban the pocket veto, scrap the Rules Committee, and prohibit binding caucuses.

Bledsoe sent the Knox bill to the House State Affairs Committee, an infamous "killer" committee, where it was rejected on a party-line vote less than two weeks later (*The Denver Post* 1988a). However, the Democrats promised to take the question directly to the people, announcing a coalition made up of retiree groups, organized labor, and government reformers that would work to collect signatures to place the amendment on the November 1988 ballot (Roberts 1988b).

Sensing growing public frustration, the Republicans worked quietly behind the scenes to give Democrats a greater voice in the legislative process. The party introduced its own bill to ban binding caucuses and allowed Democrats greater input into the formation of the budget. Although each of the nearly two dozen Democratic amendments to the document was rejected, Representative Ruth Wright, the Democratic minority leader from Boulder, acknowledged a "more open" budget process (cited in Hilliard 1988). Indeed, despite the very public disagreements over the governor's two big initiatives, *The Denver Post* concluded that 1988 was "one of the most productive sessions in recent memory" (*The Denver Post* 2008b). However, GAVEL supporters argued that the Republican abuse had not ended. Pointing to the deaths of three recent bills in committee—a proposed

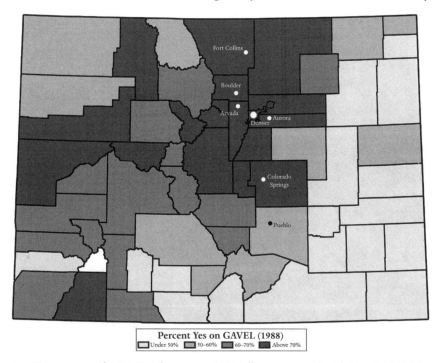

Percent Yes on GAVEL (1988)
▢ Under 50% ▨ 50–60% ▨ 60–70% ▬ Above 70%

7.1. Voter support for GAVEL, by county, 1988 (all maps created with Maptitude 5.0 by Caliper Corporation)

heating rebate for seniors, a plan to give deaf people special telephone equipment, and a bill to deregulate independent service stations—they pushed ahead with the campaign (Roberts 1988b).

As the November vote approached, no coherent campaign to oppose the amendment emerged. Although the Chamber of Commerce had initially considered taking a position against GAVEL, its board ended up endorsing it. The Republican leadership in the house argued publicly that the amendment would do little to improve the legislative process but did not campaign heavily against it. A few days before the vote, Bledsoe authored an editorial in *The Denver Post* in which he argued that weakening partisan control would only empower lobbyists and lead to pork-fueled logrolling on the budget (Bledsoe 1988).

On election day, voters did not heed the speaker's warning. By overwhelming margins, they voted in favor of GAVEL. Yet the statewide landslide masked somewhat surprising geographic patterns of support for the measure (see figure 7.1). Despite the amendment's partisan genesis, there appeared to be little relationship between voters' support for Democrats and their vote on the GAVEL measure. In figure 7.2, which shows the Democrats' share of the two-party vote

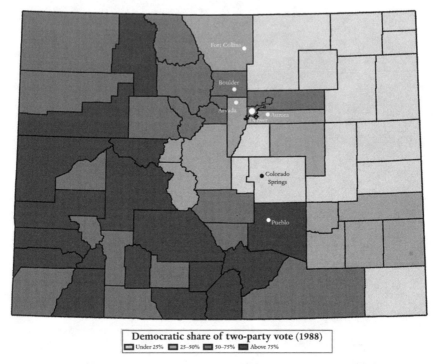

Democratic share of two-party vote (1988)
Under 25% 25–50% 50–75% Above 75%

7.2. Percentage of vote won by Democratic candidates, 1988 congressional elections

in the 1988 congressional elections, there appears to be little overlap between Democratic strongholds and areas of strong pro-GAVEL sentiment. Indeed, there is only weak correlation between county-level support for the amendment and the vote share won by congressional Democrats (Pearson's r = 0.24). Instead, the election results suggest that GAVEL tapped into a constituency in support of broader political reform that crossed partisan lines.

Two other amendments that appeared on the same ballot—a measure to overturn the state's ban on public funding for abortion (figure 7.3) and a dramatic proposal to limit property taxes, known as Amendment 6 (figure 7.4)—seem to be strong predictors of county-level support for GAVEL. Although the two measures ostensibly moved policy in radically different directions, support for each was strongly and positively correlated with support for the legislative overhaul (Pearson's r = 0.77 for the abortion measure; r = 0.64 for tax limitation). The figures help explain this puzzling pattern by locating the centrist group of voters who, uniting with Democrats from across the state, pushed GAVEL to victory: the initiative outperformed Democrats most strongly in Denver and its suburbs. The legislative reform initiative polled strongly in these areas, although in 1988

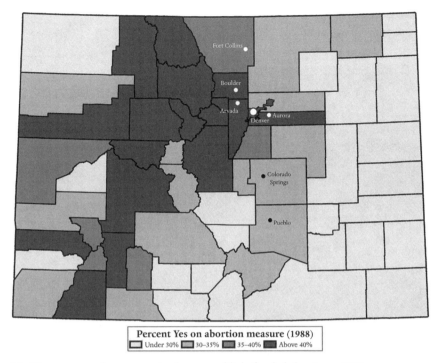

Percent Yes on abortion measure (1988)
☐ Under 30%   ▨ 30–35%   ▩ 35–40%   ▮ Above 40%

7.3. Voter support for overturning ban on publicly funded abortions, 1988

Democratic congressional candidates performed poorly in the state's capitol and metropolis.

Who were these voters who backed Republicans for the US Congress but voted to loosen the GOP's hold on the state legislature? Without individual-level polling data on the initiatives, it is difficult to tell with perfect certainty, but geographic voting patterns provide important clues. Figures 7.3 and 7.4 suggest that they were fiscal conservatives but social moderates. They strongly supported the abortion measure—which increased women's access to abortion—but also supported the tax cut. These Denver-area moderate Republicans were the voters whose state legislators were harmed by majority party control of the General Assembly. It was their fiscally conservative, socially moderate representatives whose bills were being buried in committees. They voted to give their legislators a voice with GAVEL. The analysis of roll call votes in the next section shows that they succeeded in part in this legislative aim. The wider history of transformation in Colorado politics shows that GAVEL was a skirmish in the larger fight within the Colorado Republican Party, revealing the division between Denver-area social moderates and more conservative rural Republicans that would later split the party and harm its electoral fortunes.

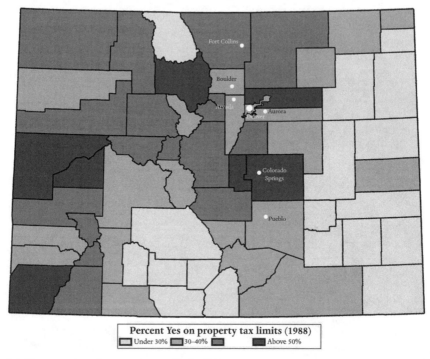

Percent Yes on property tax limits (1988)
☐ Under 30% ☐ 30–40% ☐   ■ Above 50%

7.4. Voter support for property tax limit, 1988

GAVEL'S IMMEDIATE IMPACT

Supporters of GAVEL hoped it would weaken the majority party's grip on the legislature by taking away its control of the agenda and preventing committee chairs and the speaker from pocket vetoing bills. Such indirect control can be especially important when the government is divided and a majority party in the legislature cannot rely on the governor to veto bills that may slip past its grasp because of poor party discipline. If GAVEL reduced the majority party's ability to manipulate the floor agenda to pursue party goals, it would have resulted in changes in the types of bills that received consideration on the full legislative floor and in the way legislators voted on them.

Scholars have noted that one powerful method of influence available to the majority party is negative agenda control—the power to prevent bills the majority party opposes from reaching the floor. This is particularly important if the majority party cannot count on all of its members to vote against these bills on the floor and fears that some may cross the aisle and provide the votes necessary for passage. Pre-GAVEL, bills opposed by the bulk of the majority party would simply be buried in committee, never reaching a final floor vote. After

GAVEL passed, committee chairs were required to bring all bills up for a vote, thus loosening the speaker's grip on the agenda (Ferrandino 2009). This allowed the moderates in the Republican Party to unite with the minority Democrats and pass bills over the opposition of most Republicans. If they did so frequently, we should expect to see a shift in voting patterns that followed the procedural change enacted by GAVEL.

Fortunately for the purposes of this analysis, little else changed in Colorado politics during this time, providing a clean "natural experiment" with which to measure the impact of GAVEL. Republicans retained the same tight grip on the state legislature that they had held since 1976, controlling the house by a 40–25 margin in 1987–1988 and the senate by a 25–10 edge and losing just one seat in each chamber during the next session (National Conference of State Legislatures 2002). With term limits not yet enacted, fifty house members served in both the 1987–1988 and 1989–1990 sessions.[2] Of the fifteen new members, eight were from the same party as the legislator they replaced. Roy Romer continued as governor, Speaker Bledsoe led the house throughout the transition, and district boundaries remained unchanged (Straayer 2000). Both before and after the passage of GAVEL, committees could kill bills by taking a public vote, but this required that a majority of committee members—rather than simply the chair, as in the pre-GAVEL days—wanted to keep it off the floor. Using this political stability to isolate the impact of a shift in agenda control, this chapter tracks changes from the 1987–1988 session—held just before the passage of GAVEL— to the 1989–1990 session, in which it was first implemented.

ROLL CALL VOTES

One way to measure the impact of majority party control over the agenda is to look at how effectively that party can block the passage of bills it opposes. This is what scholars call "negative agenda control" (Cox and McCubbins 2005). When a bill passes despite opposition from the majority of a party's members, it is called a "roll." Majority rolls refer to bills that pass over the opposition of the majority of the majority party (in Colorado, the Republicans). That is, a majority roll occurs when most Republicans vote against a bill that still ends up passing. Minority rolls refer to bills that pass over the opposition of the majority of the minority party (in this case, the Democrats). In other words, a minority roll occurs when most Democrats vote against a bill that ends up passing. A majority roll indicates that the majority party cannot keep bills its members oppose off the agenda if party leaders are afraid these bills still have a chance of securing approval on the floor. Pre-GAVEL, the Republicans should have been rolled rarely, if at all, and Democrats should have been rolled more frequently. Post-GAVEL, when the Republicans in the majority saw their agenda control

TABLE 7.1. Changes in roll call voting in Colorado's house, pre- and post-GAVEL

	Majority Party Controls Floor Agenda, 1987–1988 Session	Majority Party Does Not Control Floor Agenda, 1989–1990 Session
Number of majority rolls (Republican Party)	**6** **(1.4%)**	**22** **(4.8%)**
Number of minority rolls (Democratic Party)	73 (16.6%)	64 (14.1%)
Number of majority disappointments (Republican Party)	0	1 (0.2%)
Number of minority rolls (Democratic Party)	0	2 (0.4%)
Leftward policy shifts, calculated by probit	**59** **(13.5%)**	**110** **(24.2%)**
Leftward policy shifts, calculated by Optimal Classification	173 (39.4%)	220 (48.4%)

Notes: Percentages are calculated based on the number of contested roll calls on bills initially assigned to a "making good public policy" type of committee and subject to a simple majority vote. Using the probit method, a bill is categorized as a leftward policy shift if a probit model estimating the effect of each legislator's first-dimension ideal point on his or her likelihood of supporting the bill yields a negative, significant coefficient. Using Optimal Classification output, a bill is categorized as a leftward policy shift if a nay vote is the predicted choice above the projected midpoint on the line defined by a normal vector intersecting the two-dimensional estimated cutting plane at a right angle, indicating that legislators who were more conservative on the first dimension opposed the bill to the status quo. Boldface indicates that the difference between the proportions observed in the agenda-controlled and the control-free sessions is statistically significant at the 95 percent confidence level in a one-tailed test.

weakened, one would expect (and this analysis does find) that the Republicans would be rolled more frequently (see table 7.1). Since Democrats never exercised control over the agenda in this period, their roll rates should have changed very little.

Voting records from the lower house of the General Assembly provide evidence that GAVEL weakened the majority party's control over the agenda. Majority rolls increased from 1.4 percent of all contested votes in the 1987–1988 session (six votes) to 4.8 percent of all contested votes in the 1989–1990 session (twenty-two votes). This statistically significant difference suggests that GAVEL was at least somewhat successful in loosening the Republicans' grip on the flow of legislation in the house. Minority roll rates changed very little, from 16.6 percent of all contested votes in 1987–1988 (seventy-three votes) to 14.1 percent in 1989–1990 (sixty-four votes), suggesting that GAVEL, as expected, had little influence over the Democrats' ability to control the agenda by holding back bills the party opposes.

Another way parties attempt to influence policy outcomes is through their ability to induce fellow partisans to support bills favored by most of the party.

Building a sufficiently large coalition behind the party's preferred legislation is known as whipping. One way to assess the effectiveness of a party's whip organization is to consider "disappointments"—bills supported by a majority of a party's members but that do not receive enough votes to pass on the floor. Because party leaders generally know where members stand on a piece of legislation as a result of their votes in caucus and the information generated by the whip organizations, it is unlikely that leaders would willingly call votes on bills they know would fail.

Weakening party whipping power by eliminating the binding caucus was the key goal of GAVEL supporters, although there is little evidence that they succeeded. Pre-GAVEL, the majority party used the strong binding caucus to ensure passage of its preferred policies, thus reducing the number of potential disappointments. GAVEL attempted to ban the binding caucus, potentially opening opportunities for moderate Republicans to vote with the minority Democrats and thus preventing the passage of bills supported by more conservative majority party members. There were no disappointments in the 1987–1988 session, but in 1989–1990 there was one Republican disappointment and two Democratic disappointments (see table 7.1). This rather small, statistically insignificant change suggests that GAVEL did not reduce the influence of the majority party whip organization.

Of course, legislators often self-censor bills they know will not pass the legislature or that might be vetoed by the governor. In addition, legislators suffer many disappointments in committee votes that would not appear in floor votes. One of the unique rules of the Colorado General Assembly is that a legislator can introduce a limited number of bills (six per session in the late 1980s; currently five). This strict limit on legislative traffic makes the GAVEL requirement of mandatory bill hearings possible and also forces legislators to be very judicious with the types of bill they ultimately introduce (Ferrandino 2009).

POLICY MOVEMENTS

Politics in America is often discussed in spatial terms because decisions and policy shifts typically occur along a single liberal-conservative dimension (Downs 1957; Poole and Rosenthal 1997). One effect of party agenda control is to limit the kinds of policies legislators can introduce by allowing the majority party to kill bills that attempt to shift policy away from its preferred location in this one-dimensional space. In any legislature, individual lawmakers can be lined up in order along this dimension, with the most liberal member on the left and the most conservative falling on the right. It is useful to think about each party's "ideal point" on this dimension as the location of its median member. In this framework, the minority party (Democrats in Colorado during the time period included in this analysis) is situated closer to the left (liberal) side of the spectrum, while the majority party (Republicans) lies closer to the right (conservative) end. The ideal point of the median legislator in the house falls somewhere in between. In a legislature with no party agenda control, the median legislator in the chamber can amend every bill to move it to his or her ideal point and obtain passage by picking off the most moderate members of each party. The role of the majority party leaders is to prevent this from happening for bills opposed by most of their party members.

It is useful to consider how a proposed bill would shift policies relative to the status quo. When the status quo is located at the extremely liberal or the extremely conservative end of the political spectrum, most proposed bills will pass with bipartisan support because almost all members will prefer nearly any policy to the rather unpalatable status quo. In most legislatures, as is the case in Colorado, according to Representative Mark Ferrandino, most bills pass with bipartisan support (Ferrandino 2009). For a subset of bills, however, votes can become contentious. Specifically, status quo policies located near the minority party's ideal point are often targeted by the majority party as it attempts to move policy closer to its preferred location. Votes on bills that attempt to change these status quos often result in minority rolls.

However, the same is not true of status quo policies located near the majority party's ideal point. Because most members of the majority party prefer these policies to bills that seek to move policy in a different direction, the majority party can exercise its negative agenda control to block votes on these bills and prevent majority rolls. Therefore, when the Republicans, as the majority party, exercised effective control over the agenda (Colorado pre-GAVEL), the party's leaders could block votes on bills that attempted to move policy in a more liberal direction. Indeed, they should have generally allowed votes only on bills that would have moved policy in a more conservative direction, toward the Republicans' ideal point.

If agenda control is removed, however, the Republican majority may no longer be able to exclude bills that move policy in a more liberal direction from the agenda. When these bills come up for a vote, the median member of the house is able to form a two-party coalition, made up of moderates from both parties, to assure its passage.

This dynamic provides for a key test of GAVEL's impact on the majority party's control over the legislative agenda. As expected, the number of bills moving policy in a more liberal direction, away from the Republican median, increased by roughly 10 percent after the passage of GAVEL (see table 7.1). The number of bills moving policies to the left increased from 13.5 percent of all contested floor votes in 1987–1988 (59 votes) to 24.2 percent of all contested votes in 1989–1990 (110 votes). Indeed, GAVEL appears to have been successful in allowing both more moderate policies to reach the floor and a moderate cross-party coalition to adopt policies opposed by conservative Republicans.

IDEOLOGICAL DISTRIBUTION OF LEGISLATORS

As a final measure of the way GAVEL changed legislative politics in Colorado, this chapter shows that weakening the majority party's control over the legislative agenda in the house helped reshape something as fundamental as the apparent ideological distribution of legislators, even when their constituents' preferences did not change. This conclusion is drawn from the changes in roll rates and policy movements described previously. Since agenda control allowed the majority party leaders to keep bills preferred by the moderate two-party coalition off the floor, centrists in the Republican Party were denied many opportunities to show their maverick streaks on such legislation. Few bills that split Colorado's moderate Republicans from conservative Republicans ever reached a final floor vote prior to GAVEL, making it difficult to tell exactly who was a moderate and who was a conservative. If ideological positions derived from floor votes were plotted on a liberal-conservative dimension, centrist Republicans would thus look a lot like other, more conservative members of their party in the 1987–1988 session. Indeed, majority party agenda control would have increased the partisan divide between the parties, making Colorado look more polarized along party lines than it actually was.

After GAVEL, moderates in the Republican Party could occasionally display their moderation. When they could ally themselves with moderate Democrats against a majority of their colleagues in the Republican caucus, these votes would change their positions on the state's ideological map. Their ideological positions, as gauged from their roll call votes through a statistical technique pioneered by Keith Poole (2005), would shift. Centrist Republicans would appear a little closer to the Democrats, with whom they could sometimes unite, and further away from conservative Republicans, with whom they would sometimes differ. However, because moderate Republicans continued to vote with fellow Republicans more than with Democrats, these centrists would not cross the partisan divide. But their behavior would narrow the divide, leaving the legislature as a whole looking less polarized.

To test these expectations, this analysis begins by situating every legislator at his or her preferred location along the liberal-conservative dimension based on his or her votes on contested roll calls. The ideal points are estimates on two dimensions[3] using the Optimal Classification (OC) method (Poole 2005), implementing the procedure separately for the two sessions. We can then compare relative scores and the overall ideological distribution for the pre- and post-GAVEL sessions in Colorado.

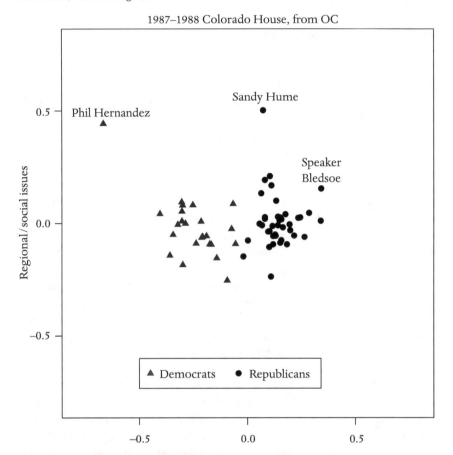

1987–1988 Colorado House, from OC

7.5. Pre-GAVEL party polarization in Colorado, 1987–1988

This analysis reveals that these fairly polarized legislatures—no Democrat is located to the right of any Republican in either session—appear even more polarized when the majority party controls the agenda. The ideological maps of Colorado in figures 7.5 and 7.6 demonstrate this visually, and the decrease in polarization is confirmed by looking at the differences in party means and medians.

Prior to GAVEL, Colorado's house appears fairly polarized, with very few legislators from either party located in the middle of the liberal-conservative ideological dimension. Figure 7.5 displays this dimension on its horizontal axis, with the vertical axis representing a different (and less important, according to statistical diagnostics) dimension. With the exception of a socially liberal alliance between Denver-area liberal Democrat Phil Hernandez and Boulder-area

1989–1990 Colorado House, from OC

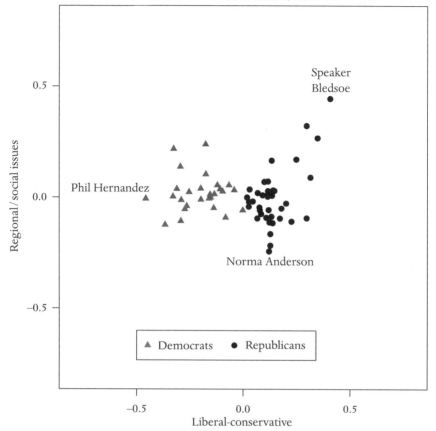

7.6. Post-GAVEL party polarization in Colorado, 1989–1990

Republican Sandy Hume, Democrats and Republicans appeared far away from each other in this agenda-controlled session. Figure 7.6 shows that the parties moved closer to each other after GAVEL reduced Republican leaders' control over the agenda. Even though the distance between Hernandez and Republican speaker Bev Bledsoe remained fairly large, many members of each party were located in the middle. The figure reveals more Ds and Rs, signifying the ideological locations of members of each party, bunched around the middle (marked by 0.0 on the horizontal axis). Measuring the distance between the mean ideal points for each party along the dominant first dimension confirms that the party caucuses moved a little closer together. Before GAVEL, the average Republican and the average Democrat were 0.39 units apart on this ideological scale. Afterward, the divide between the parties shrunk to 0.34. (The difference between party medians shrank from 0.37 to 0.31.) GAVEL did not unite the two parties in Colorado, but it did give more moderates the chance to display their centrism on a few dozen bills, thus subtly shrinking the partisan gulf.

ADAPTATIONS TO GAVEL

Perhaps the most interesting result from the voting roll call analyses presented previously is the creativity Republican leaders used to maintain their influence— although no longer dominance—of the legislative process after the passage of GAVEL. Although the majority's roll rate on bills increased in the 1989 session, it remained significantly lower than the Democratic minority's rate. Indeed, the historical record suggests that the Republican leadership quickly adapted to the post-GAVEL world, using new—and, in some cases, old—tools to limit the agenda and maintain control over the caucus. Most notably, majority leaders continued to assign bills to unfriendly committees in the hope that public committee votes against these bills (in the place of pocket vetoes by committee chairs) would prevent them from reaching the floor. However, majority party leaders also made use of several other tools at their disposal.

KILLER SCHEDULE

In addition to GAVEL, voters adopted another significant reform measure on the 1988 ballot: a new 120-day limit for each year's legislative session. To complete its work within the tight schedule, the General Assembly enacted a series of rigid deadlines for each step in the legislative process. These deadlines gave Republican leaders new opportunities to exert their influence over the agenda. While GAVEL required a vote on each bill, committee chairs retained authority over when the vote would be scheduled. By keeping disfavored bills off the calendar until the last possible minute, the chairs could ensure that even those bills voted out of committee would reach the floor too late to meet other deadlines (Lorch 1991: 234). Although late bills could be introduced, they needed the blessing of a three-person late-bills committee. Two-thirds of the committee's membership consisted of the speaker and the majority party leader (Straayer 2000: 88).

POWER OF APPROPRIATIONS

With the Rules Committee dissolved by GAVEL, the Republican leadership made increasing use of the House Appropriations Committee, which reviewed every bill that promised to spend funds from the public treasury. Increasingly, substantive policy bills that did not carry a price tag were also sent to the committee, where a Republican majority could vote to postpone them indefinitely and thus avoid a floor vote. Indeed, Democratic leaders protested loudly that the Appropriations Committee had become the new Rules Committee (Straayer 2000: 121). More recently, with the Republicans now in the minority, they have voiced the same complaint.

New Caucuses

While Republican leaders found new ways to control the agenda, their grasp over the party caucuses was unimpeded, perhaps explaining the dearth of party disappointments identified in the earlier analysis. In both houses, party leaders stuck to the legal requirements of GAVEL but found new ways to conduct old business. In the senate, Republicans began taking "straw votes" to signal where each member stood on a bill. The party insisted on having eighteen favorable straw votes before ending discussion of each section of the 1989 budget. In the house, the caucus took frequent recesses, during which party whips collected "commitments" from members. Infuriated, Democrats sent staff members to videotape their opponents' meetings. In the spring of 1989, the good government group Common Cause filed a lawsuit claiming that the Republican leaders had violated the binding-caucus ban in their consideration of the budget. The suit was quickly dismissed. A higher court later reversed the decision, but by then a new speaker had ended the practice of holding binding caucuses.

CONCLUSION

Bledsoe's 1990 retirement, and the succession battle that followed, signaled the beginning of a new era in Colorado politics. With the division among its moderate and conservative wings growing, the leadership elections became a factional struggle for the Republican Party. Although the caucus elected the conservative Chuck Berry as Bledsoe's successor, the Republicans picked a moderate as Berry's floor leader. Rancor among the top ranks, combined with Berry's more accommodating attitude toward the Democrats—including his decision to debate the budget on the floor rather than in the party caucus—greatly weakened the Republican leadership's control over the house, thereby empowering a bipartisan floor coalition of moderate Democrats and Republicans.

This change within the halls of Colorado's statehouse, along with others such as term limits and TABOR, reverberated throughout state politics. GAVEL played a small but nonetheless important role in signaling the divide between socially moderate Republicans—especially those in Denver and its suburbs—and more conservative Republicans from Colorado Springs and the state's rural areas. As the other chapters in this book demonstrate, this split within the GOP was part of what led to the party's electoral losses in recent years. While GAVEL did not create the divide, it allowed these ideological differences to play out on the floor of the General Assembly instead of remaining bottled up in committees.

At the same time, the initiative accomplished its more narrow legislative aim of opening up Colorado government to a broader range of proposals. Many of those proposals may die, but they now do so with a public vote. Today's legislators understand and, in at least one case, appreciate its legacy. Representative Mark Ferrandino, a member of the Joint Budget Committee who, through his position, could wield more power were it not for GAVEL, nonetheless supports the initiative. He stated: "If you asked me if I'd vote for GAVEL today, I think in terms of democracy and fleshing out ideas, I think it is a good thing that you can't just pocket veto ideas. GAVEL has allowed more ideas to come forward and be debated and fleshed out. Some turn out to be bad ideas and [do] not go anywhere, but there are a lot of ideas that get majority support, and are good for the state of Colorado, that would never have seen the light of day" (Ferrandino 2009).

NOTES

1. In the 1970s the "binding" caucus allowed a majority of the Republican Party to bind other party members to vote with them on the floor, contrary to the preference these members may have expressed in the caucus. However, this power was only exercised several times.

2. After five senators resigned because of the demands of long sessions, Colorado legislators themselves placed an initiative on the 1988 ballot cutting their sessions from 140 to 120 legislative days, according to Rich Jones (1992: 129). This change occurred at the same time as the passage of GAVEL, but it is difficult to see why it might substantially affect any of the aspects of legislative behavior studied here.

3. In both cases, politics appears to be primarily fought over one dimension. Consequently, most of our analysis in this section is based on members' estimated ideal points on the first dimension. Still, it is important to estimate ideal points in two dimensions so the rare bills that bring divisions along the second dimension are forced to provide information about first-dimension divisions.

REFERENCES

Bledsoe, Carl "Bev." 2009. Telephone interview with Vladimir Kogan, November 17.

Cox, Gary W., Thad Kousser, and Mathew D. McCubbins. 2010. "Party Power or Preferences? Quasi-Experimental Evidence from American State Legislatures." *Journal of Politics* 72: 799–811.

Cox, Gary W., and Mathew D. McCubbins. 2005. *Setting the Agenda: Responsible Party Government in the US House of Representatives*. New York: Cambridge University Press.

Cronin, Thomas E., and Robert D. Loevy. 1993. *Colorado Politics and Government: Governing the Centennial State*. Lincoln: University of Nebraska Press.

The Denver Post. 1988a. "Legislative Changes Die in House." January 22, 8C.

———. 1988b. "A Solid Legislative Record." May 22, 4G.

Dias, John. 1989. "Take Off the Gloves, Democrats Tell Romer." *The Denver Post*, May 29, 1A.

Downs, Anthony. 1957. *An Economic Theory of Democracy.* New York: Harper and Row.

Ferrandino, Mark. 2009. Telephone interview with Thad Kousser and Mike Binder, November 10.

Hilliard, Carl. 1988. "$4.4 Billion Budget Gets Speedy House OK." *The Denver Post*, April 22, 2B.

Jones, Rich. 1992. "The State Legislatures." In *The Book of the States, 1992–1993, Vol. 29.* Lexington, KY: Council of State Governments, 119–142.

Lorch, Robert Stuart. 1991. *Colorado's Government: Structure, Politics, Administration, and Policy,* 5th ed. Niwot: University Press of Colorado.

National Conference of State Legislatures. 2002. *Elections Data Tables,* electronic format. Denver: National Conference of State Legislatures.

Paige, Woody. 1988. "Bledsoe Needs to See the Light." *The Denver Post*, February 26, 1B.

Poole, Keith T. 2005. *Spatial Models of Parliamentary Voting.* New York: Cambridge University Press.

Poole, Keith T., and Howard Rosenthal. 1997. *Congress: A Political-Economic History of Roll Call Voting.* Oxford: Oxford University Press.

Roberts, Jeffrey A. 1988a. "Dems Hope GAVEL Loosens Republican Lock on Legislature." *The Denver Post*, January 12, 1B.

———. 1988b. "Coalition Opens Campaign to Curb Party in Power." *The Denver Post*, May 11, 2B.

Schroeder, Bill. 2009. Telephone interview with Mike Binder, November 19.

Straayer, John A. 1990. *The Colorado General Assembly.* Niwot: University Press of Colorado.

———. 2000. *The Colorado General Assembly,* 2nd ed. Niwot: University Press of Colorado.

Strickland, Ted. 2009. Telephone interview with Mike Binder, November 17.

CHAPTER EIGHT

Disparate Impact: Term Limits, Female Representatives, and the Colorado State Legislature

Courtenay W. Daum

On January 1, 1991, the state of Colorado initiated term limits restricting service in the Colorado State Senate to two consecutive terms, for a total of eight years, and the Colorado House of Representatives to four consecutive terms, for a total of eight years. All legislators in office during the 1991–1992 legislative term were term-limited out of office beginning January 1, 1999. More than a decade has passed since the first state representatives and senators were term-limited, and ample data are now available to examine the effect of term limits on elections and representation in Colorado. While there are many interesting research questions related to term limits, this chapter focuses attention on their effects on female candidates and politicians. Political scientists initially expected that term limits would be advantageous to female candidates by reducing the benefits associated with male incumbency and thus enhancing electoral opportunities for women; they believed female representation would increase in states with term limits (Jewell and Whicker 1993).

The evidence, however, indicates that term limits have not had the intended effect on women's representation. Instead, female representation actually declined in many states following the implementation of term limits. This chapter examines the impact of state legislative term limits on female legislators and candidates in the state of Colorado. Specific attention will be focused on how Republican female legislators and candidates have fared relative to their Democratic counterparts in terms of representation and elections in the era of term limits. Existing research suggests that Republican female candidates may confront different challenges than those female Democrats face as a result of different levels of party support during the recruitment stage and the primary and general elections. This chapter examines the recruitment and election of women from the Republican and Democratic Parties in the state of Colorado since the implementation of term limits to answer these questions: Does the early conventional wisdom that women will benefit in states with term limits hold true in the Colorado legislature more than ten years after the implementation of term limits? Has female representation increased or decreased in the Colorado State House and Senate in the era of term limits? Have female Democrats and Republicans fared differently in the era of term limits? Are Democratic women more likely to enter primaries than Republican women? Are Democratic women more successful in winning election than Republican women?

EXISTING RESEARCH

TERM LIMITS: NEW OPPORTUNITIES OR NEW OBSTACLES FOR WOMEN'S REPRESENTATION?

Proponents of term limits argued that they would promote the development of citizen legislatures that more accurately reflect the demographics and interests of the electorate by decreasing opportunities for individuals to become "career" legislators (see, e.g., the pro–term-limit advocacy group US Term Limits' website banner that reads "Citizen Legislators, *Not* Career Politicians" [US Term Limits 2009; original emphasis]). Term limits would restrict incumbents' terms and force open-seat elections at regular intervals, thereby providing opportunities for new individuals to be elected to office. Political scientists initially speculated that term limits would be advantageous for women seeking election to state and national office because they would reduce incumbency advantage by restricting the number of terms an individual can serve in a single office (Jewell and Whicker 1993). Because women were legally and systematically excluded from running for elected office for centuries, incumbents have tended to be males, and incumbents benefit from name recognition, fundraising advantages, the perks of office, and similar factors when running for reelection. As a result of these various advantages, when incumbents run for reelection they tend to win. Political scientists have therefore identified incumbency advantage as one of the biggest obstacles to women's representation in legislative offices (e.g., Burrell 1994; Darcy, Welch, and Clark 1994).

In addition, others suggested that term limits would make elected office less attractive to males, thereby providing women with additional opportunities to run and to win election (Jewell and Whicker 1993: 708). Term limits make it much more difficult to make a career from serving in elected office. Individuals are restricted in the amount of time they can serve in a single office; while there are always opportunities to run for other offices, term limits may increase the competition for higher offices. For example, state senates have fewer seats than state houses, and the competition for election to the senate may increase as a result of term limits. Consequently, term limits will inevitably force some politicians out of elected office.

Yet the evidence indicates that initial expectations about the effect of term limits on women's representation were inaccurate. According to extant research, there has been no significant increase in female representation in states with term limits. In fact, Susan Carroll and Krista Jenkins (2001) found that during the 1998 and 2000 elections, more female representatives were forced out by house term limits than were elected to fill the seats vacated as a result of those limits. One of the explanations for this development is that many of the house seats vacated by women in state legislatures that have term limits were not contested by women in open-seat elections (Carroll 2001a; Carroll and Jenkins 2001). In fact, the seats women occupied in state houses prior to term limits were often won by males once female representatives were term-limited out of office. Contrary to expectations, women do not appear to be more motivated to run for election to house seats vacated by incumbents than they had been to run for election to state houses prior to term limits (Carroll and Jenkins 2001).

In contrast, Carroll and Jenkins (2001) found that women fared better in winning election to state senates in the era of term limits. Many of the women who were term-limited out of state houses decided to run for seats in the state senate and were able to draw on their previous campaign and electoral experiences to win election. Thus early research on the impact of term limits indicates that their implementation affected women's representation in state houses and state senates in different ways. If, however, women's representation in state houses continues to decrease in the era of term limits, then it seems likely that their representation in state senates will decrease as the number of women in the pipeline for senate seats declines over time. Thus it is necessary to revisit the initial research on term limits and women's representation to examine the long-term effects.

DESCRIPTIVE REPRESENTATION: DO FEMALE LEGISLATORS MAKE A DIFFERENCE?

Existing research indicates that female legislators exhibit different behavior in leadership positions (Dodson and Carroll 1991; Dolan, Deckman, and Swers

2007; Kathlene 1994, 2001; Rosenthal 2000), prioritize different policy issues—including women, children, families, and social welfare issues (Carroll 2001b; Dolan, Deckman, and Swers 2007; Thomas 1994), and exhibit more support for women's issues and women's rights than do their male counterparts (Carroll 2001a). In addition, female legislators are more likely than male legislators to seek out committee assignments that enable them to work on women's issues and are more inclined to sponsor legislation addressing issues of concern to women (Darcy, Welch, and Clark 1994; Swers 2002). Thus women's presence (or absence) in a legislative body may have significant ramifications for the types of policies discussed and produced. In particular, so-called women's issues are more likely to be addressed in legislative bodies with a critical mass of female legislators. As a result, the relationship between term limits and women's numerical representation is an area worthy of further analysis.

RUNNING FOR OFFICE: OBSTACLES TO WOMEN'S CANDIDACIES

Kira Sanbonmatsu's (2002, 2006) research indicates that it is important to disaggregate female legislators by party to identify and analyze the different obstacles Democratic and Republican women must confront when considering and executing a run for elected office. For example, Republican primary electorates tend to be more conservative than the general election electorate, and female candidates from both parties tend to be more liberal than male members of their parties. The intersection of Republican women's more liberal political ideologies and a more conservative Republican primary electorate may work to the disadvantage of female Republicans, whereas Democratic women's more liberal ideologies may work to their advantage in primaries with a more liberal Democratic electorate (Lawless and Pearson 2008). In particular, Sanbonmatsu (2002: 805) suggests that greater attention needs to be focused on the different parties' recruitment strategies and how they, in turn, impact the opportunities for women to run for, and win election to, office.

For example, it has been suggested that the decline of the party organization has been advantageous for women seeking election to office because party bosses and leaders are no longer able to single-handedly select candidates and systematically exclude women (Jewell and Whicker 1993: 707). Yet the move from party-centered to candidate-centered or group-centered campaigns has not entirely eliminated the parties' gate-keeping functions. It is thus important to analyze the role parties play in recruiting and supporting candidates for office, especially in states with term limits where open seats occur more frequently and competitive primaries subsequently become more common.

Of particular interest is the individual party's recruitment of, and support for, female candidates in primaries. Carroll and Jenkins (2001) conclude that one of the explanations for the decline in women's representation in state houses with term limits is the absence of women competing in primaries. They believe recruitment of female candidates plays a significant role in a woman's decision to run for the state house:

> Women who run for state legislatures are less likely than their male counterparts to be "self-starters." Women more often than men seek office only after receiving encouragement from others . . . The lack of an obvious and automatic pool of women candidates for the state house and the fact that relatively few women are self-starters suggest the critical importance of recruitment efforts if women are to translate the opportunity presented by term limits into gains in the number of women serving in state houses. In the absence of greater efforts to identify and recruit women candidates, the evidence from the 1998 and 2000 elections suggests that term limits could actually prove detrimental to women's representation at the state house level. (Carroll and Jenkins 2001: 16)

In fact, the evidence indicates that community and political leaders are more likely to encourage a male in a position to run for elected office than they are a similarly situated female (Lawless and Fox 2005). Thus one explanation for the decline in women's representation in state houses with term limits may be that women are not entering primaries because they are not being recruited by party leaders or do not believe they will receive sufficient support from the party if they do decide to run. As a result, it is helpful to examine women's representation in party primaries.

RESEARCH DESIGN

Colorado is an interesting case study for examining the impact of term limits on women's representation in the state legislature because historically the state has had high levels of female representation relative to other states. In the years prior to term limits, women were well represented in the Colorado State House and Senate. Thus it is possible to compare the fate of female candidates and the representation of women in the pre–term-limit and term-limit eras. This analysis covers a twenty-year period (1989–2009) and examines the representation of females in Colorado's thirty-five senate districts and sixty-five house districts for each year in that span. These eleven legislative terms were selected for analysis because the first batch of legislators was term-limited out of office in 1999, and for purposes of comparison it is useful to include a similar number of elections for the pre– and post–term-limit eras. In addition, a year-to-year comparison is useful because occasional midterm appointments contribute to fluidity in the General Assembly membership.

TABLE 8.1. Total number of women in the Colorado state legislature, 1989–2009*

Pre–Term Limits		Post–Term Limits	
Year	Total Number of Women	Year	Total Number of Women
1989	29	1999	34
1990	29	2000	34
1991	31	2001	34
1992	31	2002	34
1993	35	2003	33
1994	35	2004	34
1995	31	2005	33
1996	31	2006	32
1997	35	2007	34
1998	35	2008	36
		2009	37

*Note: The Colorado legislature is composed of 100 individuals: 35 senators and 65 representatives.
Source: Center for American Women and Politics 2010.

ANALYSIS

Do Term Limits Lead to an Increase in Women's Representation?

The data suggest that term limits in Colorado did not have a significant effect on the total number of women elected to the state legislature. An examination of a twenty-one-year period beginning with the 1989–1990 term and ending with the 2009–2010 term indicates that women constituted approximately one-third of Colorado state legislators in most years. The 1999–2000 term is the first in which state legislators were term-limited out of office, yet, as table 8.1 illustrates, the number of women elected to the Colorado state legislature does not appear to be negatively or positively impacted by the term limits.

A more careful examination of the data, however, indicates that the fates of Democratic and Republican women differed in the era of term limits. Notably, as table 8.2 illustrates, the total number of Democratic women elected to the Colorado state legislature has increased significantly since term limits took effect in the 1999–2000 term. In contrast, the election of Republican women has not been aided by term limits. In fact, the overall number of Republican women elected to the Colorado state legislature has drastically decreased in the era of term limits, from a high of twenty women in the 1997–1998 term to a low of six in the 2005–2006 and 2007–2008 terms. From the data alone, it is difficult to discern if term limits negatively impacted Republican women or if something else

TABLE **8.2.** Total numbers and percentages of female Democrats and Republicans in the Colorado state legislature, 1989–2009

Year	Female Democrats	Percentage of Total Democrats	Female Republicans	Percentage of Total Republicans
1989	11	30	18	29
1990	11	30	18	29
1991	14	36	17	28
1992	14	36	17	28
1993	19	40	16	30
1994	19	40	16	30
1995	15	38	16	27
1996	15	38	16	27
1997	15	39	20	33
1998	15	39	20	33
1999	15	38	19	32
2000	15	38	19	32
2001	20	44	14	26
2002	20	44	14	26
2003	22	49	11	20
2004	23	51	11	20
2005	27	51	6	13
2006	26	49	6	13
2007	28	48	6	15
2008	30	50	6	15
2009	30	51	7	17

Sources: Center for American Women and Politics 2010; Colorado Legislative Directories 1989–2009.

accounts for the substantial decrease in their overall numbers in the Colorado state legislature.

The minimal increase in women's representation in the Colorado state legislature in recent years is entirely accounted for by the increase in the election of Democratic women. Since the 2003–2004 term, Democratic women have accounted for approximately 50 percent of Democratic legislators, and their overall numbers have increased steadily since term limits. In contrast, the overall number of Republican women elected to the Colorado legislature began to decline steadily when term limits took effect in the 1999–2000 term, and the number only increased by one in the 2009–2010 term.

TABLE **8.3.** Female representation in Colorado's house and senate, 1989–2009

Year	Total Number of Women in Senate	Percentage	Total Number of Women in House	Percentage
1989	7	20	22	34
1990	7	20	22	34
1991	8	23	23	35
1992	8	23	23	35
1993	8	23	27	42
1994	9	26	26	40
1995	10	29	21	32
1996	10	29	21	32
1997	10	29	25	39
1998	10	29	25	39
1999	12	34	22	34
2000	12	34	22	34
2001	10	29	24	37
2002	10	29	24	37
2003	9	26	24	37
2004	10	29	24	37
2005	11	31	22	34
2006	11	31	21	32
2007	10	29	24	37
2008	10	29	26	40
2009	12	34	25	39

Sources: Center for American Women and Politics 2010; Colorado Legislative Directories 1989–2009.

Similarly, an analysis of data for the house of representatives and the senate indicates that the overall number of women serving in either house has not changed drastically as a result of term limits. As table 8.3 indicates, the total number of women elected to the house remained fairly constant during the approximately twenty-year period included in this analysis. The total number of women in the senate exhibits more variation, from a low of seven (20 percent of all senators) in the 1989–1990 term to a high of twelve (34 percent of all senators) as recently as the 2009–2010 term. In the pre–term-limit era, an average of 8.7 women served in each term, whereas in the term-limit era an average of 10.6 women served as senators in each term. Thus term limits appear to have had a moderate impact on the number of female senators. The increase in the

TABLE **8.4.** Numbers and percentages of female Democrats and Republicans in the Colorado State Senate, 1989–2009

Year	Number of Female Democrats	Percentage of Female Democratic Senators	Number of Female Republicans	Percentage of Female Republican Senators
1989	2	18	5	21
1990	2	18	5	21
1991	3	25	5	22
1992	3	25	5	22
1993	3	19	5	26
1994	4	25	5	26
1995	5	31	5	26
1996	5	31	5	26
1997	5	33	5	25
1998	5	33	5	25
1999	5	33	7	35
2000	5	33	7	35
2001	7	39	3	18
2002	7	39	3	18
2003	8	47	1	6
2004	9	53	1	6
2005	9	50	2	12
2006	9	50	2	12
2007	9	45	1	7
2008	9	45	1	7
2009	11	52	1	7

Sources: Center for American Women and Politics 2010; Colorado Legislative Directories 1989–2009.

number of female senators in the era of term limits may reflect an increase in the number of viable female candidates competing in senate elections as a result of women being term-limited out of the house.

Again, however, it is important to examine the differential impact term limits appear to have had on Democratic and Republican women. Since term limits were instituted, the number of female Democratic senators has increased steadily, whereas the number of female Republican senators has decreased. Since the 2003–2004 term, female Democrats have accounted for approximately 50 percent of the Democrats in the senate, and in the 2009–2010 term they comprised 52 percent of the Democrats and nearly one-third of the entire senate membership. In contrast, as illustrated in table 8.4, there were five Republican women in the senate in each of the five pre–term-limit terms included in this analysis, accounting for 21 percent to 26 percent of the Republicans in the senate; since term limits there have been an average of 2.6 Republican women per term. In fact, since 2007 there has been only a single Republican female senator.

An examination of the fate of individual senators and candidates indicates that every Republican female senator term-limited out of office was replaced by a male, while more than half of the female Democratic senators term-limited out of office were replaced by women. Thus term limits appear to have reduced the representation of Republican women in the senate but not that of female Democrats. For example, long-serving female Republican senators such as Dottie Wham, Mary Anne Tebedo, and Sally Hopper were term-limited out of office in 1999 or 2001, and each was replaced by a male. While it is difficult to know whether these women would have been reelected to office absent term limits, given their lengthy track records and incumbent status it seems likely that term limits abruptly halted their legislative careers and contributed to a decrease in the number of Republican women in the senate.

Furthermore, each of these women was the chair of a standing senate committee—Health, Environment, Welfare and Institutions (Hopper), Judiciary (Wham), and State, Veterans and Military Affairs (Tebedo)—at the time she was term-limited out of office; Senator Wham was the chair of the Joint Capital Development Committee as well (Colorado Legislative Directory 1999, 2001). Considering the few Republican women serving in the senate relative to their male counterparts, Senators Hopper, Wham, and Tebedo's leadership of these senate committees is noteworthy both symbolically and in terms of the substantive representation of women's interests.

In addition, as previously noted, female legislators tend to behave differently than their male counterparts when assigned to leadership positions. For example, women tend to be facilitative leaders, and they prioritize different issues than male legislators do (Dodson and Carroll 1991; Dolan, Deckman, and Swers 2007; Kathlene 1994, 2001; Rosenthal 2000). As a result, the presence of women in leadership positions may substantively affect policy development and produce legislation that reflects the policy priorities of women and women's interests. Thus term limits did not simply reduce the number of Republican women in the Colorado Senate, they also removed women from senior leadership positions where they had the opportunity to make distinctive contributions and shape policy and legislative outcomes in ways that could be advantageous to female constituents.

In contrast, the first female Democratic senator term-limited out of office in 1999 was Joan Johnson, and she was replaced by a female Democrat. Similarly, four of the remaining eight female Democrats term-limited out of office were replaced by women. Thus while term limits ended the state legislative careers of both Republican and Democratic women, female Democrats have had better success in retaining those seats previously occupied by women and gaining additional seats in the senate as well. Yet similar to Republican women, female Democratic senators have also been term-limited out of office while serving in leadership positions. For example, Joan Fitz-Gerald was elected president of the senate in 2005 but resigned from the senate halfway through her final term to run for the US Congress (Colorado Legislative Directory 2005). Senator Peggy Reeves was one of three senators serving on the powerful Joint Budget Committee at the time she was term-limited out of office in 2004, and Senator Moe Keller was chair of the Joint Budget Committee in her final term in the senate (Colorado Legislative Directory 2009).

Similar to the senate, in the Colorado House of Representatives the total number of female Democrats has increased over time in the era of term limits, and Democratic women have accounted for close to or more than 50 percent of the Democrats in the house since 2001. In contrast, the number of Republican women in the house has declined significantly in recent years. In the pre–term-limit era, an average of 12.4 Republican women served per term compared with an average of 8.2 per term since term limits took effect. Since 2005, as seen in table 8.5, the number of Republican women in the house has decreased to the single digits, with a low of four women in the 2005–2006 term.

Republican women term-limited out of office have been replaced overwhelmingly by males. For example, in 1999, when term limits first went into effect, five of the six Republican women term-limited out of the house were replaced by males; the other, Republican Jeannie Faatz, was replaced by a female Democrat, Fran Coleman. In contrast, Democratic women term-limited in the house have more often than not been replaced by women from the same party. Thus term limits appear to have precipitated a decline in the number of Republican women in the house. While female Democrats have been able to retain nearly 70 percent of the seats occupied by term-limited Democratic women, Republican women have been able to retain only 13 percent of those offices.

Similar to the senate, the effect of term limits on Republican women in the house was initially more severe than it was for Democratic women. For example, in 1999, when term limits first went into effect, six Republican women were term-limited out of the house in comparison to three female Democrats. Five of the Republican women forced out of the house in 1999 had been serving longer than the four terms permitted by term limits, compared with one Democrat. As a result, it appears that a greater number of "career" Republican female representatives initially were forced out by term limits than was the case for Democrats. For example, Representative Norma Anderson was first elected to the house in 1987, and during her final term she was the house majority leader. Similarly, Representatives Mary Ellen Epps and Shirleen Tucker came to the house in 1987,

TABLE 8.5. Numbers and percentages of female Democrats and Republicans in the Colorado State House of Representatives, 1989–2009

Year	Number of Female Democrats	Percentage of Female Democratic Representatives	Number of Female Republicans	Percentage of Female Republican Representatives
1989	9	35	13	33
1990	9	35	13	33
1991	11	41	12	32
1992	11	41	12	32
1993	16	52	11	32
1994	15	48	11	32
1995	10	42	11	27
1996	10	42	11	27
1997	10	42	15	37
1998	10	42	15	37
1999	10	40	12	30
2000	10	40	12	30
2001	13	48	11	29
2002	13	48	11	29
2003	14	50	10	27
2004	14	50	10	27
2005	18	51	4	13
2006	17	49	4	13
2007	19	49	5	19
2008	21	53	5	20
2009	19	50	6	22

Sources: Center for American Women and Politics 2010; Colorado Legislative Directories 1989–2009.

and each was chair of a standing house committee—Health, Environment, Welfare and Institutions (Epps) and Local Government (Tucker)—when she was forced out by term limits (Colorado Legislative Directory 1998).

While term limits did not have a significant effect on the overall number of women serving in the Colorado legislature, a number of long-term female Republican representatives and senators were forced out of office as a result of the limits. At the same time, more female Democrats than Republicans were elected to the house and senate in recent elections. While women in the Colorado legislature used to be similarly represented by the two parties, in the twenty-first century the gap between the number of Republican and Democratic women has grown rapidly, and as of 2009 there were twenty-three more female Democrats than Republicans. But the question remains: did term limits increase opportunities for Democratic women at the same time they decreased opportunities for Republican women, or is there an alternative explanation for these developments?

WOMEN IN THE PIPELINE

One explanation for the recent increase in the number of female politicians in the United States is that the number of women in the pipeline has increased as more women run for and win election to local, county, and state offices, thereby positioning them to be competitive in elections to higher offices (e.g., Carroll and Jenkins 2001; Darcy, Welch, and Clark 1994; Dolan and Ford 1998; Duerst-Lahti 1998). Consistent with this theory, term limits may place more women in the pipeline for higher office as both male and female politicians are term-limited. Essentially, term limits could work to the advantage of women in two ways. First, by term-limiting men out of office, more opportunities are created for women to compete for open seats, thereby positioning them in the pipeline. Second, as women themselves are term-limited out of lower offices, they may take the opportunity to run for higher offices, thereby forcing themselves into and through the pipeline more quickly than may have occurred absent term limits. For example, it is logical for women term-limited out of the Colorado House of Representatives to seek election to the Colorado Senate so they can continue their political careers.

Term limits in Colorado do not appear to have had the same effect on Republican and Democratic women in the pipeline. In fact, term limits seem to have limited opportunities for Republican women, whereas the increase in female Democrats in the senate may be attributed in part to the influx of viable female candidates term-limited out of the house. Since the implementation of term limits, Democratic women in the house have made the transition to the senate in greater numbers than Republican women. Thirteen female Democratic representatives ran for and won election to the senate in the era of term limits, including four women who had been term-limited out of the house. In contrast, only four Republican women were elected to the senate after serving in the house in the term-limit era. Thus term limits ended the state legislative careers of many term-limited female Republican representatives. These women were either unsuccessful in their attempts to get elected to the state senate or opted out of running for office. In contrast, Democratic women appear to have had greater success capitalizing on open-seat opportunities in the senate to further their state legislative careers. In fact, the increase in the number of female Democratic senators appears to be a direct result of women in the house successfully running for the senate. So while term limits appear to have successfully pushed Democratic women through the pipeline, the same cannot be said of Republican women in the Colorado legislature. One explanation for the different fates of Democratic and Republican women in Colorado politics in recent years may rest with the changing internal dynamics of the state Republican Party.

CHANGING NATURE OF THE REPUBLICAN PARTY

Female Republican legislators have frequently found themselves the targets of aggressive intra-party attacks during primaries and general elections. Former senate president Joan Fitz-Gerald attributes this phenomenon to the "Republican Party's 'march to the right': Republican women who were more moderate didn't stand a chance with the right-wing juggernaut" (quoted in Bartels 2006). Thus one explanation for the decrease in the number of Republican women winning election to the state legislature may be the changing nature of Republican Party politics in the state. Female politicians tend to be more liberal than their male counterparts, and this is true for Republicans as well as Democrats (Darcy, Welch, and Clark 1994; Dodson 2006; Dodson and Carroll 1991; Dolan, Deckman, and Swers 2007). Existing research indicates that Republican voters of both sexes are less likely to support a female candidate than they are a male candidate (King and Matland 2003). In recent years the Colorado Republican Party has become more conservative, with many Republican candidates exhibiting a greater emphasis on social issues such as opposition to abortion, gay rights, and gun control and support for religious and moral values in the public sector (see chapter 6 in this volume). As a result, it is possible that Colorado Republican Party leaders and members may not be supportive of female candidates because they perceive them as too liberal or that Republican women are not inclined to run for office because they perceive a disconnect between their politics and those of the Colorado Republican Party. According to John Straayer:

> More than one Republican [has] commented that in the middle of the first decade of the twenty-first century, it was clear that "it was the boys" who were going after all the Republican moderates, including many of the women. Some commented that the party seemed increasingly to be dominated by a "bunch of angry white men," a posse . . . [F]or many of the more visible and vocal Republicans, the party agenda has changed. And with that has come a stunning shrinkage in the number of women Republican legislators and legislative candidates. (2006: 151)

The changing internal dynamics of the Republican Party in Colorado are exemplified by Republican representative Debbie Stafford's decision to switch her party affiliation in fall 2007. Stafford explained that, as a moderate, she no longer believed the party represented her values: "I am not leaving the Republican Party as much as I believe the Republican Party left me" (quoted in Paulson 2007).

Former Colorado house and senate Republican majority leader Norma Anderson suggested that female Republican candidates are having a difficult time competing in the party's caucuses and primaries. She explained that "her party has shifted hard right. GOP women, generally speaking, tend to be more practical and more moderate and 'can't get elected' through the caucus system, she says. Many won't even try" (quoted in Martinez 2006). Examples of moderate Republican female incumbents being challenged by conservative males in the party primary are evident in both the house and the senate. In 2006 Kiki Traylor—appointed to the senate when Senator Norma Anderson resigned with a single year to serve in her final term—was the incumbent running for reelection in Senate District 22. Traylor and two males—Justin Everett and Mike Kopp—competed for the Republican Party's nomination in the district nominating assembly, followed by a contentious primary. Traylor was supported by moderate Republicans, whereas Kopp was supported by conservative Republicans and representatives of the religious right (Straayer 2006: 135–136). Kopp ran as a pro-life, pro-gun, pro-faith Republican and portrayed Traylor as "soft on immigration, pro-abortion, a liberal and a friend of Democrats" (Straayer 2006: 138). The Christian Coalition distributed campaign literature attacking Traylor for supporting abortion rights. Kopp went on to win the Republican primary by a slim margin and the general election by a narrow margin in 2006 as well. A seat that had been occupied by moderate female Republicans for eight years was now held by a conservative Republican male. Norma Anderson has been quoted as saying, "If I had to start over again, I wouldn't get elected" (quoted in Martinez 2006).

Similarly, incumbent Gayle Berry was a moderate Republican elected to the house in 1996. In 2002, when Berry ran for reelection, she was challenged in the primary and targeted by the Christian right—an active player in Colorado Republican Party politics in recent years—which campaigned against her (Straayer 2007: 114). While Berry was reelected to serve a fourth and final term in the Colorado house, after her fourth term expired she was replaced by a male Democrat. Other female Republicans challenged by conservative males in the party primaries or targeted by conservative interest groups during the campaign include Senator Dottie Wham and Representatives Marcy Morrison and Tambor Williams. A frequent line of attack used against these women was that they were pro-choice (Straayer 2006: 157). Wham, Morrison, and Williams were all term-limited out of office, and each was replaced by a male; Wham and Williams were replaced by male Democrats and Morrison's seat was won by David Schultheis, a religious conservative who had previously challenged her in the Republican primary.

Thus it appears that the intersection of term limits and the changing face of the Republican Party in Colorado worked to reduce the number of Republican women elected to the Colorado legislature. While Republican women had constituted a sizable portion of the Republican delegation in the Colorado state houses for many years, term limits forced many moderate Republican women out of the house and senate. At the same time, new Republican female candidates were being elected in insufficient numbers to maintain the same levels of women's Republican representation in the Colorado General Assembly. Many of the Republican women who did run and win election were targeted by conservatives within their own party and were later defeated in the primary or the general election or saw their seats go to a Democrat after they were term-limited out of office.

It seems feasible that, absent term limits, moderate Republican women may have been able to retain those seats lost to Democrats. Many of the Republican women term-limited out of office were replaced by conservative Republican candidates who emphasized moral issues in the general election campaign and went on to lose to the Democratic candidates. It appears that moderate Republican women were better suited to some of these districts than were conservative males; absent a moderate Republican candidate, voters were more inclined to favor the Democrat. Thus term limits and the changing nature of the Republican Party appear to have contributed to the party's decline in the Colorado legislature by forcing moderate Republican women out of office.

Party Primary Explanation

Carroll and Jenkins (2001) found that 55.6 percent of women's Colorado house seats in the 1998 election and 66.7 percent in the 2000 election did not have a female candidate competing in the primary election to replace the female incumbent. The absence of female candidates in primaries means those seats will be uncontested by women, and when women do not run, they cannot win.

In recent years, female Democrats have been more likely than female Republicans to run for office. In 2006, forty-two female Democrats but just fourteen Republican women competed in their party primaries (Colorado Secretary of State 2006). Similarly, in 2008, forty female candidates competed in Democratic Party primaries compared with twenty-eight female Republicans (Colorado Secretary of State 2008). Yet there were a limited number of contested primaries, so nearly all of the female candidates competing in the primaries ran unopposed and were guaranteed to be their party's candidate in the general election.

An examination of the contested primaries in which a woman was one of the candidates indicates that Democratic females fared better than Republican women. In both 2006 and 2008 there were six contested Democratic primaries involving a female candidate, and a woman was victorious in each race

(Colorado Secretary of State 2006, 2008). In contrast, female Republican women won two of the five contested primaries in 2006 (and in one primary Republican Ramey Johnson defeated fellow female Republican Patricia Holloway), and a female Republican won three of the four contested primaries involving at least one woman candidate in 2008 (Colorado Secretary of State 2006, 2008). Despite the fact that Democratic women have had better success than Republican women in contested primaries in recent elections, there does not appear to be a systematic bias in favor of male candidates among primary voters. The overwhelming majority of female candidates entering primaries ran unopposed, and in those instances in which there was a competitive primary, women from both parties proved to be formidable opponents. For example, each of the three female Republican candidates who lost to a male opponent in the 2006 primaries received more than 45 percent of the vote in her race (Colorado Secretary of State 2006). Thus when women run in the Democratic and Republican primaries for the Colorado General Assembly, they tend to win.

That said, 84 percent of the female Democrats who ran for the Colorado legislature were elected to office in 2008, whereas only 31 percent of the female Republican candidates were elected. Thus while women from both parties may perform well in the primaries, Democratic women outperform Republican women in the general election. This suggests that the decrease in Republican women in the legislature in recent years may be accounted for by the smaller number of Republican women choosing to run for office, combined with the Colorado electorate's preference for Democratic candidates in the general election (as discussed in chapters 1 and 3).

CONCLUSION

The implementation of term limits in the Colorado legislature did not significantly affect the overall number of women serving in the house and senate. Contrary to initial expectations, the overall number of female legislators did not increase as a result of term limits. Yet term limits do appear to have played a role in the decline in the number of Republican women. Term limits forced a number of long-term female Republican representatives and senators out of office, and most of these women were replaced by males. In contrast, Democratic women term-limited out of office have often been replaced by women, and many Democratic female representatives were successfully elected to the senate after being term-limited out of the house. Additional research will be necessary, however, to determine why Republican women have appeared less inclined than Democratic women to run for office in recent years.

These preliminary findings are significant for a few reasons. First, the pipeline theory suggests that it is important to increase the number of women serving in lower-level political offices so women are in a position to run for higher elected offices in the future. As more women are elected to the Colorado Senate and House of Representatives, the argument follows that more women will be in the pipeline to run for governor or the US Congress, and more women will be in a position to be considered for state and national cabinet appointments. As a result, the increase in the number of Democratic women in the Colorado state legislature positions more female Democrats to run for higher office. In addition, because these women are term-limited, they may be more motivated to seek opportunities to run for the US Congress or a state executive office than would be the case if they were able to make a career out of being a state legislator. In contrast, the decrease in the number of Republican women serving in the Colorado General Assembly means there may be fewer Republican women in a position to compete for higher offices in the years to come. The situation for Republican women appears especially dire given the decrease in the number of Republican women in the Colorado House of Representatives. If election to the house places women in the pipeline for election to the senate, then the decrease in the number of Republican female representatives appears to have contributed to the decrease in Republican female senators, which subsequently puts even fewer Republican women in a position to run for statewide or national office.

Second, the fact that term limits have not contributed to an increase in the overall number of women serving in the Colorado legislature may have implications for policy outcomes. As previously noted, women bring a different perspective to the legislative process and identify different legislative priorities than do their male counterparts. Any decrease in the number of women changes the nature of the dialogue and the legislative process. While the overall number of women may be remaining steady, the decrease in the number of Republican women may have a significant effect on the Republican Party's policy priorities and political strategies in the Colorado legislature. This change in emphasis may be an intentional redirection of the Republican Party—Republicans are not recruiting or electing women because the party wants to change its policy priorities—but the evidence seems to indicate that term limits worked to push some moderate Republican women out of offices to which they would likely have been reelected absent term limits.

REFERENCES

Bartels, Lynn. 2006. "GOP Women 'Dwindling': Only Six among Republican Lawmakers in House, Senate." *The Rocky Mountain News*, August 23.

Burrell, Barbara. 1997. *A Woman's Place Is in the House*. Ann Arbor: University of Michigan Press.

Carroll, Susan J. 2001a. "The Impact of Term Limits on Women." *Spectrum: The Journal of State Government* 74(4): 19–21.

————. 2001b. "Representing Women: Women State Legislators as Agents of Policy Related Change." In *The Impact of Women in Public Office*, ed. Susan J. Carroll. Bloomington: Indiana University Press, 3–21.

Carroll, Susan J., and Krista Jenkins. 2001. "Unrealized Opportunity? Term Limits and the Representation of Women in State Legislatures." *Women and Politics* 23(4): 1–30.

Center for American Women and Politics. 2010. "State Fact Sheet: Colorado." Available at http://www.cawp.rutgers/edu/fast_facts/resources/state_fact_sheets/CO.php. Accessed June 28, 2010.

Colorado Legislative Directories. 1989–2009. *Colorado Legislative Directory*. Denver: State of Colorado.

Colorado Secretary of State. 2006. "Colorado Cumulative Report Official Results Primary Election." Available at http://www.sos.state.co.us/pubs/electronicresults2006P/. Accessed November 24, 2009.

————. 2008. "Official Publication of the Abstract of Votes Cast for the 2008 Primary and 2008 General Elections." Available at http://www.elections.colorado.gov/Content/Documents/2008_Abstract.pdf. Accessed April 25, 2009.

Darcy, R., Susan Welch, and Janet Clark. 1994. *Women, Elections and Representation*. Lincoln: University of Nebraska Press.

Dodson, Debra L. 2006. *The Impact of Women in Congress*. Oxford: Oxford University Press.

Dodson, Debra L., and Susan J. Carroll. 1991. *Reshaping the Agenda: Women in State Legislatures*. New Brunswick: Center for American Women and Politics.

Dolan, Julie, Melissa Deckman, and Michele Swers. 2007. *Women and Politics: Paths to Power and Political Influence*. Upper Saddle River, NJ: Pearson Prentice-Hall.

Dolan, Kathleen, and Lynne Ford. 1998. "Are All Women State Legislators Alike?" In *Women and Elective Office: Past, Present, and Future*, ed. Sue Thomas and Clyde Wilcox. New York: Oxford, 73–86.

Duerst-Lahti, Georgia. 1998. "The Bottleneck: Women Becoming Candidates." In *Women and Elective Office: Past, Present, and Future*, ed. Sue Thomas and Clyde Wilcox. New York: Oxford, 15–25.

Jewell, Malcolm, and Marcia Lynn Whicker. 1993. "The Feminization of Leadership in State Legislatures." *PS: Political Science and Politics* 26(4): 705–712.

Kathlene, Lyn. 1994. "Power and Influence in State Legislative Policymaking: The Interaction of Gender and Position in Committee Hearing Debates." *American Political Science Review* 88: 560–575.

————. 2001. "Words That Matter: Women's Voice and Institutional Bias in Public Policy Formation." In *The Impact of Women in Public Office*, ed. Susan J. Carroll. Bloomington: Indiana University Press, 22–48.

King, David C., and Richard E. Matland. 2003. "Sex and the Grand Old Party: An Experimental Investigation of the Effect of Candidate Sex on Support for a Republican Candidate." *American Politics Research* 31(6): 595–612.

Lawless, Jennifer, and Richard Fox. 2005. *It Takes a Candidate: Why Women Don't Run for Office*. New York: Cambridge University Press.

Lawless, Jennifer, and Kathryn Pearson. 2008. "The Primary Reason for Women's Under Representation? Re-evaluating the Conventional Wisdom." *The Journal of Politics* 70(1): 67–82.

Martinez, Julia C. 2006. "Republican Women Snubbing Politics?" *The Denver Post*. Available at www.denverpost.com/portlet/article/html/fragments/print_article.jsp?article=3979861. Accessed July 31, 2006.

Paulson, Steven K. 2007. "Debbie Stafford Switches to Democratic Party." Available at http://cbs4denver.com/local/aurora.colorado.rep.2.562605.html. Accessed January 12, 2010.

Rosenthal, Cindy Simon. 2000. "Gender Styles in State Legislative Committees: Raising Their Voices in Resolving Conflict." *Women and Politics* 21: 21–45.

Sanbonmatsu, Kira. 2002. "Political Parties and the Recruitment of Women to State Legislatures." *The Journal of Politics* 64(3): 791–809.

———. 2006. *Where Women Run: Gender and Party in the American States*. Ann Arbor: University of Michigan Press.

Straayer, John. 2006. "The Great Downhill Run." Unpublished manuscript.

———. 2007. "Colorado Legislative Term Limits: The Worst of Both Worlds." In *Legislating without Experience: Case Studies in State Legislative Term Limits*, ed. Rick Farmer, Christopher Z. Mooney, Richard J. Powell, and John C. Green. New York: Lexington Books, 99–120.

Swers, Michele L. 2002. *The Difference Women Make: The Policy Impact of Women in Congress*. Chicago: University of Chicago Press.

Thomas, Sue. 1994. *How Women Legislate*. New York: Oxford University Press.

US Term Limits. 2009. http://www.termlimits.org/. Accessed November 29, 2009.

CHAPTER NINE

One Thing after Another: Layers of Policy and Colorado's Fiscal Train Wreck

John A. Straayer

This is a story about the evolution of fiscal policy and related institutional change in Colorado over the past two-and-a-half decades. It is a story about the substantial dismantling of a governing apparatus capable of establishing policy direction and budget priorities. It is a story of a decision-making style our founders would surely have viewed with dismay, and it is the story of a state in which fiscal policy is piled upon fiscal policy in a process driven largely by the uncoordinated pursuit of special advantage by an assortment of interests and the flow of economic circumstances rather than by self-conscious choices made by elected institutional authorities. The piling of law upon law has by definition altered policy, but it has also had extraordinary institutional consequences. This is a story without an end.

If there is a current policy perspective in the academic literature that comes close to fitting Colorado, it would be that offered by Professors Christopher McGrory Klyza and David Sousa in their analysis of national environmental policy development over the past several decades. Klyza and Sousa write, "New laws affecting the management of public lands and wildlife were layered atop existing statutes and agency practices" (2008: 1). They note that environmental policy is made in a framework created by earlier policies that were made in their own particular framework, resulting in the "layering of contradictory policy commitments" (ibid.: 3, 8–9) and generating "frustration on all sides" (ibid.: 11). The result, they conclude, is that environmental policy in the United States "will likely continue to be a mix of train wrecks and next-generation success stories" (ibid.: 309). This layering of policy upon policy in a manner that leads to a train wreck comes close to describing the manufacture of fiscal policy in Colorado. Given the current state of Colorado's policy and politics, however, "next-generation success stories" are questionable (see Bell Policy Center 2011; Center for Colorado's Economic Future 2009, 2011).

To some extent, public policy is always produced in incremental fashion—responding to shifts in public opinion, heavily flavored by the successes of special interests, and replete with unanticipated consequences. Sometimes shifts in public opinion, stunning events, or the emergence of new leadership push policy in radically new directions. 9–11 did this, as did the Great Depression of the 1930s and the 2008–2010 financial unraveling. But we can usually identify institutions and processes of a fairly enduring nature and longstanding policy directions that persist absent sudden and unexpected change. There is generally some measure of continuity with respect to decision-making institutions and the deciders.

Through the employment of Colorado's initiative process, albeit with some help from Colorado's legislature, a long string of groups operating in varying political and economic circumstances has collectively created a budgetary arrangement that (1) leaves elected authorities without the capacity to establish and pursue statewide priorities with any sense of continuity by depriving them of fiscal authority and resources and (2) stimulates the continual flow of proposals for ever more modifications of the law designed to dodge or bypass choices made earlier. Actions taken to change policy have impacts on institutions as well and, in turn, stimulate efforts to change policy even more, and on and on it goes.

Currently, Colorado is operating with multiple and conflicting constitutional provisions that restrict both revenues and spending and require expenditures. Such provisions apply to the state as a whole as well as to local governments. One measure, the Taxpayer's Bill of Rights (TABOR), limits annual revenue growth to the level of the prior year plus additional increments for inflation and population growth or to student population increases in the school districts and real property value growth in other local jurisdictions. Until 2009, a statutory measure (Arveschoug-Bird) limited state General Fund appropriation increases to 6 percent over the prior year. Still another measure requires new spending in the single-largest government sector, the K–12 schools, in an amount equal to the prior year plus inflation and student population growth. In addition, the combination of federal and state policy plus political reality drives growth in spending for Medicaid and corrections. The legislature can reduce taxes, and it has done so, but the legislature cannot raise taxes or extend those that expire. Only voters can do so, and Colorado voters have proven to be tax averse, although endowed with a healthy public service appetite.

DIRECT DEMOCRACY IN COLORADO

Like two dozen other states, most of them west of the Mississippi River, Colorado adopted direct democracy procedures roughly 100 years ago in the midst of the Progressive Era. Colorado's provisions are arguably among the most citizen-friendly in the nation. To place a measure on the ballot, citizens must gather the signatures of registered voters in a number equal to 5 percent of the total vote for secretary of state in the immediately preceding election (Colorado Constitution V, l; see also chapter 4 in this volume). They are permitted to employ paid signature gatherers, the signature hunters need not be registered voters, and there are no geographical distribution requirements for the signatures. In 2010, roughly 85,000 signatures would have qualified a measure for the fall election ballot.

The initiative process has been used extensively in Colorado, and its use has accelerated in recent years. A total of 210 initiated measures have appeared on the ballot in the state's history. From the initial use of direct democracy in 1912 to 1970, 49 percent of the 210 initiated measures appeared on the ballot. Voters have faced the remaining 51 percent since 1970, with 17 percent of the 210 appearing in just the past eight years. Direct democracy in Colorado has become an increasingly inviting industry.

Ballot measures in Colorado have addressed a wide range of issues over the decades, from election reform, land use, and schools to such social matters as abortion and gay marriage. But the largest single category has involved measures addressing taxes, tax policy, and related fiscal matters. The use of the initiative and referendum to tinker with state money is not new, dating back nearly 100 years. What is new is the use of the process, mostly the initiative, to pass measures that substantively alter fiscal policy and, with it, the budget process itself.

Since 1978, when California voters approved Proposition 13—which severely limited increases in property taxes—both an anti-tax and anti-government political element in the states and the enactment of various tax and spending limitations have increased. And so it has been in Colorado. Over the past two-and-a-half decades, voters have approved both citizen-initiated and legislatively proposed measures that have produced an extraordinarily complicated fiscal policy, one broadly viewed as seriously dysfunctional (Center for Colorado's Economic Future 2009).

An assortment of constitutional and statutory provisions now places the state in a situation in which, as a former house speaker described it, the state is "driving with one foot on the brake and one foot on the gas" (quoted in Patton 2008). Some laws require spending, while others restrict both revenues and spending (Colorado Legislative Council 2003). No single policy did this, and the multiple measures that have collectively created the current state of affairs came about as a result of no singular vision. As Henry Ford said about history, it has been "just one damn thing after another," and as America's founders who cherished representative government might well have added, "what the hell are you doing?"

FISCAL RESTRICTION—THE FOOT ON THE BRAKE

In Colorado's history there have been four significant limitations on the ability of the state government to collect revenues and to spend; the two major ones remain today. Two designed to restrict appropriations, and thus spending, were enacted by the legislature itself. The first was adopted in 1977 and was known by its now deceased author, Democratic state senator James Kadlecek. The Kadlecek Amendment, which was statutory and thus subject to legislative suspension or modification, stipulated that annual state General Fund appropriations could not exceed the level of the prior year by more than 7 percent. The amendment did not impact revenues and did not apply to capital expenditures.

In 1990 the legislature, at the behest of Republican state senator Mike Bird and Republican house member Steve Arveschoug, adopted another statutory measure; this one dropped the allowable annual General Fund appropriation increase to 6 percent. Again, the measure did not impact capital spending and initially was subject to legislative change. The 2009 General Assembly eliminated the Arveschoug-Bird limit.

The other two limiting measures are constitutional, not statutory; thus upon adoption they were, and remain, beyond the reach of the legislature. The first, called the Gallagher Amendment after its senate sponsor, Democrat Dennis Gallagher, was referred to the voters by the legislature. The second, TABOR, was initiated by Douglas Bruce, a Colorado Springs resident who moved to Colorado from Southern California and brought with him antipathy toward the government and experience in California's anti-tax/anti-government wars.

Voters adopted the Gallagher Amendment in 1982, not long after California adopted Proposition 13. Like the California measure, the amendment was a reaction to displeasure with the property tax. Colorado had long experienced extreme county-to-county variability in county assessor property valuations, a practice that skewed the tax burden across the state. Similar to the situation in California, there was resistance to a rising residential property tax burden that, in turn, was a product of rising property values (also see chapter 10 in this volume).

The primary purpose of the amendment was to put a lid on residential property taxes and equalize assessments statewide. Gallagher established a statewide ratio between revenues from residential property taxes (45 percent) and those from commercial properties (55 percent). It also set an assessment rate of 29 percent of market value for commercial properties and an initial rate of 21 percent of market value for residences. The value of property was to be reassessed every two years, and to maintain the 45–55 percent ratio (adjusted a bit for new construction and oil/gas extraction values), the assessment rate on residential properties could float. That is, if statewide growth in the value of residential properties exceeded that of properties on the commercial side, the 21 percent of market value assessment rate for residences could decline (Colorado Legislative Council 2003).

And decline it did. As the aggregate value of new residential property ran ahead of commercial value increases year after year, by 2008 Colorado homeowners' domiciles were assessed at roughly 8 percent of market value. This was and remains a very good tax situation for homeowners, but it is not good for businesses, which carry by far the greater burden.

From the adoption of Gallagher in 1982 until passage of the TABOR revenue-limiting constitutional amendment in 1992, local governments could maintain a fairly constant inflow of property tax revenue or even increase that revenue when needed. As the assessment rate on residences declined, they could simply increase the mill levy to compensate for the assessment reduction and keep tax revenue levels neutral. Or they could increase the levy if so authorized by state law or run a ballot measure if the law required. Thus regarding tax revenue flows, Gallagher was of limited concern to local governments or to the state, for that matter.

But then came another major fiscal measure, the Taxpayer's Bill of Rights, in 1992. TABOR created its own independent set of impacts on the government, but, in addition, it altered the way Gallagher affected both local governments and the state. TABOR was a lengthy and complicated measure with a variety of provisions, but the major ones were to require public votes in any jurisdiction that wanted to raise a tax, institute a new one, or continue a tax that was set to expire. TABOR simply took away the government's authority to raise taxes. Governments, both local and the state, were free to cut taxes, but they could not create new ones.

TABOR also set limits on the revenue governments could collect and keep. For the state, the limit each year was the number from the previous year plus percentage increases for inflation and population growth. For the schools districts it was the prior year's number plus inflation plus student head-count increases. For other local governments it was the prior year's number plus inflation plus the value of growth in new properties.

One way to characterize TABOR's institutional impact is to say that it virtually replaced government finance and appropriations committees with finance committees composed of every registered voter within a jurisdiction: the state, a school district, a city, a county, or a special district. With respect to the government's most central power, the power to lay and collect taxes, TABOR eliminated representative government and replaced it with direct democracy.

As noted earlier, TABOR also changed the impact of the Gallagher Amendment. By requiring a popular vote to adjust tax rates or tax revenues upward, TABOR compromised the ability of local governments to adjust mill levies in accordance with downward-trending residential assessment rates so as to maintain existing tax revenue totals. One effect of this was that many local authorities, leery of going to the ballot with tax measures, saw their revenues decline relative to what would have been the case absent TABOR. When that happened in school districts whose mill levies were further depressed by a 1994 change in the 1988 School Finance Act, the state's burden for funding K–12 schools grew.

Colorado's constitution and the School Finance Act set the level of overall state government financial responsibility for the schools. Thus as the Gallagher-TABOR interaction along with School Finance Act strictures on district mill levies reduced the local share of financial responsibility, the state's share grew. Whereas local government tax collections once constituted 60 percent of the total K–12 budget, by 2010 that amount was below 40 percent. This situation created a growing financial load for the state, which—thanks to TABOR—was also under pressure because of the revenue limit. Of course, the 2008–2010 recession left the state with an enormous budgetary shortfall, but the long-term consequences of TABOR's revenue limitation remain.

The interactions of Gallagher, TABOR, and the School Finance Act are clearly complex and difficult to explain. But they are essentially this: as Gallagher pushed residential property assessment rates down, local government officials could compensate for potential revenue losses by increasing the millage rate. That is, they could do so until TABOR (1992) required popular votes on mill levy increases and the School Finance Act shortly thereafter required mill levy reductions whenever revenues exceeded the TABOR cap. Then, even if voters approved the expenditure of revenues in excess of the TABOR limit, the mill levy still declined. As a consequence, the property tax–based share of school funding shrunk and the state's share grew, placing growing pressure on the state budget (Center for Tax Policy 2005).

TABOR contains a number of additional provisions, including government authority to hold tax-related elections in odd- as well as even-numbered years, a requirement for reserves, and the ability of the state to declare as "enterprises" those departments whose budgetary reliance on state appropriations is 10 percent or less. Later in this chapter I discuss how these provisions have impacted the state. It will suffice to say at this point that together, Gallagher, TABOR, and—until 2009—the 6 percent annual appropriations increase limit transposed Colorado's system of representative government into something rather different. No longer do elected officials control state and local financing.

Two political maneuvers by the General Assembly that track back to TABOR have further complicated Colorado's fiscal situation and limited legislative influence on state and local finances and, thus, public policy. For several years after the 1992 adoption of TABOR, state revenues exceeded the TABOR limit, thereby requiring taxpayer refunds. Many legislators thought it made little sense to collect money and then give it back. So during the 1999, 2000, and 2001 sessions, the General Assembly enacted a series of tax cuts, most notably reductions in the state sales and income taxes. Of course, while the lawmakers had the authority to make cuts, TABOR barred them from reversing the reductions. When the 2001 recession hit, the state's fiscal problems were all the more severe given the tax cuts. Over the course of the next decade the tax cuts cost the state over $1 billion in revenue, a figure that grows with time.

On the heels of TABOR, the General Assembly also chose to ask voters to extend the "single-subject" rule that applies to legislative bills to future ballot measures as well. Lawmakers discovered after TABOR passed that it was a multifaceted and complicated measure containing "sleeper" provisions about which many—perhaps most—voters were unaware. To prevent this from happening again, a single-subject measure was referred to the voters in 1994 and easily passed. This single-subject measure has turned out to be a problem rather than a solution, however, because untangling the multiple constitutional provisions that lie at the core of the state's fiscal policy and fiscal problems can only be done one item at a time.

The limits embedded in these multiple statutory and constitutional measures have thus put the brakes on state and local governments in several ways. Revenues are limited, and, as a consequence, so is spending. The authority to manage the fiscal system, at both the local and state levels, has been largely stripped from elected officials and resides instead in "finance committees of millions."

Additional factors that have greatly affected Colorado's finances, ones unrelated to direct democracy, include the decades-long pattern of providing an assortment of tax credits and sales tax exemptions. As of 2011, these exemptions and credits totaled over 100 in number and deprived the state's General Fund of roughly $2 billion annually, with roughly half of that total related to food and prescription drugs (Colorado Legislative Council 2009, 2011).

Examples include sales tax exemptions for the sale of food purchased for home consumption, insulin, prescription drugs, straw for livestock bedding, farm auction closeout sales, low-emitting vehicles, bingo and raffle equipment, and many more. In addition to the host of sales tax exemptions, a continual flow of legislative enactments has provided tax credits and rebates. Various laws have provided credits for child care, plastic recycling, low-income housing, long-term care, alternative fuels, conservation easements, and a long list of others. In the aggregate these credits run into the hundreds of millions annually and into the billions through time. Each credit now has its own constituency, and reversing the process would be very difficult politically.

SPEND—PLACE THE OTHER FOOT ON THE GAS

While Gallagher, TABOR, and (until 2009) the 6 percent annual appropriations growth limit have kept a foot on the fiscal brakes, both political and legal factors drive the state in the opposite direction. State Medicaid spending is growing and is driven largely by federal policy and case load. The Corrections Department budget has grown as well, and for both legal and political reasons it is difficult to control. Existing sentencing policies and a general increase in crime have expanded the prison population (albeit with some reduction in 2010), and efforts to ease up on criminal law carry political risk. Further, any changes made now have a delayed impact on the prisoner population and corrections costs.

Beyond the continuing and inescapable budgetary pressures from Medicaid and the Corrections Department, in 2000 voters adopted a constitutional measure known as Amendment 23. This provision drives the cost of the K–12 school system, the single largest slice of the state budget. The amendment was placed on the 2000 ballot through the initiative process by a consortium of groups that included teachers, school administrators, school boards, parents, and other traditional supporters of elementary and secondary education. It passed by a 53–47 percent margin.

Amendment 23 fixes the required level of K–12 spending growth in the state constitution. Each year the General Assembly is required to set funding at the level of the prior year plus an increase for student population growth and, for the decade ending in 2010, another 1 percent designed to compensate for perceived funding shortages during the years and decades prior to 2000. (In the context of the 2010–2011 budget crunch, the legislature did reduce K–12 funding, in a controversial move.) The amendment contains several other provisions, such as the establishment of an "education fund" to be filled with a fraction of annual state income tax revenues (Colorado Legislative Council 2003).

The net result of the combination of Medicaid, the Corrections Department, and Amendment 23 has been to lock into the annual budget process political and legal requirements for spending that consume between 70 and 80 percent of available state General Fund revenues. Essentially, spending decisions with respect to most of the General Fund budget are beyond the legislature's control.

Although financially small by comparison to Amendment 23 or even Medicaid and the Corrections Department, another constitutional provision locks up most proceeds from state-sponsored gambling operations for a variety of parks, trails, and open-space programs and keeps the money completely away from the legislature. When state-sponsored gambling was initially authorized in 1980, revenues were dedicated to a conservation fund for use by cities and counties for outdoor and recreation projects, but the provision allowed some of the funds to be used for capital construction. In 1982 the legislature authorized a lottery system, and in 1988 it expanded that system to include electronic games (Lotto), directing some of the revenue to the payment of bonds for new prisons. Then in 1992 park, trail, and open-space advocates succeeded in passing a constitutional measure that effectively locked up much of the gambling money for their preferred programs. The revenues are distributed by a board, known as GO-CO (Great Outdoors Colorado), with the legislature completely out of the picture (see also chapter 10).

COPING—FISCAL CRASHES AND LEGISLATIVE PATCHES

Each of the measures described earlier, those that restrict revenues and spending and those that demand increases in spending, became public law within its own particular political and economic circumstances. The consequences of all or any of these measures were never assessed against the others. Collectively, however, they frame the fiscal policy of the state and its budget process.

The results of making policy in this fashion first became painfully clear in 2001, when Colorado and the nation entered a fairly deep economic recession, and again in 2009–2010 in the wake of the most serious economic downturn in half a century. The combination of Colorado's multiple and conflicting fiscal policy provisions and the economic downturn set in motion a long parade of actions designed to patch the system.

As the 2001 recession hit, General Fund revenues fell from $6.55 billion in 2000–2001 to $5.57 billion the following year, a decline of 15 percent. Much of the decline was in income tax revenue. General Fund revenues did not climb back above the 2000–2001 figure until seven years later, in 2007–2008, only to sink again in 2009–2010 (Colorado Legislative Council, quarterly revenue estimates).

This enormous loss of revenue had three important effects. First, as the revenue total declined, so did the level of allowable state revenue in subsequent years. Until the passage of Referendum C in 2005, TABOR pegged the amount of allowable revenue at the level of the prior year plus adjustments for inflation and population growth, as explained previously. Thus with an economic downturn, the amount the state could collect and spend was ratcheted down. Second, insofar as appropriations fell in tandem with revenue decreases, the total in allowable appropriations in the out-years fell as well. Third, with the state short of money, program areas that were either legally or politically unprotected took the brunt of the budgetary hits. With the K–12 schools and both Medicaid and the Corrections Department protected legally and politically, the cuts came in higher education, transportation, and human services.

REPAIR WORK—PATCHES AND EVASIONS

A parade of efforts began, each designed to provide a partial escape from the fiscal policy box Gallagher, TABOR, Amendment 23, the 6 percent limit, and other measures had created. Some were made or promoted by the General Assembly and some by various groups. Some were successful and some were not. When successful, they added further complications to an already muddled policy and budgeting process.

2002–2004—CASH FUND RAIDS, RECESSIONS, AND FEES

In the recessionary years 2002–2003 through 2003–2004, the legislature essentially raided scores of cash funds. This was done both because of a desire to minimize the damage to programs that severe budget cuts would create and to keep the appropriation level from falling (ratcheting down) and thus creating a reduced base for future years. Over seventy transfers were made from roughly fifty-three funds. They ranged from a tobacco litigation settlement cash fund to funds of unclaimed property and major medical insurance. Collectively, the transfers totaled around $1.5 billion. Unsurprisingly, the transfers drew criticism from groups that had stakes in the funds. Lawsuits challenging the actions followed as well, but the courts upheld the legislature's authority to move the money.

Even with the transfer of well over $1 billion into the General Fund, budget cuts ensued, described euphemistically as "expenditure reductions." For fiscal year 2002–2003 the reductions totaled $537 million, with $201 million more the following year. Since each reduction required a change in statute, sixty-nine bills were run in 2003 alone. To partially counter these reductions, a few bills were run to create "revenue enhancements." Collectively, they raised just $2.3 million. Examples include one allowing simulcasting of dog races; another set a tax amnesty period for scofflaws (Colorado Legislative Council undated).

In addition, during the 2002–2004 period, the legislature enacted thirty-seven measures authorizing increases in dozens of fees and created many more. New fees and fee increases, unlike new taxes, are not subject to the TABOR-required statewide popular vote. Collectively, these maneuvers raised $69 million, which cushioned the impact of the budget cuts and bolstered the appropriations total on which future allowable increases would be based. But even with all these efforts to shore up the General Fund, total allowable appropriations were lower in 2004–2005 than in 2002–2003.

2004—MONEY LAUNDRY

Under TABOR, college and university tuition was counted as "state revenue." In years when state tax revenues were sufficient to reach or exceed the TABOR limits, additional tuition receipts—whether from expanded enrollment or increased rates—were simply rolled into the pool of excess revenues that were then rebated to taxpayers as tax credits. In addition, extra tuition receipts had the effect of displacing General Fund tax revenues that could otherwise have been retained and spent on other state programs.

The lengthy and complicated TABOR measure contained a provision whereby the state could declare an agency to be an "enterprise" if less than 10 percent of its total revenues were derived from direct state appropriations. The first agency to be declared an "enterprise" was the Colorado Division of Wildlife, which is funded largely by hunting and fishing license fees. Prior to gaining enterprise status, the agency could not raise fees, since in good revenue years extra collections added to the state surplus. When designated an "enterprise," Fish and Game license income no longer counted as state General Fund revenue. This released the agency to hike its fees and made additional room for general tax revenues under TABOR's revenue cap.

It occurred to legislators that, with some ingenuity, this enterprise provision in TABOR could be employed as a loophole in higher education financing. Thus in 2004 a bill was passed creating what is now called the College Opportunity Fund, which basically functions as a money laundry. Rather than make appropriations directly to colleges and universities, the state sends its higher education allocation to a state agency—the Colorado Student Loan Program—and establishes a per-student dollar figure as a voucher. Students then select a school, the agency is notified of their choice, and the agency funnels the student vouchers to the school in the form of a "purchase" of a product. The vouchers are for resident undergraduates; for graduate education and other institutional costs, including to some extent undergraduate education, the state appropriates money as "fees for service."

This scheme artificially drives direct state appropriations to colleges and universities below 10 percent of their revenue total, thus qualifying them for "enterprise" status. This designation then frees schools to raise tuition and at the same time clears out room under the TABOR revenue cap for additional general tax revenues (Straayer 2004). While it works as intended during good revenue years, the extra room under the cap is of little consequence in economic downturns such as the one the state faced during 2008–2011.

2005—Referenda C and D

In spite of the fiscal adjustments made with cash fund transfers, initiation of more fees, and the creation of the higher education money laundry, the state found itself on the brink of a financial cliff in 2004 and 2005. With the economy recovering somewhat, there was promise of improved revenues, but since the base had declined during the recessionary downturn, the depressed levels of both allowable receipts and appropriations promised further deep—even draconian—reductions in funding for higher education, health care programs, and transportation. Perversely, the state would simultaneously be making major cuts and refunding hundreds of millions in tax revenue.

Several efforts during the 2004 legislative session to fabricate a ballot measure asking voters to release the TABOR cap failed. But in 2005, with the budget crisis ever more imminent, the Republican governor and several Republican legislators teamed up with the Democratic speaker of the house and his party to refer a measure to the voters asking them to approve a five-year "timeout" on the TABOR revenue limit. The referred measure also stipulated that henceforth, when state revenues fell, the highest prior revenue year would constitute the floor for future calculations of the cap, thus eliminating TABOR's ratchet effect. This ballot measure was known as Referendum C. A companion measure, Referendum D, asked that, above a certain level, new tax receipts be employed for highway projects.

Referendum C passed by a 52–48 percent margin, but D narrowly failed. It was hard-fought, with the Republican governor, Republican moderates, the business community, and most Democrats in support and the larger slice of the Republican Party—along with an assortment of general anti-tax/anti-government groups—in opposition.

The passage of Referendum C allowed the state to keep all of the money collected through existing tax law for a period of five years. No additional taxes were enacted, and the 6 percent per year appropriation increase limit remained in place. For three years after 2005, state revenues improved significantly. As a result, rather than imposing further budget reductions, the state was able to provide some new money for higher education and other state programs, and resources beyond the 6 percent General Fund increase were funneled into transportation and other capital expenditures.

But Referendum C expired in 2010 and the TABOR revenue lid returns, although with a very depressed economy its limitations had no immediate consequences. In the 2008 election, voters were given the option of altering the constitution to alleviate the contradiction between TABOR, which limits revenue, and Amendment 23, which drives spending, but they voted the measure down.

2007—Stop the Mill Levy Slide

The basic law that drives funding for the K–12 schools is called the School Finance Act. The act was originally passed in 1988 and was designed to equalize funding for schools districts across the state. It is passed in amended form each year. In 1994, two years following passage of TABOR, the act was changed to include a provision requiring school districts to reduce the mill levy so as to reduce property tax revenues when the existing levy generated more money than the district could keep under TABOR's cap. Other local governments could give the money back in a form of temporary mill levy reduction, but under the School Finance Act the schools had to lower the mill levy; once lowered, it stayed lowered per the Finance Act requirement.

Between the 1992 enactment of TABOR and 2007, 175 of the state's 178 school districts passed what are called "de-Brucing" measures that allow the district to keep and spend revenues in excess of the TABOR limit in a given year. Still, the mill levy had to be dropped to reduce the prospects of revenue excesses occurring again the following year. Thus in spite of local voter approval of erasing the TABOR revenue lid, the School Finance Act drove mill levy rates lower and lower. The lower they went—more so and more quickly in growing jurisdictions—the greater the state's share of total school funding costs became. In addition, the variance in district-to-district levies grew, with the richest districts enjoying the lowest mill levies.

Pressed to do so by newly elected Democratic governor Bill Ritter and in the context of state budgetary pressures, the legislature amended the School Finance Act in 2007 to freeze school district mill levy rates in the 175 districts that had voted to erase the TABOR revenue cap. This was fully in keeping with the TABOR provision for voter overrides of the revenue lid, and it did away with the statutory School Finance Act requirement to lower the mill levy, voter approval of "de-Brucing" notwithstanding.

The impetus for this action is clear. The state was operating in a fiscal vise composed of TABOR, Amendment 23, the 6 percent annual appropriation increase limit, and growing costs for the Corrections Department and Medicaid. Funding for transportation, higher education, and other programs was in short supply. The local school district mill levy freeze was designed to stop the decline in the local share of school costs and, in fact, would even increase that share as aggregate property values grew. As a consequence, the state's share of school funding would drop, and more money would be available for other state activities.

Colorado's anti-tax and anti-government elements attacked the mill levy freeze with a vengeance, just as for years they have promoted revenue and spending limits and fought efforts to find revenue to support most public programs. A lawsuit was filed claiming that the mill levy freeze constituted a tax increase and should thus have been put on the ballot for a statewide vote. In 2008 a Denver district court agreed with the plaintiffs and found the law to be unconstitutional. This decision was appealed, and in 2009 the state supreme court validated the legislative action, saying that since voters approved the TABOR override, the change to the School Finance Act was constitutional. Democrats, including the governor, applauded the decision; Republicans decried the outcome as a policy decision by a partisan Democratic court (*Mesa County Board of County Commissioners v. State of Colorado* 2009).

As it turned out, the 2008–2010 recession pushed local property values down, thus depressing local school district tax revenues. This, in turn, has left it to the state to backfill the gap, albeit a gap that would have been larger without the freeze.

THAT'S NOT ALL, FOLKS

The 2002–2004 draining of cash funds, the passage of Referendum C, the higher education money laundry, and legislation to stop the mill levy decline were perhaps the most significant efforts to cope with the state's fiscal policy puzzle. But they were by no means the only efforts that sought to impact revenues or expenditures legislated, initiated, or referred to voters by the General Assembly. Increasingly, ballot measures contain wording that exempts new revenues from TABOR's limit, restricts the legislature's authority to touch new funds, or both.

In 2003 the legislature referred to the voters a proposal to change the Gallagher Amendment to freeze the residential assessment rate at 8 percent. It lost by a large margin. That same year an initiated measure sought to raise money through expanded gambling to provide funds for tourism promotion; it, too, lost. A 2005 initiated proposal to raise tobacco taxes with revenues devoted to health care and tobacco-use cessation made it to the statewide ballot, where it passed.

The 2008 state ballot contained eighteen measures, several of which were intended to impact fiscal policy. Two of them were related to the use of oil and gas revenues, one of which would have provided funds for higher education scholarships and one of which would have diverted money to improvements on Interstate 70; both were defeated. One measure that carried the illusion of "free" money for education by expanding gambling and dedicating the resultant tax revenues to community colleges passed.

In 2008–2011 another deep recession hit Colorado, aggravating existing fiscal problems and again sending the legislature scrambling for ways to cope. During its 2009 session, the legislature enacted several bills designed to patch the fiscal system. One imposed hundreds of millions of dollars in new fees on hospitals to leverage federal Medicaid money and expand health care coverage. Another raised automobile registration and rental car fees, with the hundreds of millions in resulting revenues earmarked for highways. Still another did away with the Arveschoug-Bird 6 percent limit on annual General Fund appropriation increases, although it did nothing to erase the TABOR revenue/spending cap. The 2010 General Assembly passed a series of controversial measures to roll back some existing tax breaks.

Looking back through time, one finds more cases of fiscal tinkering, with some efforts intended to shrink revenue and some designed to raise revenue. In 1978, 1988, 1990, and 2000, various initiated measures proposed to limit revenues, spending, or both in much the same way as TABOR. They all failed. Initiated measures in 1992, 1993, 1994, 2000, and 2001 proposed some form of new taxes for causes ranging from health and smoking cessation to the K–12 schools, science and math grants, tourism promotion, and the study of a fixed-guideway transportation system running from Denver's International Airport to the mountain ski areas. These, too, failed.

Still other unsuccessful proposals Colorado voters faced included ones to create a K–12 school voucher system (1998), to withdraw tax-exempt status for certain religious properties (1996), to allow the state to incur a multiyear debt to pay for non-state prisons (1995), to allow the Great Outdoors Colorado program to borrow against anticipated revenues to buy open-space land (2001), and to permit video lottery games at horse and dog racing tracks (2003).

Among the victories was a 1992 vote that authorized "T-Rex," which permitted borrowing against anticipated federal gas tax receipts for a major Denver interstate expansion project. Successful measures in 1980 and 1988 had authorized state-sponsored lottery games, followed by an expansion of the games to produce revenue to build more prisons; a 2000 vote secured all future funds for outdoor programs. Other initiatives created a property tax break for seniors (2000), expanded that break for veterans and the disabled (2006), and authorized participation in a multi-state lottery (2001). Each of these measures directed revenues to specific purposes, leaving the legislature with no discretion as to the use of the funds. In the General Assembly the Republican-controlled house continued efforts to reinstate several repealed tax exemptions.

If Colorado voters have not had enough chances to function as a "finance committee of millions" over the past several decades, they will have plenty more opportunities to do so in the future. The 2010 statewide ballot, for example, contained three initiated measures, each designed to further constrict revenues and legislative fiscal flexibility.

WHAT HAVE WE CREATED?

The decades-long parade of enactments, many of the most significant of which came by way of citizen initiatives, has left the state without an institutional apparatus capable of setting anything like an integrated and forward-looking policy direction. The measures were designed to promote policies, but they have had long-lasting impacts on the institutions as well. Gallagher targeted property tax reform, Amendment 23 was meant to help the K–12 schools, TABOR and the 6 percent limit were designed to control government growth, and so forth. But these enactments and others have altered the way policy is made, as well as impacting policy itself.

Thus both the institutional and policy consequences of the various enactments have been significant. On the institutional side, the state legislature and local governing boards have been stripped of much of their fiscal authority. Elected officials can reduce or eliminate taxes but not raise them. At the state level, the legislature's appropriations discretion has been severely constricted. Spending priorities are largely pre-set by constitutional provisions, federal requirements, Corrections Department policy, and the specific-use dedication of gambling taxes and are driven in part by the ebb and flow of the economy and tax revenue. Then, in good revenue years, the TABOR limit must be addressed. The complex maze of policies pushes in opposite directions, both limiting resources and requiring expenditures and leaving the state without a predictable revenue flow and endlessly vulnerable to further cuts or revenue confiscation by measures pushed by political hobbyists or special interests. To a significant extent, representative government is a thing of the past.

The policy consequences are evident in the erosion of state funding in several areas, most notably higher education and transportation. With budgetary allocations to the K–12 schools, Medicaid, and the Corrections Department substantially beyond the control of the legislature and the governor, higher education and transportation remain major areas of "discretionary" spending. The proportion of the state General Fund budget dedicated to higher education has gone from over 17 percent in 1992 to less than 9 percent in 2010–2011; during budget preparation for the 2011–2012 cycle there was talk of eliminating public support for colleges and universities altogether. Indeed, state appropriations for higher education continue to shrink.

In combination with the ebb and flow of the national economy, the state's fiscal policy has produced a volatile revenue flow. During the past decade, revenue gains and losses compared with the prior year have ranged from an almost 15 percent drop in 2001–2002 to a 13 percent gain in 2005–2006 and then a 10.5 percent drop in 2008–2009. Fiscal year 2011–2012 is projected to show a gain of 9.7 percent over 2010–2011, but with the wild shifts of the past, one is tempted to view projections as little better than guesses (see Center for Colorado's Economic Future 2009; Colorado Legislative Council, quarterly revenue estimates for various years).

Colorado ranks forty-eighth in the nation in state support for higher education. In real dollars, per-pupil support is 23 percent less than it was ten years ago, and tuition in state-supported colleges and universities is 29 percent higher than the national average. Support per student is 26 percent of the Wyoming amount and less than half that of New Mexico, Utah, Arizona, Alabama, Arkansas, and Louisiana. It is just 53 percent of the figure in Mississippi and 54 percent of the national average. In personal income, Colorado ranks fifteenth in the nation and is in the bottom third in combined state-local tax burden. Comparatively, it ranks high in personal income and low in state taxes. Colorado enjoys one of the best-educated citizenries in the nation because of the importation of citizens who were educated elsewhere (Metro Denver Economic Development Corporation 2009).

State roads and bridges have also suffered. A recent report by the Colorado chapter of the American Society of Civil Engineers gave the state a C+ for its infrastructure, noting that "population growth and deferred maintenance are combining to stress Colorado's highways [and] bridges" (quoted in Olinger 2009a). The April 20, 2009, edition of *The Denver Post* reported that "about half of Colorado's highway miles are poor, but CDOT [the Colorado Department of Transportation] is billions short for repairs" (Olinger 2009b).

One more policy consequence has been the proliferation of fees, which, unlike taxes, remain under the control of the legislature and do not require voter approval. As noted earlier, an explosion of new fees and fee increases occurred following the 2001 recession, and that pattern has not abated, with forty-one new fee bills enacted in the 2008 session and even more in 2009. The resultant revenues only marginally compensate for the general tax revenue losses, but they further complicate the fiscal system and do nothing to restore legislative fiscal flexibility. They have, however, often further solidified voter irritation with the government and resistance to the elimination of current constitutional revenue restrictions.

Both public and private sector leaders have routinely expressed deep concern about the predicament. Legislators in both parties have called for more support for higher education, transportation, and health care. So have business sector leaders, who see these areas as essential to maintain a favorable business climate and a productive workforce. But with revenues legally limited and most spending legally mandated, the state government lacks the capacity to do much of what is broadly viewed as important, even essential.

CAN HUMPTY-DUMPTY BE FIXED?

There are several legal paths out of the current "one foot on the gas, one foot on the brake" conundrum, but none has been politically viable. One is to do what many local governments have done, and that is to ask voters to "de-Bruce." TABOR allows voter overrides of revenue limits; and many cities, counties, and school districts have received voter permission to spend excess TABOR revenues for specific projects—street repairs, for example. But except for the 2005 passage of the Referendum C five-year suspension of the state revenue limit, there have been no successful efforts to eliminate the state-level revenue limitation.

A second path is to amend the constitution to eliminate, or at least moderate, conflicts among the provisions that simultaneously limit revenues and demand spending. Amendment 59, on the 2008 ballot, pushed in that direction; it sought to largely eliminate the conflict between TABOR's cap and the spending requirements of Amendment 23. But voters rejected the proposal. As noted earlier, there have been less sweeping efforts to keep some excess TABOR revenue for specific purposes—math and science projects (2000) and highways and higher education facility maintenance (1998), for example—but voters rejected these as well.

A third way out of the fiscal box would be to convene a constitutional convention and rewrite fiscal policy from scratch. This idea has been discussed from time to time but has yet to gain traction. Many groups fear that it is impossible to predict the result. Some interests worry that provisions that benefit them now might disappear. Others worry about what might be injected into a new document. This uncertainty, plus a constitutional procedural calendar that would push the conclusion of a convention out several years, has precluded such an effort.

There may be ways to soften the fiscal problem short of a complete overhaul of fiscal policy or without any constitutional tinkering. As noted earlier, the General Assembly has enacted dozens of sales tax exemptions and tax credits. Sales tax exemptions have been statutorily granted to everything from cigarettes to Internet access, aircraft component parts, child care, and bull semen. Their current aggregate value is in the range of $1.6 billion annually. The 2009 state supreme court decision upholding the mill levy freeze contains language that leads some to believe the state could take back these sales tax exemptions and tax credits to generate more revenue and could do so without a vote of the people— as long as overall state revenues do not exceed the TABOR lid of prior year plus inflation plus population growth (*Mesa County Board of County Commissioners v. State of Colorado* 2009).

The idea of recouping billions of dollars per year and, in the process, irritating scores of groups that now benefit from the tax breaks may not be in the cards politically. Even if a few of the exemptions and credits were withdrawn by statute, as happened in 2010, the increased tax revenue remains at a level that constitutes another patch rather than a fulsome fix of fiscal policy.

NEXT-GENERATION SUCCESS STORY—WILL THERE BE ONE?

Here is a sampling of *Denver Post* headlines in 2009: "Fix our budget mess" (attorney general editorial, March 19), "Higher ed leader sees disaster ahead" (August 24), "State doors barred as furloughs begin" (October 9), "Building-repair budget falls apart" (October 15), "Billions short on state goals" (October 16), "Voters aren't in mood for taxes" (editorial, November 6), "Like a Gordian knot, state budget fit to be tied" (November 11), "State nears cliff on budget" (November 22), "State deficit even deeper" (December 19), and "Colorado's growing pains only going to get worse" (December 31).

Two extensive studies, one conducted by the University of Denver and the other by the Denver Metro Chamber of Commerce Economic Development Corporation, described the impact of the state's dysfunctional fiscal policy—which is aggravated by term limits—and called for reform (Colorado Economic Futures Panel 2007; Metro Denver Economic Development Corporation 2005). Denver Metro Chamber of Commerce executive vice president Tom Clark told the summer 2009 legislative fiscal stability commission that higher education and transportation are top priorities for businesses when they consider coming to, or staying in, Colorado (author present).

One might surmise that with broad agreement on the need for better fiscal treatment of higher education, transportation, and health programs, there would be a sufficiently large and robust political force to drive the state to undertake a fiscal policy repair job. But two interrelated political factors have thus far proven to be insurmountable barriers to reform.

The first is the success and continuing role of the anti-tax, anti-government forces in the state. The image of TABOR author Douglas Bruce was significantly tarnished by his very short (one year) and undignified (behavior that drew institutional censure) stint in the Colorado House of Representatives, but TABOR itself has come to be viewed fairly broadly as sacrosanct. TABOR places the question of taxes in the hands of voters, and arguments that compromise citizen control are a very difficult sell. When some political voices point to TABOR as a problem, others quickly take the opposite position and chastise TABOR critics for not trusting voters and for threatening to deprive them of future tax refunds. In his 2009 State of the State Address, for example, Governor Bill Ritter mentioned a need to reform TABOR. The Republican house minority leader quickly cited that remark as a particularly disappointing part of the speech.

The second, and related, political factor that works against fiscal reform is the mix of ideology and political ambition within the Republican Party and the impact this has in creating caution on the Democratic side. The ideological part is in keeping with the party's general antipathy toward large government.

This general ideology-based support for revenue and spending limits is reinforced by both party and individual ambition. Republicans lost majorities in both state legislative chambers in 2004 for the first time in over forty years, and their numerical deficit grew in 2006. In 2006 the governorship shifted back to the Democratic side as well. Republicans made a net gain of 1 seat in the 100-member institution in 2008. A major Republican goal in 2010 was to capture a majority in at least one legislative chamber or to take back the governorship so the party would have bargaining power in the 2011 redistricting process. The party thus never missed a chance to blast the Democrats, most notably for any initiative or even any discussion of loosening revenue and spending limits. (Republicans did capture a 1-vote majority in the house in 2010.) Furthermore, personal ambition and political success in the Republican Party hinge in part on ensuring that the most active and most conservative elements in the party are placated. Any hint of a willingness to reform fiscal policy and possibly threaten TABOR can be political suicide.

What about the Democrats? With precious few Republicans to work with in reforming fiscal policy, Democrats have been largely on their own. They have therefore exposed themselves to the "big government" critique, and a Republican anti-tax and attack strategy has intimidated them to some extent. Just as the Republicans want their legislative majority back, the Democrats have been intent on holding their power, which has meant avoiding a frontal attack on TABOR. There was broad Democratic support for the 2009 elimination of the 6 percent annual General Fund increase limitation, but it was accompanied by private worries about the 2010 electoral consequences. Further, even with impending fiscal troubles having been in plain sight for over a decade and in the context of draconian 2009 and 2010 budget cuts, few legislative- or executive-branch Democrats pressed for fundamental fiscal policy change; they, like the Republicans, saw the 2010 election on the horizon.

Given the narrow victory for Referendum C in 2005, the defeat of several money measures in 2008, and continued support for revenue and spending limits by the vast majority of Republican leaders, any reform may require a fiscal disaster of major proportions to focus public attention on the connection between the current muddled fiscal policy and the difficulties in funding colleges and universities, transportation, and health care. In the meantime, efforts remain patchwork as the governor and some legislators push for new fees, seek more federal money, and even talk about selling some of the state's physical property. In the wake of the 2009 state supreme court Mesa County decision, there have been several repeals of sales tax exemptions and tax credits.

Republicans continue to praise revenue and spending limits and, along with many Democrats, stick to fairly conservative mini-fixes, fearful of potential negative political consequences administered by the party base. Predictably, nearly every move the Democrats have made in an effort to patch the system has brought sharp Republican criticism despite the institution of new fees by the Republican legislature in 2001–2002. Former senate minority leader Josh Penry may have been correct when he described the band-aid approach to budgeting as eviscerating TABOR "on the installment plan" (quoted in Hoover 2009). Colorado's fiscal train wreck has become the focal point for increasingly partisan warfare.

Ironically, past efforts to cope with budgetary crises may have contributed to the difficulty of enacting any comprehensive fiscal fix. During the 2000–2001 economic downturn, the legislative raid of cash funds softened the impact and led many voters to believe there were indeed rabbits in the budgetary hat. The 2005 passage of Referendum C temporarily steered the state away from the edge of a fiscal cliff and again allowed voters to breathe a sigh of relief. If the national fiscal stimulus package eases the negative consequences of the 2008–2011 downturn, Colorado may yet again push meaningful fiscal policy reform down the road. To repeat from the chapter's opening paragraph, this is a story without an end.

REFERENCES

The Bell Policy Center and others. 2011. *The Road to 2011.* Available at http://www.bell-policy.org/content/road-2011. Accessed April 30, 2011.

Center for Colorado's Economic Future. 2009. "Colorado's State Budget Tsunami." University of Denver *Issue Brief* (July).

———. 2011. "Summary of Preliminary Report, General Fund Revenues and Expenditures: A Structural Imbalance."

Center for Tax Policy. 2005. "Implications of the Budget Ratchet for Colorado's Budget, FY 2001–02 through FY 2009–10." October. Available at http://centerfortaxpolicy.org/reports/Ratchet_study.pdf. Accessed April 30, 2011.

Colorado Constitution. Article V, Section 1 (initiative).

———, Article X, Section 3. Uniform taxation (Gallagher Amendment).

———, Section 17. Education—funding (Amendment 23).

———, Section 20. The Taxpayers Bill of Rights.

Colorado Economic Futures Panel. 2007. *Final Report: Principles for Progress: Shaping the Economic Future of Colorado.* Denver: University of Denver. Available at http://www.du.edu/economicpanel/report/pdf/final-highres.pdf. Acessed April 30, 2011.

Colorado Legislative Council. 2003. *Publication No. 518: House Joint Resolution 03–1033 Study.* September. Denver: Colorado General Assembly.

————. 2009. *State Sales and Use Tax Exemptions*. July. Denver: Colorado General Assembly.

————. 2011. *State Income Tax Credits and Rebates*. January. Denver: Colorado General Assembly.

————. Various years. Quarterly revenue estimates. Denver: Colorado General Assembly.

————. Various years. *State Ballot Information Booklet*. Denver: Colorado General Assembly.

————. Undated. *Tax and Finance*. Denver: Colorado General Assembly.

Hoover, Tim. 2009. "Justices: Measure Didn't Violate TABOR." *The Denver Post*, March 17. Available at dphttp://www.denverpost.com/news/ci_12928774. Accessed April 30, 2011.

Klyza, Christopher McGory, and David Sousa. 2008. *American Environmental Policy 1990–2006: Beyond Gridlock*. Cambridge: MIT Press.

Mesa County Board of County Commissioners v. State of Colorado. 2009. Supreme Court Case 2008 SA 216.

Metro Denver Economic Development Corporation. 2005; updated annually. *Toward a More Competitive Colorado*. Denver: Metro Denver Economic Development Corporation.

Olinger, David. 2009a. "Colo. Infrastructure Gets C+." *The Denver Post*, January 7. Available at http:www.denverpost.com/news/ci_11389115. Accessed April 30, 2011.

————. 2009b. "Well-Traveled Roads, Bridges in a Fix." *The Denver Post*, March 20. Available at http://denverpost.com/news/ci_11954452. Accessed April 30, 2011.

Patton, Zach. 2008. "Comity Captain." *Governing* (November). Available at http://www.governing.com/poy/Andrew-Romanoff.html. Accessed April 30, 2011.

Straayer, John. 2004. "Colorado's Higher Education Vouchers: A New Trend or Budgetary Desperation?" *Spectrum: Journal of State Government* 77(4): 34–37.

Suthers, John. 2009. "Fix Our Budget Mess." *The Denver Post* guest commentary, March 19. Available at http://denverpost.com/opinion/ci_11945111. Accessed April 30, 2011.

Scores of reports from media sources, *The Rocky Mountain News, The Denver Post, The Colorado Statesman,* and others gathered over three decades; direct observation of the Colorado General Assembly over the same time period; and continual examination of annual state budgets and appropriations reports.

Chapter Ten

Financial Architecture of Post-Republican Colorado

Scott Moore

The most recent comprehensive review of Colorado's public finances found that "approximately 80 percent of the State's total revenues were earmarked" (Colorado Office of the Governor 1959: 131). Specifically, 57 percent of the state's revenues were earmarked by the state constitution, while another 23 percent were earmarked by statute (ibid.). The practice of earmarking fixes expenditure programs in perpetuity and privileges some state functions over others. Programs supported by earmarks are not subject to the same annual consideration and competition for funds that define legislative budget processes. Agencies and beneficiary groups develop proprietary interests in earmarking, and these programs are slow to adapt to efficiencies or changed conditions, if they ever do. Moreover, one of the effects of earmarks is to stimulate the development of even more earmarks. As a result, various organized interests have developed sophisticated political campaigns to guarantee themselves a fixed piece of the revenue pie, including increased use of the ballot initiative process.

This chapter assesses the implications of funding earmarks and their impacts on the structure of Colorado's state government.

Several institutional developments involving earmarking will be examined, including the development of the State Highway Department and its gasoline tax earmarks as well as conservationists' efforts to create a state lottery, earmarking the proceeds for conservation purposes. Both the gasoline tax and the state lottery developed as a result of a tense dialogue between the state legislature and organized interests that culminated in the use of the ballot initiative. Following this, the chapter examines the proliferation of constitutional earmarking in recent years in the context of financial restrictions on state taxes and expenditures that resulted from the Taxpayer's Bill of Rights (TABOR), as advocates for program spending have increasingly sought constitutional earmarks and other devices to defend and expand public expenditures for state programs. Across these historical and contemporary domains we see a tendency toward ever more constitutional and statutory earmarking, which the implementation of TABOR has intensified. Finally, I argue that reforming TABOR has been, and will likely continue to be, done by a succession of both statutory and constitutional earmarking events, which will not undo TABOR but rather will redo many of its restrictions over time.

DEMANDS OF REPRESENTATIVE DEMOCRACY

The idea of automatic allocations dominating state government expenditures is a significant departure from the ideals of republican democracy. According to Alan Rosenthal, legislative judgment is superior to executive decision-making and direct ballot democracy: "In republican theory, deliberation is crucial to the governmental process. The framers of the constitution intended to establish a legislative body that would restrain public demands and through deliberative processes arrive at reasoned settlements" (1998: 40).

Echoing Madison's *Federalist 51*, Rosenthal adds that "legislatures can 'refine and enlarge' the public views by passing them through the medium of a chosen body of citizens" and can serve as a bulwark against destructive majorities (ibid.). Legislatures can assemble public sentiments across the broad spectrum of opinion, reason contentious issues to a common solution, and legislate with a cautious appreciation of long-term consequences, risks, and costs. A deliberative process also leaves open the possibility of adjustment and refinement in light of the results of legislation. Furthermore, representatives' visibility and stature hold them accountable for their decisions.

Earmarking revenues, however, privileges some governmental functions and shields their expenditures from the deliberative process altogether. The arm's-length treatment of administrative agencies also isolates chunks of public authority from all but intermittent deliberation (Lowi 1979). These developments threaten to undermine the legislative process and performance, as articulated by Madison. Although TABOR is perhaps the most consequential factor in the process of removing government functions and expenditure choices in Colorado, there is a long history of prior examples, including highway funding, discussed in the next section.

EARMARKING FUNDS FOR STATE HIGHWAYS

Well into the second decade of the twentieth century, roads were primarily the responsibility of Colorado's counties. State law passed in 1885 provided that each county commission appoint and compensate a road overseer to organize crews to build and maintain roads. The state authorized counties to impose extra levies for road building and permitted citizens to contribute labor in lieu of road tax payments. County road poll taxes were also employed at the option of the counties. After 1905, the political efforts of state road advocates focused on creating a Highway Commission that would plan and propose construction of a state network of highways. A period characterized by experimentation and multiple funding arrangements—with federal grants and a ballot initiative serving as catalysts for administrative innovation—followed. By the end of the 1920s, Colorado had created a Highway Commission that had extraordinary financial and operational independence from the rest of the state government.

Legislative bills to create a Highway Commission foundered until 1909, when the Colorado Auto Club and the Good Roads Association were incorporated into the Rocky Mountain Highway Association. Their luminary founders signified involvement by important Denver commercial and banking interests (Stone 1918: 579–580). The 1909 bill created a three-person commission and provided for a secretary-engineer. With an initial $56,000 appropriation, commissioners designated routes of state concern and set standards for constructing and improving them.

The bulk of this first appropriation ($46,500) was set aside for the counties, a strong harbinger of a pattern to come. The counties remained the main axis of road building, and legislation required that they match state funds and assume responsibility for the construction of roads. Every state dollar was to be matched by two county dollars. Many counties did not participate because they lacked such funds (Hafen 1931; Wiley 1976). In addition, the financial basis of the state government discouraged a robust effort. Notably, the fund structure and appropriations patterns were heavily fragmented into separate funds to be drawn upon by highly specific appropriations. For example, the General Fund was the largest single fund, but it was fed exclusively by the state property tax mill levy collected by the counties. The state also had an insurance tax for the Insurance Fund, and proceeds from the sale, lease, and rent of lands granted by Congress's 1875 Enabling Act filled separate School Land Funds. The Colorado

Revised Statutes (1908) record several funds created by the state legislature, some of which originated in the territorial period, with each fund only supporting specific programs. They included the Game Fund, the Brand Inspection Fund, the University Fund, the Bounty Fund, and the Military Poll Tax Fund, to name a few. The existence of these separate funds limited competition for their use and assured transparency for a legislature unwilling to surrender control of the state's limited revenues.

Legislative appropriation from state funds was also complex. The legislature produced three kinds of appropriations bills, ranging from the general and inclusive to the highly specific (e.g., a specific county road or a specific building for a state institution). The General Assembly made road appropriations one road at a time, with each bill designating the county in which each road was situated. For example, Colorado's 1907 Session Laws record passage of seventeen separate appropriations laws for each of seventeen wagon roads. Relatively nonrestricted funds, such as the Internal Improvement Fund, were objects of fierce competition and supported several types of improvements (e.g., reservoirs and canals), of which roads were only a part. Highway supporters contested for these funds, sometimes successfully and other times not.

Legislation enacted in 1913 increased the earmarked road funds and insulated decisions about their uses in new ways. The Highway Commission was reorganized, a State Road Fund was created, and money could be drawn from the fund as needed, without specific authorization from the General Assembly. Internal Improvement monies were transferred to the State Road Fund; half the proceeds from vehicle registration fees fed the State Road Fund, with the other half distributed to the counties. Still, these funds were insufficient to support a robust road-building effort.

Institutional customs and interests also vexed a system whose designers urged the adoption of a 4,380-mile state road network, to be built over a twenty-year period (Merchant 1955b). From a rational engineering perspective, the county-centered system of management, punctuated by politically driven allocations of state road funds, produced eccentric plans paired with irregular execution (Wiley 1976). When it came to highway finance, then, state legislators were unreliable partners, as allocations from the Internal Improvement Fund were bound up in political trading (Merchant 1955a).

A long-term highway-building project was secured by the passage of an earmarked state gasoline tax in 1919. This tax carried a series of fortuitous implications. First, it did not upset the state government's overall tax structure. Claimants to the state property mill levy and the Internal Improvement Fund would not be slighted by a self-funded roads program. Second, the initial tax rates were low enough to elide opposition. In any case, the gas tax was paid in small driblets, not as a lump sum. Advances in refining caused average gas prices to drop from twenty-nine cents to seventeen cents per gallon during the 1920s. As a result, states raised gas tax rates without incident. During this time, Colorado counties secured a 50 percent share of gasoline revenues. In Colorado and the other states that had adopted a similar tax, rifts within the highway coalition were commonly expressed as negotiations over the distribution of gas revenues, not over the tax itself. Rural interests, which wanted farm-to-market roads, feared they would be left out by allocations that rewarded denser urban counties (Burnham 1961). With "unit" or county-based legislative districts, Colorado's rural counties enjoyed particularly strong political leverage.

If the highway movement had any detractors, their objections would have stemmed from jealousy. In 1926, highway advocates feared a legislative raid on "their" gasoline and vehicle fee revenues and sought to seal them off from legislative diversion through the ballot initiative process. The measure failed at the polls by a margin of two to one (Elofson 2007). But after the General Assembly diverted a total of $4.3 million in 1933 and 1934 to fund relief and public pensions, it referred a successful constitutional measure in 1934 to prohibit itself from diverting gas tax revenues again.

Over the course of this formative period, 1913–1935, the state Highway Department had evolved into a "political nexus," linking successive state engineers, local governments, contractors, automobile enthusiasts, and commercial truckers into a coalition that supported highway construction and improvement (Dunn 1978). The commission had only two administrative heads between 1913 and 1930, each serving over eight years. This leadership durability helped sustain trust and cooperation within the highway community that were vital to its internal consensus and its insularity from "outside" influence.

Regardless of the rigor of the engineering knowledge brought to bear on the original state highway system, it would be a mistake to paint the governing of highway funds and highway planning as apolitical. An expanding pie of revenues gathered by an unobtrusive, modest tax provided direct material benefits to contractors, shippers, and city builders and helped off-load some of the costs of state roads that traversed counties.

The arrangement fits the pattern James Wilson (1980) has identified as clientele politics, wherein the bulk of decision-making is intramural. A limited range of officials and private claimants cooperated in a political dance of mutual accommodation. Oversight and gentle persuasion from the legislature advanced legislator-specific interests in roads without creating controversy or requiring that legislators take responsibility. External perturbations, in the form of assertive governors who did not favor the status quo arrangements of these "independent operators," did not occur until the late 1930s and 1940s (City Club of Denver 1940; Kobs 1972).

In short, there is perhaps no better example of a Colorado program with exclusive and robust funding and the support of a diverse array of supporters with so strong a proprietary interest in sustaining it as the formative period of Colorado's highway program. Constitutional earmarks and strategic prodding by highway supporters through the initiative process were decisive in the development of this successful agency.

It is noteworthy that highways' privileged financial position endured far beyond this formative period of development. Indeed, highway funding has acquired newer earmarks beyond the constitution's gasoline tax earmark. For example, diversions of sales and use tax revenues to the Highway Users Tax Fund (HUTF) were engineered by the 1979 Noble Bill. Named after its western slope author, Senator Dan Noble, the bill transferred $323 million to the HUTF from sales taxes raised from the sale of vehicles, tires, parts, and accessories through 1986–1987. A "phase-out" of the Noble Bill raised another $65 million through June 1991. For fiscal years 1995–1996 and 1996–1997, the General Assembly diverted another $234 million from general revenues for highway construction (Colorado Legislative Council 1996). In another remarkable legislative feat, with Senate Bill (SB) 97–1, the General Assembly diverted nearly $1.4 billion in sales tax revenues between 1997 and 2009—an arrangement superceded in part by a 2009 vehicle registration fee bill (SB09–108) that provided more stable revenues at the $200 million–per-year level.

PRESERVATIONISTS SPIN THE WHEEL OF FORTUNE

Just as the "road lobby" managed to construct a semi-independent slice of government, largely walled off from legislative control and complete with its own funding stream, so did the "outdoor lobby" a half century later. Today this edifice is known as GO-CO, or Great Outdoors Colorado.

The origins of GO-CO reach back to the 1970s. Between 1960 and 1980 Colorado's population grew by nearly 55 percent. Farms and ranches, historic structures, and place-defining landscapes were routinely converted to residential and commercial uses. State and local governments lacked sufficient park and recreation facilities, and existing parks were suffering from overuse. The tourism industry was said to be at risk as distinctive landscapes were overlaid and interspersed with development.

Following a protracted legislative lobbying and public consultation effort, preservationists believed they had found a solution with the 1980 passage of Amendment 2, a constitutional referendum authorizing the creation of a state-supervised lottery. In 1980 the word "lottery" was inextricably paired with parks, preservation, and open space in the public mind because preservationists had campaigned for passage of the lottery on that basis. Part of the advocates' case for using the lottery as a source of funding was that it would not crowd out expenditures for other public programs, such as schools, and other operational costs of government that were supported by general taxes.

Experiences in other states led proponents to expect that a lottery could (after prizes and administration) yield between $8 million and $27 million per year, barely a blip in the state's $2.5 billion budget in 1980–1981 (Colorado Legislative Council 1980). Still, in relative terms, $8 million was a lot of new money for parks. The same year's appropriation for the Parks Division was just over $4.9 million, and the entire Department of Natural Resources appropriation was $39.3 million (Colorado Joint Budget Committee 1981).

In 1982 the General Assembly enacted implementing legislation (SB 82–119) to create a Lottery Division and establish a statutory formula for distributing proceeds. Parks and conservation advocates were disappointed. The law allocated 50 percent of lottery proceeds for state capital construction projects while limiting parks to 10 percent and the state Conservation Trust Fund to 40 percent of the proceeds. The following year the legislature further hobbled Amendment 2 by diverting (with HB 83–1320) lottery funds dedicated to capital construction to general budgetary ("deficit reduction") purposes. Another bill (SB 83–401) authorized the use of lottery funds for the Division of Parks' general operating expenditures.

Advocates of the original Amendment 2 may well have marveled at the meager results from the constitutional amendment they had promoted in 1980. Although the measure left substantial discretion to the General Assembly, parks and open space were getting lost in the service of capital construction and deficit reduction. By mid-1986 the lottery was producing revenues of $29 million per year, but capital construction was getting nearly half of that amount while parks' spending was supporting operations, not the creation of new parks. Further, the legislature retained control over whether to renew the lottery and other state-sponsored games of chance. As a result, in 1988 the General Assembly created "Lotto" under the authority of Amendment 2, using the proceeds for capital construction, mostly within the prison system. Forty percent of the lottery proceeds were dedicated to the Conservation Trust Fund, but the distribution of funds to local governments lacked oversight with respect to actual use for preservation.

Preservationists believed they had been "had." The General Assembly continued to shrink the state's income tax base, a task begun in earnest with the 1977 indexation of the tax code's eleven brackets—which cost the treasury $405 million over the first five years. The General Assembly also passed a succession of bountiful income tax credits in 1979, 1980, and 1981, worth a combined $232 million (Colorado Legislative Council 1984). Even though the state's budget needed no further pressures or complications, in 1985 the General Assembly passed stiffer criminal penalties (SB 85–1320), setting off a costly campaign of prison construction (Colorado Legislative Council 2001a). It appeared that "deficit reduction" was a fig leaf for legislative preference, not an imperative demanded by the elusive machinations of the economy.

It is not as if legislative budgeters were ogres seeking to usurp public intent. The diversion of lottery funds was (literally) permitted by the language of the lottery amendment, and the stated conservation priority was also clear. The legislature's institutional complexity and the specialization of its parts explain why a single legislature can pursue multiple independent agendas to cut taxes, increase prison spending, and divert funds. Sympathetic leadership might have merged the divergent legislative streams into a consistent whole, but regardless, the Joint Budget Committee was performing its sometimes dismal constitutional obligation to ensure that expenditures do not exceed revenues. Within the reactive mind-set of budget balancing, lottery funds seemed like "a lot" for parks and conservation. That thinking made it much easier for the Joint Budget Committee to divert funds to spare colleges and schools from deeper immediate cuts.

Meanwhile, a new consensus was evolving within the preservationist community. During the 1980s the public discussion concerning the goals and tools of public conservation policy had matured significantly. Preservation interests morphed from parks acquisition to open space—a more ambitious, subtle, and inclusive concept. In the late 1980s Governor Roy Romer empanelled a Citizens Committee that reported enthusiastic support for a broad range of conservation tools and uses, including trails and river greenways, recreational reservoirs and river uses, state parks, natural resource interpretation and watchable wildlife, wildlife and environmental education, city and county parks, and the preservation of open space and natural areas (Great Outdoors Colorado 1990).

Partnerships with state agencies and private entities were recommended, as were changes in property laws expanding conservation easements to support land preservation. Armed with a consensus that held broad appeal across a broad spectrum of disparate environmental, recreational, tourism, and ranching interests, advocates of a new dedicated funding arrangement under new authority sought help from the legislature. Legislation proposing to amend the state constitution to build a trust fund of half a billion dollars from a dedicated 0.25 percent state sales tax and half of all lottery proceeds emerged with powerful Republican sponsorship. It failed in the Senate Finance Committee, however.

In the summer of 1992, a group that became known as the "Great Outdoors" coalition acquired sufficient petition signatures to place a November 1992 constitutional initiative on the ballot that would take the control of lottery revenues away from the General Assembly. Fifty-seven percent of voters supported the measure, designated as Amendment 8. It created a Great Outdoors Colorado Trust Fund, free from the legislative appropriations process. The Trust Fund board would be appointed by the governor and would not be subject to any order or resolution of the General Assembly regarding its organization, powers, revenues, and expenses. Existing capital construction funding obligations would continue to be met for five years. Thereafter, 40 percent of proceeds would be distributed to the Conservation Trust Fund for local governments, and 10 percent would be allocated to state parks. Finally, 50 percent of the proceeds, up to $35 million (adjusted annually for inflation), would be allocated to the Great Outdoors Colorado Trust Fund. Surpluses over this amount go to the state's General Fund (Colorado Legislative Council 1992).

As with the highway lobby a half century earlier, the conservationist-preservationist nexus succeeded dramatically. The nexus freed a substantial independent revenue stream for a preferred use. Since 1992, GO-CO's inflation-indexed annual revenue cap has grown from $35 million to $55 million. As of December 2009, GO-CO had committed over $650 million for nearly 3,000 projects across the state. These projects include both small and large community park acquisitions and improvements, as well as collaboration with the state Parks Division to improve and create parks and expand buffer zones around parks. GO-CO has restored historic and scenic trails and helped the Division of Wildlife protect and expand habitats, including wetlands. GO-CO has helped leverage its revenues in other ways to preserve some of the state's remaining natural landscapes, including 850,000 acres of river corridors, mountain valleys, and historic landscapes (Great Outdoors Colorado 2009). The trust fund has amplified its funding stream by working with local and international land trusts, leveraging about twice the number of dollars of investments from local governments, land trusts, and others. Conservation easements are employed as well. Partnership acquisitions with GO-CO support have preserved numerous breathtaking natural landscapes.

It might be said that the result of 1992's Amendment 8 was to produce an extensive preservation directorate beyond the dreams of the 1980 lottery referendum proponents. By inducing local governments to engage in recreation and land planning through its competitive grants programs, GO-CO has shaped its political environment, acquired allies and supporters, and engaged interested parties in a continual rhythm of meetings, conferences, and consultations. GO-CO, like the road lobby, has proved that earmarks can work to advance their advocates' interests (Colorado Legislative Council 2001b).

TABOR: EARMARKS IN REVERSE

If the road and outdoor lobbies provide lessons in earmarking—capturing—revenues, TABOR offers a lesson in doing the reverse, namely, restricting the revenue flow. But what roads, GO-CO, and TABOR have in common is their impact on representative government and the deliberative process within the Colorado General Assembly. Essentially, these developments change the architecture of state government and ultimately diminish the authority of the people's elected representatives.

At the most fundamental level, one cannot understand contemporary legislative politics and finances or what legislators, governors, lobbyists, and state administrators in Colorado do without having a grasp of the Taxpayer's Bill of Rights. A protracted property taxpayer revolt in the 1970s set the stage for TABOR's passage, but public support for TABOR in 1992 was not simply the result of dissatisfaction with property taxes. The TABOR ballot initiative intersected with a hotly contested presidential election—with previously discouraged voters mobilized by the presidential candidacy of the independent Ross Perot—and higher voter turnout as a result of the presence of several measures on a crowded ballot, including a constitutional amendment to deny civil rights protections to gay individuals (Bradford 1994); four constitutional measures dealing with limited gaming, one referred and three initiated; constitutional restrictions on black bear hunting; and, of course, the GO-CO measure.

Another factor in TABOR's passage was a strategic shift by the state's Republican Party. While Republican notables had joined in opposition to previous TABOR measures since the mid-1980s, they were notably absent in 1992. Democratic governor Romer's opposition to TABOR was neutralized by the fact that he campaigned for an earmarked 1 percent sales tax for schools that same year. In view of the fact that many were surprised by the measure's contents in later years, TABOR may have been oversimplified in the public mind such that it was seen only as requiring public approval for tax increases. In fact, TABOR contained subtle mechanics, dimly understood by many among Colorado's political establishment.

Once passed, the Taxpayer's Bill of Rights changed the axis of Colorado politics. Briefly, TABOR limits the growth of expenditures by the state and all its local governments with a formula: the percentage of population growth plus the percentage of growth in the Consumer Price Index (CPI). Allowances are made for changes in the numbers of schoolchildren in school districts. TABOR also restricts taxation levels: no tax can be established or its rate increased without a vote of the electors in the relevant jurisdiction (i.e., statewide, school district, city). These provisions are unquestionably the most restrictive tax and expenditure limitations among the US states, and TABOR has forced state officials to make a succession of adaptations that further complicate state finances (James and Wallis 2004; Martell and Teske 2007).

Beginning in 1993, the legislature interpreted TABOR to mean that a statutory appropriation limit passed by the General Assembly in 1991 was "constitutionalized" by TABOR. The statute in question is called the 1991 Arveschoug-Bird limit, which stipulated that General Fund appropriations could not grow beyond 6 percent annually. The General Fund is the backbone of the state's services and operations, with sales, excise, personal, and corporate income tax revenues flowing into it. General Fund revenues make up approximately 43 percent of the state government's appropriations and support the prison system, the universities, state school aid, welfare, Medicaid, and environmental protection. The typical Colorado state agency draws heavily on the General Fund.

From a simple common-sense perspective, TABOR has considerable surface appeal. The idea of voting on all tax increases recognizes the fundamental importance of seeking public permission for taxation. The notion that expenditures should not grow faster than inflation seems reasonable. The argument for TABOR was that by observing inflation as a limit, public expenditures would gravitate to a steady state relative to the economy. However, former Joint Budget Committee chair Bradley Young has written that TABOR is a downward ratchet on governments and that the claim that the state's inflation and population growth reflect the size of the economy is false (Young 2006; see also Lav 2008). The CPI measures only the prices of goods and does not track the size of the economy. "If the economy grows at 8 percent, not uncommon for Colorado from 1970 to 2000, and the state government is allowed to grow at 6 percent, or just two percentage points less, state government will have been reduced by 10 percent relative to the economy in just six years, 20 percent in twelve years, or 30 percent in nineteen years" (Young 2006: 9).

By holding government expenditure growth to this particular formulaic limit, TABOR shrinks the size of the government in small increments that compound over time and does not allow the government to keep pace with the economy. TABOR essentially creates a recurring tax cut, slowly strangling the state's ability to provide the public with the services a succession of state legislatures has authorized.

The use of a general inflation index as a government expenditure limit is based on misplaced reasoning. As David Bradley and his colleagues concluded: "No existing measure of inflation—neither the Consumer Price Index nor the GDP [gross domestic product] deflator nor any other measure—correctly captures the growth in the cost of the kinds of services purchased in the public sector. State governments, for instance, are major purchasers of health care, the costs of which are rising far faster than the general rate of inflation" (2005: 4).

The CPI measures price changes its "consumer market basket" and weights components as follows: 42 percent housing, 17 percent transportation, 15.4 percent food and beverages, 6.1 percent medical care, 5.9 percent recreation, 4 percent apparel, and so forth (Bradley, Johnson, and Lav 2005: 8). Governments produce and purchase a different mix of goods and services. Many of the goods and services state governments produce inflate at much faster rates than does the general CPI consumer market basket. For example, while CPI increased by 27 percent from 1993 to 2003, its education component increased 70 percent, medical services nearly 51 percent, and drugs and medical supplies 46 percent (ibid.). Finally, it is a well-respected maxim that governments' service-intensive elements tend to be relatively unyielding to technology-induced efficiencies (Baumol and Bowen 1966).

For several decades the lion's share of the General Fund supported six Colorado state departments (Courts, K–12 Education, Higher Education, Health Care, Human Services, and Corrections), whose expenditures tend to have faster-than-CPI growth profiles. Service expenditures are also related to caseload increases, which grow rather than subside during recessions. Finally, some programs grow because the General Assembly, state courts, and federal grant requirements require them to do so: costs under the federal-state Medicaid program and state criminal sentencing laws are examples.

TABOR TRIGGERS AMENDMENT 23

TABOR was designed to apply the brakes to government growth, but it has also been a catalyst for more earmarking. In the area of K–12 education, the single-largest state expenditure category, funding decreased during the 1990s. School funding advocates became alarmed at the state's failure to supplement school district funds up to targeted levels, as promised in a 1973 School Finance Act. Further, a 1988 School Finance Act, prompted by the outcome of the Luhan case (involving funding equity in the schools) in 1987, was designed to reduce school district pupil expenditure disparities. Yet when push came to shove, the funding was not there. This situation prompted Governor Romer's 1992 campaign for a dedicated sales tax increase for K–12 education.

After 1992, TABOR became the primary obstacle to honoring the General Assembly's school funding promises. Under TABOR, the legislature could not increase taxes to pay for school funding increases without crowding out funding for other vital General Fund programs. The constitutionalizing of Arveschoug-Bird (until 2009) meant that competition for funding would be stiffer. K–12 education was competing with the state's most expensive and expansive programs—the Corrections Department, Medicaid, and higher education—for funding. Meanwhile, revenue surpluses over TABOR's expenditure limits began to materialize in the economic boom of the late 1990s, when income tax and sale tax revenues soared. TABOR required that surpluses be refunded to taxpayers, and the refunds became the feature many came to identify with TABOR. By the end of June 2000, over $2.3 billion in refundable TABOR surpluses had been recorded, and anticipated refunds for 2000–2001 were estimated to be nearly $900 million (Colorado Legislative Council 2000).

In addition to claiming credit for TABOR refunds, legislators cut income tax rates twice ($276.6 million in 1999 [HB 99–1207] and $151.1 million in 2000

[HB 00–1103]), reduced the state sales tax rate from 3 percent to 2.85 percent (a cut of $79.4 million) with HB 00–1259, and passed a permanent 10 percent state income tax credit worth $38 million in its first year of implementation (2000) (HB 00–1049). In 1997 the General Assembly passed SB 97–1, which earmarked funds above the 6 percent Arveschoug-Bird–limited HUTF. The bill permitted General Fund monies to be transferred, up to a limit equal to 10.355 percent of the year's state sales tax revenues. In the three fiscal years from 1998 to 2001, SB 97–1 transferred $546.4 million to HUTF—distributed according to earmarking provisions—to augment financially strapped state, county, and city highways (Colorado Legislative Council 2000, 2001c, 2002). All of these developments reduced the funding stream for K–12 education.

In this context, the Colorado Children's Campaign (CCC), formed in the mid-1980s to advocate for better children's health and education opportunities, sponsored a signature drive to place Amendment 23 on the 2000 ballot. From the perspective of CCC and its impressive list of allies, not only had the General Assembly declined to maintain education funding, but in passing SB 97–1 the assembly had locked in funding for highways at the expense of schools by agreeing to transfer General Fund "surpluses" to the Highway User Tax Fund. The future funding of schools would be even more difficult because of the structural erosion of the income and sales taxes.

Education advocates were alarmed by the fact that increases in funding were not keeping up with inflation; that is, there was a real decline in overall school funding by 2000. The Gallagher provision in the state constitution, which limited residential property taxes, was unassailable, so advocates' clearest path to augment school funding was earmarking state revenues to force appropriations.

Amendment 23 was a precise work of draftsmanship. It mandated that the "statewide base per pupil funding" (Colorado's core state K–12 funding program) be increased by the rate of inflation plus 1 percent until fiscal year 2010–2011, when the increase would be linked to inflation only. Categorical programs (English proficiency, special education, small schools, transportation, and others) would be increased in the same way. Amendment 23 also required "maintenance of effort" to prevent the General Assembly from replacing "old" spending with "new" Amendment 23 funds. Unlike the 1992 GO-CO amendment, Amendment 23 did not create a new revenue source, but the constitutional earmark eliminated the need for education to compete for general funds. As a result of Amendment 23, competition for General Fund support would intensify as prisons, colleges, Medicaid, pollution control, and other programs fought for a more limited piece of the pie. Amendment 23 gave school funding a constitutional privilege, with the result that other programs and institutions would have to yield to its unassailable constitutional claim to the General Fund.

UNSTABLE ARCHITECTURE
....

With General Fund and overall state expenditures limited under TABOR, much of the revenue flow commandeered by privileged programs, and the aftereffects of the 2001 economic recession felt keenly, the General Assembly began to craft a patchwork of exceptions to the pattern of financing state government operations. During the 2003 and 2004 legislative sessions, it became clear that earmarks, especially Amendment 23, would crowd other General Fund programs. So the legislature began to tinker with the fiscal architecture.

In 2004 the legislature took advantage of a statutory provision that allowed the designation "enterprises" for state agencies with less than 10 percent of their revenues coming directly from legislative appropriation, thus releasing them to collect revenues that would not be counted under the TABOR limits. The legislature did this in higher education by funneling state support for colleges and universities through a College Opportunity Fund, thus reducing the level of "direct" state support for colleges. Student tuition could then be raised and would not count as TABOR revenue. This benefited the schools financially and made room under the revenue cap for more tax revenues (Moore 2004).

In 2007, with Democrats having achieved control of the house, the senate, and the governorship, the legislature adopted SB 07-199—a mill levy freeze that put an end to what had been a downward slide in school district levies and locally derived school revenues. The consequence of the slide had been the need for more and more state funding to backfill the amount that was not derived from local taxes. This controversial law generated a measure of relief for the state's strained General Fund (Moore 2007).

In 2009 the legislature made four additional moves to skirt TABOR's strictures, further altering the state's fiscal architecture in the process. One bill (HB 09-1293) imposed a fee on hospitals, thereby generating more federal program matching funds and permitting broader health care coverage for low-income patients while reducing the costs of uncompensated care for hospitals. Another law, nicknamed "F.A.S.T.E.R." (SB 09-109), imposed a series of automobile registration and rental car fees to raise money for highways and bridges. Yet another important bill gave enterprise status to the unemployment compensation section of the State Department of Labor and Employment (HB 09-1363). As was the case with higher education, this removed some revenue from under TABOR's cap. Finally, the legislature modified the longstanding Arveschoug-Bird 6 percent appropriation limit with SB 09-228. This move did nothing to increase revenue, but it did give the legislature more latitude in spending revenue that comes in under the TABOR limit (Moore 2010).

All of these legislative adaptations, or "workarounds," have changed the state's finances and rendered TABOR funding caps somewhat less relevant, but they will not necessarily enable much legislative discretion over these program funds. Legislative discretion is also challenged by program advocates understandably impatient with the loss of legislative control of finances. Organized interests within Colorado have utilized the ballot initiative process more and more frequently to advance and protect their interests. For example, Amendment 35 in 2004 established a constitutional earmark for new tobacco taxes to fund health programs. In 2008 the passage of Amendment 50 expanded casino gambling, with associated tax revenues dedicated to community colleges. It is easy to imagine that other advocacy communities will emulate these initiatives in the foreseeable future.

THE ARCHITECTURE OF COLORADO'S FUTURE

Earmarking is not new, having begun shortly after Colorado became a state. But the scale and pace of earmarking Colorado's fiscal structures have increased, as have legislative attempts to release the state from some of its inherited financial restraints. In recent years, for example, the General Assembly has partially recreated higher education as a series of public enterprises, thereby shifting costs from the General Fund to students. It has removed a volatile element from overall TABOR accounting by converting unemployment insurance to enterprise status. The assembly created new annual revenues of over $830 million through vehicle registration and hospital provider fees. These are considerable reformulations of the state's financial structure to support crucial government services. Some of these measures shrink the TABOR-accounted state government while either increasing the footprint of public services (higher education) or maintaining them at current levels (unemployment compensation insurance). One imagines that other state functions are being scouted for enterprise status to further augment the state's release from TABOR accounting, in the process making TABOR less relevant to the state's finances.

Colorado's history demonstrates a marked inclination to restrict legislative discretion over revenues, an inclination shared by a long parade of General Assemblies themselves. As previously noted, the General Assembly has been prodded to cooperate with the initiative process, as in the example of highway building. None of the state's earmarking activities, however, has taken as much discretion from the management of general government functions and pitted the supporters and beneficiaries of public spending against each other so profoundly as the Taxpayer's Bill of Rights. But perhaps the General Assembly can accommodate itself to the post-TABOR world by entertaining new roles and new governance arrangements that preserve its relevance as an institution.

Taxation is perhaps the most difficult thing representative governments do. The impulse to avoid decisions that impose burdens on constituents is powerful. In general, elected officials survive taxing decisions by deferring the impacts of their taxes to future years, denying that taxes have been imposed, deflecting the blame for taxation on others, and shifting the burden to the politically unorganized (Hansen 1983; Rubin 2010). Elected governments may tax wisely when people are not watching or when the necessity to do so is broadly accepted.

Colorado's government has never fully embraced the deliberative ideal republican theory recommends, and it is difficult to imagine how it could generate the conditions that would approximate that ideal. The impacts of TABOR have fallen unevenly, and the revenue adaptations to TABOR have privileged some programs over others, thereby shifting funding burdens. At the same time, little has occurred to warm the public to the benefits of legislative discretion per se. The tangle of state finances is now more difficult to understand and to communicate to the citizenry. There are several designs for a post-TABOR Colorado, including that of repealing TABOR and returning the state to a republican form of government with flexible finances (Principles for Progress 2004). But it is unlikely that TABOR will be undone because in spite of public vagueness about the amendment, people broadly support what they think it represents. It is far more likely that TABOR will be redone and marginalized by a succession of limited changes. It is hard to imagine that, after having pushed so many issues to the periphery of legislative discretion because of its distrust of legislatures, the electorate will invite more legislative discretion.

The "solution" to TABOR has been and will continue to be pursued along an eccentric path defined by a succession of new fees, workaround constitutional provisions through the courts, and earmarking statutory and ballot measures such as we have already seen. This sits well with the features that presently define Colorado's political landscape. Colorado's citizenry remains broadly skeptical of politics, including progressives who support more robust public services but are mindful of the General Assembly's perfidious history. Preferring representative government but unable to endure TABOR's selective paralysis of the government, program advocates have shown themselves to be strategically adroit in their desperation. For many advocates and organized beneficiaries, the commitment to representative government has become vestigial by necessity: TABOR has made the unthinkable thinkable. Impatient advocacy communities have shown a willingness to be party to controversial fee earmarks, to endorse enterprise devices, and to seek separate protection for the services they deem necessary through the initiative process. Colorado's fiscal and political future will most likely be forged by this growing and vigorous sector.

REFERENCES

Baumol, William J., and William G. Bowen. 1966. *Performing Arts: The Economic Dilemma.* New York: Twentieth Century Fund.

Bradford, Stephen. 1994. *Gay Politics vs. Colorado: The Inside Story of Amendment Two*. Cascade, CO: Sardis.

Bradley, David, Nicholas Johnson, and Iris Lav. 2005. *The Flawed Population plus Growth Formula*. Washington, DC: Center for Budget and Policy Priorities. January 13.

Burnham, John. 1961. "The Gasoline Tax and the Automobile Revolution." *Mississippi Valley Historical Review* 48: 435–459.

City Club of Denver. 1940. Pamphlet no. 24: "Financing Highways in Colorado." Denver: City Club of Denver.

Colorado Joint Budget Committee. 1981. *Long Bill Narrative, 1981–1982*. Denver: Colorado General Assembly. April 27.

Colorado Legislative Council. 1980. Publication no. 248: "Analysis of 1980 Ballot Proposals." Denver: Colorado General Assembly.

———. 1984. Publication no. 286: "Individual Income Tax Returns Filed in Fiscal Year 1982/83." Prepared by the Research and Statistics Division, Colorado Department of Revenue. Denver: Colorado General Assembly.

———. 1992. Publication no. 369: "Analysis of 1992 Ballot Proposals." Denver: Colorado General Assembly.

———. 1996. Noble Bill Transfers to the Highway Users Tax Fund. Staff memorandum, November 6. Denver: Colorado General Assembly.

———. 2000. *Focus Colorado: Economic and Revenue Forecast: March*. Denver: Colorado General Assembly.

———. 2001a. Publication no. 487: "An Overview of the Colorado Adult Criminal Justice System." Denver: Colorado General Assembly.

———. 2001b. Background Information on GOCO and on the 2001 Referred Ballot Measure Concerning GOCO's Authority to Borrow Money. Staff memorandum, October 19. Denver: Colorado General Assembly.

———. 2001c. *Focus Colorado: Economic and Revenue Forecast: March*. Denver: Colorado General Assembly.

———. 2002. *Focus Colorado: Economic and Revenue Forecast: March*. Denver: Colorado General Assembly.

Colorado Office of the Governor. 1959. *Financing Government in Colorado: Report of the Governor's Tax Study Group*. Denver: Colorado Office of the Governor.

Colorado State Treasurer. 1881–1935. Biennial Reports of the State Treasurer.

Dunn, James. 1978. "The Importance of Being Earmarked: Transport Policy and Highway Finance in Great Britain and the United States." *Comparative Studies in Society and History* 20: 29–53.

Elofson, Stan. 2007. *A Listing of Statewide Initiated and Referred Ballot Proposals in Colorado, 1912–2006*. Denver: Colorado General Assembly.

Great Outdoors Colorado. 1990. *Final Report*. Denver: Great Outdoors Colorado Citizens Committee. December.

———. 2009. "Accomplishments." Available at www.goco.org. Accessed November 22, 2009.

Hafen, Leroy. 1931. "The Coming of the Automobile and Improved Roads." *Colorado Magazine* 8: 1–16.

Hansen, Susan. 1983. *The Politics of Taxation*. New York: Praeger.

James, Franklin, and Allan Wallis. 2004. "Tax and Spending Limits in Colorado." *Public Budgeting and Finance* 24: 16–33.

Kobs, Kathryn. 1972. The Political Career of William Lee Knous. MA thesis, University of Colorado, Boulder.

Lav, Iris. 2008. *Fixing TABOR's "Ratchet" Will Not Repair TABOR: Deterioration in Colorado Largely Attributable to Formula*. Washington, DC: Center for Budget and Public Priorities. April 10.

Lowi, Theodore. 1979. *The End of Liberalism,* 2nd ed. New York: W. W. Norton.

Martell, Christine R., and Paul Teske. 2007. "Fiscal Management Implications of the TABOR Bind." *Public Administration Review* 67: 673–687.

Merchant, Frank. 1955a. "Colorado's First Highway Commission 1910–1912—Part I." *Colorado Magazine* 32: 74–77.

———. 1955b. "Colorado's First Highway Commission, 1910–1912—Part II." *Colorado Magazine* 32: 146–151.

Moore, Scott. 2004. "Colorado." Salt Lake City: University of Utah Center for Public Policy and Administration. Available at http://www.cppa.utah.edu/westernstatesbudgets. Accessed December 1, 2009.

———. 2007. "Colorado Finance Politics in 2007: Prospecting in a New Democratic Era." Salt Lake City: University of Utah Center for Public Policy and Administration. Available at http://www.cppa.utah.edu/westernstatesbudgets. Accessed December 1, 2009.

———. 2010. "The Path to Resolution: Democrats Map the Future of Colorado's State Finance Western States Budgets." Salt Lake City: University of Utah Center for Public Policy and Administration. Available athttp://www.cppa.utah.edu/westernstatesbudgets/WPSA09/index.html. Accessed December 1, 2009.

Principles for Progress: Shaping the Economic Future of Colorado. Denver: University of Denver.

Rosenthal, Alan. 1998. *The Decline of Representative Democracy.* Washington, DC: CQ Press.

Rubin, Irene. 2010. *The Politics of Public Budgeting,* 6th ed. Washington, DC: CQ Press.

Stone, Wilber Fiske. 1918. *History of Colorado, Volume I.* Denver: S. J. Clarke.

Wiley, Marion. 1976. *The High Road.* Denver: Department of Highways.

Wilson, James Q., ed. 1980. *The Politics of Regulation.* New York: Basic Books.

Young, Bradley. 2006. *TABOR and Direct Democracy: An Essay on the End of the Republic.* Golden, CO: Fulcrum.

The State of Change Changes Again

Courtenay W. Daum, Robert J. Duffy, and John A. Straayer

As illustrated throughout this volume, Colorado's politics, which for over 100 years has featured an independent citizenry, is nothing if not both changeable and resistant to one-party rule. For most of the state's history, neither the Democratic nor the Republican Party has been able to fully dominate elective politics; on the few occasions when one party has gained the upper hand, complete hegemony was short-lived. Republicans found that out in 2004, as did the Democrats in 2010.

Consistent with our argument that Colorado politics is fluid and subject to change, the state's political landscape shifted again in the months preceding the 2010 midterm elections. In this election cycle, change came in the context of continuing voter dissatisfaction with the national and state economies and the perception that the Democratic Congress and President Barack Obama were not responding adequately to the economic crisis. No matter that similar public unhappiness with the government and the bad economy had been directed at a Republican president and his party just two years earlier—an unhappiness that helped put the Democrats in charge of both chambers of the US Congress and the White House in the first place. Notably, these frustrations played a role in the emergence of the Tea Party Movement, a political development that had great significance in Colorado politics during the 2010 primary and general elections. That said, as is the norm in midterm elections, the minority party gained seats in the General Assembly and in the state's US House delegation.

At the same time, Coloradans' support for direct democracy continued unabated in 2010 with the placement of six citizen-initiated items on the November ballot. Three of the six ballot items were proposed by anti-tax smaller-government interests within the state and were intended to have a dramatic effect on state and local government revenues. All three measures failed, but nothing occurred to ease the state's fiscal predicament, which had been in the making for over two decades.

STATE RACES

STATEWIDE RACES

Of all the state contests in 2010, the race for governor was the most unusual. Unexpectedly, Democratic governor Bill Ritter announced ten months ahead of the election that he would not seek a second term. Some speculated that Ritter feared he would be defeated (*Huffington Post* 2010; Valentine 2010). Others took him at his word that his decision was based on what was best for his family. Denver mayor John Hickenlooper quickly emerged as the Democratic Party's candidate for governor. The Republican Party's gubernatorial nomination process proved much more complicated. Initially, the competition was between Colorado Senate minority leader Josh Penry and former congressman Scott McInnis. Ultimately, Penry, who had once served as an aide to McInnis, bowed out to avoid a primary that may have proven detrimental to the Republican Party's gubernatorial nominee in the general election (Crummy 2009). As a result, McInnis's only competition for the nomination was the relatively unknown Dan Maes, and McInnis quickly became the presumptive nominee.

In July 2010, with the Republican Party primary rapidly approaching, it was reported that McInnis had received $300,000 to write a series of position papers in which he plagiarized the writings of a Colorado judge. The McInnis campaign's response to the plagiarism allegations did not satisfy many Coloradans, and his campaign never recovered from the charges. In the end, Maes, a Tea Party favorite, won the nomination (Crummy 2010a).

As the Republican Party nominee, however, Maes had to contend with allegations of financial and ethical improprieties. For example, he had taken $40,000 in mileage money from his campaign—an amount widely viewed as suspicious—and he was also subject to the largest campaign reporting violation in state history. He raised over $300,000 in campaign funds, but he spent nearly $72,000 to reimburse himself for a variety of expenses, some of which were untraceable for a lack of good records (Crummy 2010b). In addition, Maes portrayed himself as a successful businessman and onetime Kansas undercover law enforcement hero, but after he secured the nomination, evidence surfaced that questioned the veracity of both claims.

Then, to further complicate the Republican Party's prospects of winning the gubernatorial campaign, former Republican congressman Tom Tancredo entered the race as the American Constitution Party candidate. Tancredo had labeled both McInnis and Maes as dead-in-the-water candidates and called upon whoever won the nomination to withdraw, thereby providing the opportunity for a more viable Republican candidate to enter the race. If the winner of the Republican primary refused to renounce the nomination, Tancredo said he would get in the race. When Maes won and refused to resign, Tancredo kept his word (Crummy 2010c; Crummy and Sherry 2010). Throughout the campaign, Tancredo blistered Maes as an incompetent who could not win the general election.

Once Tancredo entered the race, it was assumed that the Republican electorate would split its support between Maes and Tancredo, thereby handing the governorship to Hickenlooper; in the end, that proved to be true. But what might well have been a Democratic runaway turned out to be an interesting, if strange, contest. As more and more reports emerged about unusual behavior and activities by Maes and his campaign, Republicans abandoned him, and many moved to support Tancredo. In the final weeks of the campaign, Rasmussen pollsters had Tancredo within four points of Hickenlooper, while Maes, the official Republican Party nominee, appeared to be in danger of failing to get 10 percent of the vote in the general election (Malone 2010). If that happened, the Republicans would become a minor political party and be subject to restrictive campaign contribution limits in 2012. In the end, Hickenlooper won easily, with more total votes than Tancredo and Maes combined (Malone 2010).

In contrast, the contests for the statewide offices of secretary of state, treasurer, and attorney general lacked the unusual traits of the race for governor and generally reflected the national pro-Republican mood in 2010. Democratic incumbent treasurer Cary Kennedy faced Republican Walker Stapleton and narrowly lost. Similarly, Democratic incumbent secretary of state Bernie Buescher failed to survive the challenge of Scott Gessler. The only statewide executive-branch incumbent to win was Republican attorney general John Suthers, who was challenged by Boulder district attorney Stan Garnett.

DISTRICT RACES

With the governor's race all but lost early on, the Republican Party looked to capture a majority in one or both of the General Assembly chambers. To do so, Republicans needed a net gain of four seats in the senate and six in the house. Republicans were especially eager to solidify their position in the state legislature given the fact that 2011 is a congressional redistricting year. In Colorado the state legislature is charged with drawing new district lines, and Republicans were understandably motivated to win seats in the General Assembly so they would have the ability to block any attempted Democratic gerrymander. The Republicans' strategy was to target a handful of seats they identified as their best chances to win. Most were districts Republicans had dominated in the past but had lost in the Democratic upsurge in 2004 and 2006. In the end, Republicans picked up one additional seat in the senate in November 2010, leaving them the minority party by the count of 20 to 15. But Republicans did succeed in capturing the house of representatives by the narrow margin of 33 to 32. Thus the pattern of divided partisan control of state offices returned in 2010, with Democrats controlling the governorship and the state senate and Republicans filling the other statewide offices and recapturing the house of representatives.

Unless the Democrats recapture the house and hold the senate in 2012, the state house, state senate, and the governorship will have been united under one-party control for just eight of the previous forty years: 1999–2000 and 2003–2004 with Republican governor Bill Owens and an all-GOP legislature, and 2007–2010 with Democratic governor Bill Ritter and a Democratic house and senate.

The two-party gender differential that had once tilted Republican but more recently had shifted heavily in the Democratic direction changed very little in 2010. The August 2010 primary featured thirty-nine female Democratic contenders to just twenty-one Republicans. In November the ballot listed seventeen Republican women, two for senate seats and fifteen for the sixty-five house positions. On the Democratic side the total was thirty-three: eight female senate candidates and twenty-five for the house of representatives. Following the election, twelve of the forty-eight Republican members of the legislature were female, as were twenty-seven of the fifty-two Democrats. Notably, Colorado continues to rank high among the US states when it comes to the descriptive representation of women in state legislatures; 39 percent of the Colorado General Assembly was female in 2010, matching the state's historical highpoint (Colorado Legislative Directory 2011; chapter 8 in this volume).

DIRECT DEMOCRACY

Colorado's century-old love affair with direct democracy continued in 2010. The November 2010 ballot contained nine measures, six of which were citizen-initiated and three referred by the legislature. The six initiated questions addressed familiar themes such as abortion, state and local taxes and finance, and antipathy toward "big government." Four of the six citizen-initiated ballot measures proposed changes to the Colorado Constitution, while two proposed to alter statutory law. These ballot measures came from familiar sources: the tax measures from persons connected to TABOR's Douglas Bruce, the abortion proposal from the same individuals who had pushed it in 2008, and the anti–government health care amendment from Jon Caldara and his libertarian Independence Institute (Hoover 2010a).

Three measures that addressed taxes and finance would have had the effect of reducing government revenues. Collectively, they would have reduced taxes on income, property, and phone service, rolled back existing levels of auto registration fees, and severely limited the government's ability to borrow money for capital projects; at the same time, they would have imposed property taxes on such government entities as colleges and universities. Provisions in the three measures were to be phased in over several years, but the impact, had all three passed and gone into effect immediately, would have been to reduce available state general funds to the point that 99 percent of revenues would have been required to meet constitutional obligations to the K–12 schools, with just $38 million left to pay for the rest of the state government (Colorado Legislative Council 2010). The three proposals, dubbed the "ugly three" by a well-funded campaign led by the business community and supported by most members of both parties, were defeated by large margins (FitzGerald 2010).

Despite the defeat of the three tax-cut measures, the state continues to face serious budget problems. The 2010–2011 state budget remains out of balance by several hundred million dollars, and lawmakers face the prospect of being well over a billion dollars short of producing a balanced budget for 2011–2012. With a new governor and control of the legislative chambers divided, the coming years are destined to produce unparalleled challenges (Hoover 2010b).

The anti-abortion proposal defined life as existing "from the beginning of the biological development" of a human being and would have extended all existing state constitutional rights to that "person" (Colorado Legislative Council 2010). The Independence Institute's anti–big government amendment was designed to keep the state out of the business of helping to implement provisions in the 2010 national government's health care reform law. The final ballot measure was a statutory proposal to restrict conditions under which persons accused of certain crimes could be released on bail. These three measures lost as well.

As is most often the case, the three proposals from the General Assembly had fairly minor impacts. All three amended the constitution. One shifted the job of licensing gambling operations from the secretary of state to the Department of Revenue, another eliminated property taxes on minor uses of government property for private purposes, and the third provided for the state capitol to be relocated in the event of a disaster. Only the measure on capitol relocation passed. All in all, the 2010 direct democracy story was mostly a repeat of the past. Voters had a lot of homework to do if they were to vote intelligently on a fairly long list of measures. Some came from citizen groups and others from legislators. The issues addressed reflected the patterns of Colorado politics.

2010 FEDERAL ELECTIONS

Just as 2006 and 2008 were bad years for Republicans, 2010 was a bad year for Democrats, as the party lost six seats in the US Senate and sixty-three in the US House of Representatives. But Colorado's US Senate race provided a rare piece of good election day news for the party, as Michael Bennet, appointed by Governor Bill Ritter in 2009 to fill Ken Salazar's Senate seat, narrowly defeated Republican Ken Buck. In Colorado's three contested House races, however, only Ed Perlmutter won reelection. John Salazar and Betsy Markey were swept from office in their reelection bids in the Third and Fourth Congressional Districts, respectively.

US SENATE

By most measures, Colorado's Senate race should have been a cakewalk for Republicans. With the national unemployment rate hovering near 10 percent, voters had soured on congressional Democrats and President Obama, whose approval levels were under 50 percent. Polls consistently showed that Republican voters were more enthusiastic than Democrats and that unaffiliated voters, who had voted Democratic by wide margins in 2006 and 2008, now favored Republicans. Republicans also enjoyed a statewide voter registration advantage of 62,000, up significantly from their 2008 edge of 12,000 (Colorado Secretary of State 2010a).

Moreover, although Michael Bennet was a prodigious fundraiser, he began the year with significant liabilities. Perhaps most important, Bennet was a political newcomer, and this was his first campaign. Bennet, a political moderate, had been a surprising pick to replace Salazar, and his selection disappointed many Democrats who thought he was too conservative. Other Coloradans resented the fact that he had been appointed to office and had not earned it through an election. Still others were upset that the Obama administration threw its support to Bennet in a transparent effort to preempt any primary challenge. Those efforts were ultimately unsuccessful, as Andrew Romanoff, the former speaker of the Colorado house, decided to contest the primary. As a result, Bennet was forced to spend a significant amount of the money he had raised to win his party's nomination. Romanoff's candidacy also forced Bennet to tack left on a number of issues, including health care, to appeal to Democratic primary voters. By the end of the campaign, Bennet was one of the Senate's most enthusiastic supporters of the health care bill's so-called public option, which made it harder to portray himself as a moderate in the general election. Perhaps most worrisome to Democrats, the primary grew nasty as it wore on, leading to concerns that intra-party divisions would harm the eventual nominee. Bennet ultimately prevailed, but with a less than resounding eight-point margin (Johnson 2010). Republicans thus had many reasons to be optimistic about their chances to win the Senate seat in November.

But Republicans had their own problems and handed the Democrats an opportunity when they nominated Weld County district attorney Ken Buck. Buck was initially seen as having little chance of winning the nomination—he was not very well-known around the state, and he was seen as too conservative by party establishment leaders, who quickly threw their support behind former lieutenant governor Jane Norton. Although Buck's fundraising was anemic, he was helped a great deal in the primary campaign by outside groups such as Club for Growth Action, which spent nearly $2 million on an independent expenditure campaign attacking Norton's conservative credentials. Buck also garnered the support of the Tea Party Movement, which saw Norton as the handpicked favorite of state party chair Dick Wadhams and the national party establishment, which was eager to avoid a divisive primary. Because Republican primary voters in Colorado are very conservative, both candidates eagerly sought their votes and espoused positions that, while attractive to the party base, would prove problematic in a general election. Buck articulated a host of controversial positions during the primary, proclaiming his opposition to all abortions, including in cases of rape and incest. He also called for privatizing Social Security and the Veterans Administration and abolishing the Department of Education, and he questioned the constitutionality of student loans. These positions resonated with Republican primary voters but were problematic in the general election, especially among the state's many unaffiliated voters (Booth 2010; Simon 2010).

In addition, Buck's penchant for speaking first and thinking later ultimately provided an opening for Norton, who trailed Buck in most polls through the summer. A voter at a Buck campaign event asked Buck why he should vote for him. Buck replied, "Because I don't wear high heels." Buck said his answer was a joke, made in response to Norton's suggestion that he was not man enough to attack her personally, relying instead on outside groups to do his dirty work. In any event, Buck's words were captured on video, and the Norton campaign featured them in a television ad aimed at women voters. Buck's lead shrank in the final weeks of the campaign. Although he ultimately won 52–48, his "high heels" gaffe came back to haunt him in the general election (Simon 2010).

The Bennet-Buck race turned out to be the most expensive in the nation, attracting more than $33 million in total spending (Center for Responsive Politics 2010a). Bennet raised and spent $11.4 million, while Buck spent just $3.8 million (Center for Responsive Politics 2010b). The Democratic Senatorial Campaign Committee (DSCC) spent an astonishing $8.3 million, while the National Republican Campaign Committee (NRCC) spent just over $5 million. A veritable avalanche of interest groups spent an additional $20 million total, with Karl Rove's American Crossroads leading the way with just under $6 million in independent expenditures attacking Bennet. All told, six additional groups spent more than $1 million apiece in the race, and another six spent at least $500,000 (Center for Responsive Politics 2010c). The groups supporting Buck outspent those supporting Bennet by a margin of 4–1.

Polls showed Buck ahead for most of the race, albeit narrowly, but Bennet and his allies hammered him for his public statements on a range of issues, seeking to define Buck as too extreme for the citizens of Colorado. The DSCC went on the air in August with ads citing Buck's positions on Social Security and Medicare and his claim that the 17th Amendment—which allowed for the popular election of US senators—was a bad idea. More important, though, later ads by the DSCC and Campaign Money Watch were aimed squarely at unaffiliated women voters. The ads focused on Buck's opposition to all abortions, his support for a controversial ballot measure critics said would make it harder to obtain common forms of birth control, and his refusal to prosecute a rape case when he was the Weld County district attorney because he said the victim had a case of "buyer's remorse." A number of ads also featured the "high heels" video previously used in the Norton campaign ad. The goal, of course, was to portray Buck as unsympathetic to women. It worked—exit polls showed that women voted for Bennet by a 56–39 margin, while men chose Buck 54–40 (CNN 2010). According to Denver pollster Floyd Ciruli, "We saw Republican and unaffiliated women move dramatically at the end" of the campaign (quoted in Booth 2010).

In the end, Michael Bennet won the race by just under 29,000 votes. As might be expected, Bennet easily carried traditionally Democratic areas, including Boulder and Denver Counties, while Buck dominated in El Paso, Douglas, and Weld Counties, as well as the sparsely populated counties on the eastern plains. But Bennet carried the bellwether counties of Jefferson, Adams, Arapahoe, and Larimer by a few thousand votes each and thus carried the state (Colorado Secretary of State 2010c).

In an indication of the effectiveness of the Democratic attacks, exit polls showed that 54 percent of Colorado voters thought Ken Buck was too extreme. Although Buck carried independent voters by a 53–37 margin, Bennet won 60 percent of those who self-identified as "moderates." The exit polls also showed that Bennet won 94 percent of Democratic voters and 10 percent of Republicans (CNN 2010). The Republican crossover vote was large enough that it might have made the difference in the race. Although it is impossible to know for certain, it is plausible that the larger defection rate among Republicans reflected the unwillingness of Norton voters to support Buck in the general election.

The exit polls also showed that Democrats may have had a superior get out the vote (GOTV) operation. Among those casting ballots on election day, Democrats outnumbered Republicans by a 33–28 margin (CNN 2010). In addition to the Bennet campaign, the state Democratic Party, Organizing for America, and affiliated interest groups conducted an intensive GOTV effort aimed not only at turning out the base but also focusing on unaffiliated women and Latino voters. According to reports in *The Denver Post*, 1,900 volunteers knocked on 325,000 doors. In the campaign's final weeks, vote monitors from the Bennet campaign, union groups, and Organizing for America tracked early-vote totals and neighborhoods that were "underperforming" their computer models. Extra volunteers were then directed to those neighborhoods. In addition, women's groups used enhanced voter lists to call independent women considered persuadable regarding Buck's failings (Booth 2010).

Democrats also made a concerted effort to target Latino voters. Unlike Buck, Bennet aired television and radio ads on Spanish-language stations and was undoubtedly helped by Tom Tancredo's campaign for governor. Tancredo's position on a host of issues, including his vocal opposition to immigration, helped mobilize Latino groups, who worked together to target 88,000 infrequent Latino voters (Booth 2010). In the end, Latinos comprised 12 percent of the Colorado electorate in 2010, essentially maintaining their turnout rates from 2008 (CNN 2010).

The Republican train wreck in the governor's race hurt Buck as well. The Maes-Tancredo split and the continued weakness of the Republican Party meant the party's once-vaunted GOTV operation was hamstrung in 2010. This was exacerbated by the fundraising woes of the Republican National Committee (RNC) under the leadership of Michael Steele. In the past, the RNC had funded the party's GOTV operations, but the committee's anemic fundraising prevented it from doing so in 2010. In addition, the Republican Governors Association (RGA), which had been planning to spend heavily in the state, withdrew completely after Maes won the nomination and reallocated the funds to states where Republican prospects were brighter. If Buck had been able to count on the usual support from either the RNC or the RGA, the outcome might have been different. Buck's decision to ignore the Latino vote, as Bob Schaffer had done two years prior, was also a mistake.

HOUSE RACES

As noted previously, Democrats fared less well in US House races in Colorado in the 2010 election, losing two of the three contested seats. In the Seventh District, Ed Perlmutter had a few uncomfortable weeks in his campaign against Aurora city councilman Ryan Frazier but ultimately won reelection by a comfortable 53–42 margin. Frazier was initially seen as having little chance against the popular Perlmutter, but, as the year wore on, Republican prospects grew brighter nationally. Republicans also cut into the Democratic advantage in voter registration, reducing the margin to 22,000 from 36,000 just two years earlier (Colorado Secretary of State 2010a). By late summer, outside groups began running television ads, spending more than $3.5 million on the race. Leading the way on the Republican side were the American Action Network at $1.5 million and the American Future Fund, which spent $565,000; the key actors supporting Perlmutter were the National Association of Realtors ($430,000), the National Association of Realtors Congressional Fund ($296,000), and the Democratic Congressional Campaign Committee (DCCC), which made $465,000 in independent expenditures (Center for Responsive Politics 2010d.) With respect to the candidates themselves, Perlmutter spent $2.5 million compared to Frazier's $1.4 million (Center for Responsive Politics 2010e).

The most surprising result was in the Third District where, in a rematch of their 2008 contest, Republican Scott Tipton defeated incumbent John Salazar by a 50–46 margin. Salazar had defeated Tipton by 20 points in 2008; despite again having a big fundraising advantage in 2010, he was overwhelmed by the national Republican trend. Tipton, a state senator, had wooed Tea Party supporters by pledging to cut the federal government in half. Originally given little chance of winning, Tipton was helped by a surge in Republican registration, which boosted the district's Republican lead from 10,000 in 2008 to 18,000 by election day in 2010 (Colorado Secretary of State 2010a). When it became clear that Salazar was in trouble, the DCCC diverted money from some other races, including that of Betsy Markey in the Fourth District, in an unsuccessful attempt to save the seat. The DCCC spent $1.2 million, while the NRCC spent $850,000. The biggest spender among outside groups was Americans for Job Security, which spent $500,000 attacking Salazar (Center for Responsive Politics 2010f). Republicans successfully nationalized the race, and Salazar fell victim to voters' unhappiness with the federal government.

Although Republican Cory Gardner's victory in the Fourth District was not surprising given the national results, the margin of his victory (52–41) over Betsy Markey was unexpected. Markey, who had carried Larimer County by 34,000 votes over Marilyn Musgrave in 2008, won the county by just over 300 votes in 2010 (Larimer County Clerk 2008, 2010). Markey also carried Boulder County, but by a smaller margin than she had in 2008. Gardner won the rest of the district easily, despite being outspent by Markey $3.2 million to $2.1 million (Center for Responsive Politics 2010g). In her 2008 victory, Markey received nearly 179,000 votes overall, compared to Musgrave's 140,000. But turnout in midterm elections is generally much lower than in general elections, and in 2010 Gardner won the district even though he captured just 138,000 votes—fewer than Musgrave had in losing two years earlier. But the electorate in 2008 was much larger and less Republican than was the case in 2010, and in a district where Republicans outnumber Democrats by 43,000, that was more than enough to explain the result (Colorado Secretary of State 2010a). Unaffiliated voters make up one-third of the district's voters, and Markey needed to at least repeat her 2008 performance to have a chance to win. She was unable to do so in 2010.

Although the district attracted more than $3 million in outside spending, the total fell far short of what most observers had expected. In the end, the NRCC led the way, with $925,000 in independent expenditures. The Chamber of Commerce also spent $500,000 supporting Gardner, while Women Vote! ($677,000), Majority Action PAC ($241,000), and the Service Employees International Union ($205,000) were the biggest spenders on the Democratic side (Center for Responsive Politics 2010h). The Democratic National Congressional Committee had reserved nearly $800,000 in television ads, but it shifted that money to other races after concluding that Markey could not win.

DÉJÀ VU: THE STATE OF CHANGE

In just the first decade of the twenty-first century, Colorado politics at both the national and state levels shifted from Republican dominance to Democratic dominance and, in the 2010 election, back in the Republican direction. Given the national political picture—a Democratic president facing a divided US Congress, an opposition party that has stated its singular goal for the next two years as guaranteeing that President Obama is a one-term president, and continued economic uncertainty nationwide—and severe budgetary problems within the state, the future of Colorado politics is increasingly difficult to predict. At this point it is unclear which party will have national momentum in 2012, and questions remain about the long-term viability and influence of the Tea Party Movement in both Colorado and nationally. With a history of political change and an independent voting public, one-third of which is affiliated with neither major party, Colorado politics remains difficult to predict—and endlessly interesting.

REFERENCES

Booth, Michael. 2010. "Teamwork, Tenacity Help Propel Bennet in Senate Race in Colorado." *The Denver Post,* November 11. Available at http://www.denverpost.com/election2010/ci_16518314?source=rss. Accessed November 11, 2010.

Center for Responsive Politics. 2010a. "Outside Spending, 2010 Senate Races." Available at http://www.opensecrets.org/outsidespending/summ.php?cycle=2010&disp=R&pty=A&type=G. Accessed November 16, 2010.

———. 2010b. "Total Raised and Spent, 2010 Colorado Senate Race." Available at http://www.opensecrets.org/races/summary.php?id=COS1&cycle=2010. Accessed November 16, 2010.

———. 2010c. "Outside Spending, 2010 Race: Colorado Senate." Available at http://www.opensecrets.org/races/indexp.php?cycle=2010&id=COS1. Accessed November 16, 2010.

———. 2010d. "Outside Spending, 2010 Race: Colorado District 07." Available at http://www.opensecrets.org/races/indexp.php?cycle=2010&id=CO07. Accessed November 19, 2010.

———. 2010e. "Total Raised and Spent, 2010 Race: Colorado District 07." Available at http://www.opensecrets.org/races/summary.php?id=CO07&cycle=2010. Accessed November 19, 2010.

———. 2010f. "Outside Spending, 2010 Race: Colorado District 03." Available at http://www.opensecrets.org/races/indexp.php?cycle=2010&id=CO03. Accessed November 19, 2010.

———. 2010g. "Total Raised and Spent, 2010 Race: Colorado District 04." Available at http://www.opensecrets.org/races/summary.php?id=CO04&cycle=2010. Accessed November 19, 2010.

———. 2010h. "Outside Spending, 2010 Race: Colorado District 04." Available at http://www.opensecrets.org/races/indexp.php?cycle=2010&id=CO04. Accessed November 19, 2010.

CNN. 2010. "CNN Politics, Exit Polls, U.S. Senate, Colorado." Available at http://www.cnn.com/ELECTION/2010/results/polls/#COS01p1. Accessed November 14, 2010.

Colorado Legislative Council. 2010. "2010 State Ballot Information Booklet" (*Blue Book*). Denver: Colorado Legislative Council.

Colorado Legislative Directory. 2011. Denver: Colorado General Assembly.

Colorado Secretary of State. 2010a. "Total Registered Voters by Congressional District, Party, and Status." Available at http://www.sos.state.co.us/pubs/elections/VoterRegNumbers/2010/October/ByPartybyStatus.pdf. Accessed November 16, 2010.

———. 2010b. "Elections, 2010, Primary Elections Results." Available at http://www.sos.state.co.us/pubs/electionresults2010/primary/ColoradoReport.html. Accessed December 16, 2010.

———. 2010c. "Official Results, General Election." Available at http://www.sos.state.co.us/pubs/electionresults2010/general/coloradoreport.html. Accessed December 16, 2010.

Crummy, Karen. 2009. "Penry Explains Exit from Colorado Governor's Race." *The Denver Post*, November 11. Available at http://www.denverpost.com/politics/ci_13759041. Accessed September 25, 2010.

———. 2010a. "Storm over Possible Plagiarism in McInnis Writings Escalates." *The Denver Post*, July 15. Available at http://www.denverpost.com/ci_15509569. Accessed November 28, 2010.

———. 2010b. "Maes' Campaign Has Reimbursed Family $71,658." *The Denver Post*, October 20. Available at http://www.denverpost.com/campaign/ci_16382376?IA

DID=Search-www.denverpost.com-www.denverpost.com. Accessed November 29, 2010.

———. 2010c. "Tancredo Warns McInnis, Maes to Quit GOP's Governor's Race or He'll Run." *The Denver Post*, July 23. Available at http://www.denverpost.com/ci_ 15582443?IADID=Search-www.denverpost.com-www.denverpost.com. Accessed November 29, 2010.

Crummy, Karen, and Allison Sherry. 2010. "GOP, Tea Party Leaders Back Away from Maes." *The Denver Post*, September 3. Available at http://www.denverpost.com/ campaign/ci_15979509?IADID=Search-www.denverpost.com-www.denverpost. com. Accessed November 29, 2010.

FitzGerald, Drew. 2010. "Colorado Firms Spend Millions Fighting Tax-Cutting Measures." *The Denver Post*, July 23. Available at nhttp://www.denverpost.com/search/ ci_15582081. Accessed November 29, 2010.

Hoover, Tim. 2010a. "Group Claims Bruce Illegally Funded Petition Drives for Anti-Tax Ballot Measures." *The Denver Post*, October 19. Available at http://www.denverpost. com/search/ci_16373273. Accessed November 29, 2010.

———. 2010b. "Ritter Unveils $19.1 Billion Colorado Budget for 2011–12 Fiscal Year." *The Denver Post*, November 3. Available at http://www.denverpost.com/news/ci_ 16501789. Accessed November 29, 2010.

The Huffington Post. 2010. "Bill Ritter's Retirement Announcement: 'Intensely Personal' Decision Will Free Him to Make 'Tough Decisions.' "Available at www.huffington-post.com/2010/01/06/bill-ritter-retirement. Accessed November 15, 2010.

Johnson, Kirk. 2010. "Incumbent Backed by Obama Wins Colorado Primary." *The New York Times*, August 10. Available at http://www.nytimes.com/2010/08/11/us/ politics/11primaries.html. Accessed November 23, 2010.

Larimer County Clerk. 2008. "2008 Larimer County General Election Official Results." Available at http://www.co.larimer.co.us/elections/2008general.htm. Accessed November 19, 2010.

———. 2010. "2010 Larimer County General Election Official Results." Available at http://www.co.larimer.co.us/2010election/1448.htm. Accessed November 19, 2010.

Malone, Patrick. 2010. "Public Polls Dead Wrong on Dead Heat for Governor." *The Pueblo Chieftain*, November 7. Available at http://www.chieftain.com/news/local/ article_8e7685e8-ea2a–11df-b62d–001cc4c03286.html. Accessed November 29.

Simon, Stephanie. 2010. "Democrats See Hopeful Signs in Colorado Race." *The Wall Street Journal*, August 12. Available at http://online.wsj.com/article/SB1000142405 2748704216804575423673158908584.html. Accessed November 23, 1010.

Valentine, Elizabeth. 2010. "Democratic Ritter's Exit from Colorado's Gubernatorial Race Causes Stir." Available at http://www.associatedcontent.com/article 2561457 /democraticritters_exit. Accessed November 15, 2010.

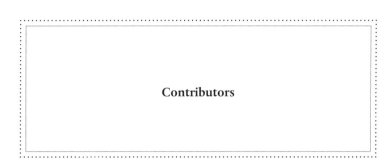

Contributors

Mike Binder is a doctoral student in the Department of Political Science, University of California, San Diego.

Courtenay W. Daum is assistant professor of political science, Colorado State University. She specializes in public law and gender politics. Professor Daum's publications include *Women in Congress: Descriptive Representation and Democratic Governance*; *Women as Leaders in Congress*; and *Women in the 107th Congress: The Past Meets the Future.*

Scott Doyle is the clerk and recorder in Larimer County, Colorado. A Republican, he was first elected in 2002. Doyle has been the recipient of numerous awards, including the Election Administration Best Practices Award and the Public Official of the Year prize from the National Association of County Recorders, Election Officials and Clerks.

Robert J. Duffy is professor and chair, Department of Political Science, Colorado State University. Professor Duffy's areas of academic specialization include American politics and policy and environmental policy. His publications include *The Green Agenda* and many articles and book chapters, including several on national political races in Colorado.

Vladimir Kogan is a doctoral student in the Department of Political Science, University of California, San Diego.

Thad Kousser is associate professor of political science, University of California, San Diego. He specializes in American politics and state government and politics. Professor Kousser's publications include *Term Limits and the Dismantling of State Legislative Professionalism*.

Robert D. Loevy is professor of political science, Colorado College. His specialties include American politics and state and local government. Professor Loevy's publications include *The Flawed Path to the Presidency* and *Colorado Politics and Government* (with Tom Cronin).

Seth E. Masket is associate professor of political science, University of Denver. His academic areas include political parties and state legislatures. Professor Masket's publications include *How Informal Party Organizations Control Nominations and Polarize Legislatures*.

Scott Moore is associate professor of political science, Colorado State University. His areas of specialization include public administration and state and local politics. Professor Moore's publications include articles in *Administration and Society* and *The Natural Resources Journal*.

Kyle Saunders is associate professor of political science, Colorado State University. Professor Saunders specializes in American politics, political parties, and elections. His publications include *Is Polarization Really a Myth* and several articles and book chapters on national elections in Colorado.

Daniel A. Smith is associate professor of political science, University of Florida. He specializes in American politics and direct democracy. His publications include *Educated by Initiative: The Effects of Direct Democracy on Citizens and Political Organizations in the American States* (with Caroline Tolbert).

John A. Straayer is professor of political science, Colorado State University. He specializes in Colorado and legislative politics. Professor Straayer's publications include *The Colorado General Assembly*.

Index